John Stuart Blackie

The Language and Literature of the Scottish Highlands

John Stuart Blackie

The Language and Literature of the Scottish Highlands

ISBN/EAN: 9783337159597

Printed in Europe, USA, Canada, Australia, Japan

Cover: Foto ©Thomas Meinert / pixelio.de

More available books at **www.hansebooks.com**

THE
LANGUAGE AND LITERATURE
OF
THE SCOTTISH HIGHLANDS

BY

JOHN STUART BLACKIE

PROFESSOR OF GREEK IN THE UNIVERSITY OF EDINBURGH.

"The way to a mother's heart is through her children; the way to a people's heart is through its language."—J. P. RICHTER.

EDINBURGH
EDMONSTON AND DOUGLAS
1876

TO HER GRACE

ELIZABETH DUCHESS OF ARGYLL

This Volume

IS

WITH SINCERE ESTEEM AND

GRATEFUL REGARDS

DEDICATED

BY

THE AUTHOR.

CONTENTS.

PREFACE.

THIS book is an humble attempt to break down the middle wall of partition which I have found to exist fencing off the most cultivated minds in England and in the Lowlands of Scotland from the intellectual life and moral aspirations of the Scottish Highlanders. This partition, so unnatural between kindred races, appears to me to have grown up from a combination of unhappy circumstances, which has rudely torn away one remote limb of the empire from the sympathy of the rest, but is kept up mainly now by the neglect with which all classes have conspired to treat the Caledonian branch of the great Celtic family of languages. For this neglect our Scottish philologers, who ought to have seen more sharply, and our Highland upper and middle classes, who ought to have felt more truly, are chiefly responsible. From a residence of some years in the Western Highlands, and a habit of feeling the

pulse of various persons and classes in reference to
Celtic matters, I became deeply convinced that some
attempt should be made to remedy a state of things
so disgraceful to our character as an educated people;
but I certainly should never have presumed to take
this office upon myself, had I not seemed to recognise
certain advantages in my position at the present junc-
ture which might give my advocacy greater weight
than would justly belong to many a more competent
champion.   How far I have succeeded in the attempt
those who know may judge; in the meantime, I only
wish to return special thanks to those gentlemen learned
in Celtic lore, without whose aid I should never
have succeeded in working my way through the difficulties which a poetical translator from the great Gaelic
classics at this time of day cannot fail to encounter.
The names of the Rev. Dr. Clerk of Kilmallie, the
Rev. Alexander Stewart of North Ballachulish, the
Rev. Duncan M'Innes, Oban, and Duncan Clerk,
Esq., Oban, not to mention the assistance derived in
some cases from Pattison and other previous labourers
in the same field, will serve as a sufficient guarantee
to the public that I have in no case planted my foot
within the prickly preserves of the old Gaelic Muse
without good guidance.   As to the general style of

the translations, I have endeavoured to follow the spirited freedom of Dryden and our old masters, rather than the curious literalness which has been lately fashionable. While anxiously retaining every feature of the original that was in anywise characteristic, I have been throughout indifferent to mere words which, if expressed, had no particular beauty, and, if omitted, left no appreciable blank.

ALTNACRAIG, OBAN,
October 1876.

LANGUAGE AND LITERATURE

OF

THE HIGHLANDS OF SCOTLAND.

CHAPTER I.

LANGUAGE.

A chànain sgapach
Thapaidh bhlasda, ghrinn
Thig le tartar
Neartmhor o bheal cinn !—MACDONALD.

JOHN BULL is, as all the world knows, a very clever fellow, and has done not a few notable things in his day that will be talked of in history as long as the temples of the Greeks and the roads of the Romans; but with all his cleverness and all his practicality he has made not a few great blunders in public matters, most of which have not even a flash of brilliancy to redeem their stupidity. Among these great blunders may certainly be reckoned three —Ireland, the Education of the People, and the Scottish Highlands. All these blunders, however various in their character, seem to flow from one common cause, of which the positive side is an excess of individual freedom, and the negative a defect of social organisation. We are in the habit of leaving too many things to shift for themselves, till, like an unweeded garden, they grow up into an intolerable nest of nettles, by which being stung and fretted we immediately commence reforming and re-tracing our steps in a fashion extremely furious, and therefore not exactly wise; sometimes altogether futile, being too late. The blunder which was perpetrated in the Highlands, in the shape, first, of rank population which no man cared to weed, and then of a systematic depopulation which no man cared to moderate, was the natural result of the overstrained idea of personal freedom, especially in matters of landed property, hereditary in Englishmen, acting in concert with certain political misfortunes and certain economical crotchets which specially affected that part of the British dominions. These causes, working quietly, and without any attempted check, for more than a century, have caused the Highlands generally to fall into a state of neglect and disregard which every man wise to estimate the worth of the Celtic element in our mixed population must lament. No doubt Walter Scott with his Rob Roy, Robert Burns, to a certain extent, with his Highland Mary, and Wordsworth with his Inversnaid Beauty, did something to revive the kindly feeling towards the Highlands which the political rancour inherited from the Rebellion of 1745 and the dogmatic prejudices of Dr. Johnson had done their best to extinguish; but this revival, like the Jacobite songs of Hogg and others, was more in the way of sentimental sympathy than of practical aid; and so it came to pass that, in the middle of this nineteenth century, we found our Highland economy drifted into a condition, if less fretful and less noisy, not much less lamentable than that of Ireland. In our haste to make money, the besetting sin of a commercial people, we had surrendered ourselves to the despotic sway of economical reforms, crudely conceived and harshly executed, proceeding upon the false idea that, if only the absolute amount of certain products were increased, no regard was to be had to the quality or the distribution of the producing population ; and the infatuation of this one idea had, in many cases, proceeded so far as to leave large districts of the country absolutely without anything to represent a middle class, save the factor, the doctor, and the parish minister. Landlords, once the centre of a kindly circle, found society everywhere except at home ; and as for the land, once green with furrowed slopes, and happy with smoking cottages, the only thing to be done for it was to stock it largely with sheep or deer, to reap large rentals, at no expense, from Tweedside farmers or London millionaires, with an absolute immunity from the possibility of poor-rates and poachers. Of course, the state of things was not everywhere so bad ; there were noble gentlemen who knew how to combine warm devotion to mountain sports with the kindly care of a hereditary tenantry ; but if any proprietor of land, whether to pay his own debts, or to save himself from poor-rates, or to humour a heartless factor, chose to clear the land of its people, and stock it with sheep or deer, there was no law to hinder him ; and public opinion, which might have complemented the deficiency of feudal law, partly from the remoteness of the region where these acts, equally inhuman and impolitic, were committed, partly from the servility of the local press, writing too often in the interest of lairds and lawyers, partly from the pernicious influence of the selfish maxim, " that a man may do what he likes with his own," partly, no doubt, in the way of reaction from the exaggerated statements and unfounded outcries of agrarian agitators without fairness, and economic speculators without sense,—from all these causes public opinion did nothing to preserve the Highlanders; accustomed itself rather, comfortably, to the idea that the sooner these barren regions, half redeemed from the primeval waters, could be disembowelled of all human population, and left in the undisturbed possession of sea-gulls and stags and salmon, so much the better. The troops of Saxon tourists who spread themselves annually into the glens and over the Bens of old Caledonia, had, of course, nothing to do with the results of economical mismanagement, stowed far away, if registered at all, in dry statistical tables and unapproachable Blue-books; it was mountains they came to see, not men; and the sheep upon a thousand hills without a single human dwelling in view, would, to their holiday associations, more readily have suggested a sonnet of Arcadian blessedness than a pamphlet of agrarian dissatisfaction. Nor were the Highlanders themselves altogether dissatisfied,—those of them at least who had begun to live like the Swiss, by making a show of their mountains and hanging on the skirts of the rich English Nimrods who, at certain seasons of the year, came to represent their old chiefs. Meanwhile the real life-blood of the people was being drained away; halls once resonant with rich social merriment, and reverberant with the traditions of a chivalrous and high-souled manhood, were dumb as death, or replaced by more pretentious edifices, which were Celtic in nothing but the ground on which they stood; the language and the music, which even till now had stirred the stoutest hearts and raised the most effective war-cry in our great British battle-fields, was treated everywhere with contempt, and deemed worthy of culture by only the more discerning few of those who naturally spoke it; everything Celtic was looked upon as destined to a hasty extinction, most worthily treated when either kicked violently out of the world, or painted all over with such a thick coat of Saxon whitewash that its distinctive features could no longer be recognised; and it was generally agreed, in influential quarters, that the only euthanasia for the fragment of the Celt that yet remained in the country was to get the Teut on his back, and be ridden out of his identity, as the Poles are by the Russians.

But the Highlanders, though they may have received sometimes treatment from the lords of the soil not a whit better than the Poles have done when sent to Siberia, were not exactly in the position of that misfortuned people; nay, not even as the poor Irish, whom the insolence of the vulgar English mind delighted to stigmatise as "aliens in blood, in language, and in religion," and treated them accordingly. The unfortunate political skits of a misguided loyalty in 1715 and 1745 had long been forgotten, and so many mighty captains of Celtic name had since then, from the rising to the setting sun, defended the boundaries of our broad empire in moments of peril, that the general feeling towards the Gaels remained that of kindliness and of admiration. Such a feeling never existed in Ireland towards the Irish. At the very moment when the sons and grandsons of the brave men who fought at Badajos and Waterloo were being shovelled in shoals from their native glens to leave a parish without a people, and gratify the selfish ambition of some scheming factor or the fancies of some doctrinaire economist, Highland colours were still seen flaunting in our regiments and at periodical aristocratic gatherings, Highland bagpipes sounded the pibroch of the clan through the old familiar glens, and feats of Celtic strength and agility were performed before groups of elegantly-dressed English ladies with admiration and applause; and though this, of course, was only a shadowy, soulless mimicry of the old life, and rather a playing at Highlanders than being honestly Highland, still even this superficial recognition of a noble but unfortunate nationality sprung from a germ of kindly sentiment that might, in some happy moment, shape itself into a deed. Here and there also there were found in the hills genuine heads of the old stock, who, like the Macpherson of Cluny, were Highlanders in their core as well as in their kilt, and not only on a gala-day, but every day of the week, and every hour of the day; and when one was lucky enough to come shoulder to shoulder with such men, there shot an electric influence from their presence with a fervour and a freshness that might melt, for the moment, the impenetrable mail of the most dogmatic economist. These things were signs of lusty life amid the general decrepitude into which the Highlands had been allowed to fall by its natural protectors. Then there was one goad of a decidedly practical character, that at length came to prick the flesh of the lords of the glen, and induce them to think that they had proceeded somewhat thoughtlessly with their cheap remedy of expatriation. All lairds have not exclusively sheep-farms, and such lairds required labourers; but the labourers were not to be found : they had retired in troops to America, where they hoped to be treated, and generally were treated, with more consideration than they had been at home. This affected the pocket, which is the grand avenue by which the hearts of a certain class of human beings in this couutry can be reached. But there was another influence also,—an influence of an intellectual character, that now began to act in favour of the Highlanders. Partly by the natural " process of the ages," partly by a stirring contagion from the continental world, with which England since the peace in 1816 was always drifting into closer connection, a change came over the spirit of John Bull's speculative faculty; and from a narrow traditional conservatism of all kinds of respectable prejudice, he bolted right out into the large field of broad historical sympathy, after

the manner of the Germans.   One fruit of this we recognise
in Grote's democratic History of Greece, another in the new
estimate of Cromwell and Frederick the Great put into
vogue by the master-touch of Carlyle's brawny brush, and
a third in the thoughtful soul and genial evangelic significance which Jowett and those who laboured with him
engrafted into the barren verbalism which had so long
lorded it over the scholarship of Oxford.   It was, in the
nature of things, scarcely possible that this new habit of
looking behind and beyond the curtain of narrow English
traditions should fail to affect in some appreciable degree
the long-neglected languages and literatures of the Celts
in these islands.   And accordingly we find the names of
Skene, M'Lauchlan, Clerk, Cameron, Robertson, and others
in Scotland, Stokes, Reeves, O'Curry, and O'Sullivan in
Ireland, teaching the better class of English readers to give
up their cherished habit of looking at our early history
only from a Saxon point of view, and to plant themselves
dramatically into the centre of Celtic life, whence alone the
true character of our mixed civilisation can be understood.
With regard to Wales, Nicolas, Stephens, and other Cymric scholars, were not less active; and though Arnold,
always happy to poke into the ribs of dogged old Philistin-
ism, failed in his attempt to induce the Oxford authorities
to found a Celtic chair in their University, there was more
of hope and encouragement in such an application having
been made at all in that quarter, than of discouragement
in its refusal.[1]   Specially in the present age a new claimant
for the regards of the learned world came upon the stage,
which worked powerfully in favour of the long-neglected
Celtic element.   I mean Comparative Philology; and this

[1] This was written before a formal proposal was made by Jesus College
to found a Celtic Chair in the University of Oxford, which I understand
from the newspapers has now been realised.

science, though capable of being pursued in a way as thorny and forbidding and purely technical as the most arid specialties of the old classical scholarship, had the good fortune to have its cause pleaded in this country by an accomplished foreigner, who united the extensive reading and accurate research of his country with a cultivated eloquence and a popular power which no native writer on the same subject has rivalled. Philology was now made palatable to the ladies, and nothing the worse for that; for a good pudding deserves a good seasoning, and with the ladies the seasoning is always an indispensable element of the compound. Along with the charms of Max Müller's exposition, the travelling habits of the age soon opened up a new vein of popular research, which drew deep from Celtic sources. I mean in the department of topographical etymology. Taylor in England, Joyce in Ireland, and Robertson in Scotland, following in the tract of Forstemann, Butmann, and other learned Germans, furnished a new sort of intellectual recreation to the more educated class of tourists, in the etymological analysis and historical interpretation of the countries and cities through which they passed. People heard with surprise now for the first time that rivers and mountains and vales, untrodden for many centuries by foot of Celt or Sclav, bore upon their visage the most undeniable evidence of a Celtic or Sclavonian baptism; and an intelligent curiosity was gratified to find that the familiar name of some romantic crag or brook or mountain hollow was a condensed expression of the most striking pictorial features of the scene. The old grey stone on the old brown moor, previously only an old grey stone and nothing more, turned out, when its Celtic designation was wisely deciphered, to be a record of some awful piety, heroic achievement, or rueful scene of human sorrow that our forefathers had enacted there. In short, thoughtful travellers made the discovery that to travel wisely, even the dead languages once spoken in transmuted homes deserved some kindly regard, much more the living language of a race, stout, fervid, chivalrous, and gallant above their compeers, and whose virtues were not the less real because unhappy circumstances had doomed them to shine in a corner. Nor was it in the direction of topography only that comparative philology opened up to fresh-minded inquirers a new and interesting field of research. Proper names of persons had their etymological history no less than names of places; and a very cursory inspection of the Glasgow Directory raised to a certainty the awakened suspicion that not a few of those who counted themselves Saxons, whose ancestors had spoken English for centuries, and who were accustomed to join with zest in ridiculing the peculiarities of the High-landers, were themselves, in every syllable of their names, as in every drop of their blood, undeniable Celts. Any shepherd-boy in the glens, however innocent of school-training, could tell a Lowland gentleman bearing such a name as *Glass*, that if he had really been of Lowland descent his name would have been *Gray;* or if he bore the name of BAIN, that his designation, with a real Lowland pedigree, would have been WHITE; and so forth. Thus may many a modern Greek, if you scrub the Hellenic polish from his skin, be declared to be an Albanian or a Sclavonian. And in the same way the "perfervid genius of the Scots" which burns in the heart of a Chalmers, a Guthrie, and a Mac-leod, when probed to the bottom, may appear to be really a Celtic fire, while your pure Saxon shall be proved to be a stout and solid but a lumpish creature comparatively. And the result of a scientifically conducted philologico-ethnogra-phical inquiry may be that in the great living machine which we call society in Scotland, it is the Saxon who supplies the iron and the wood; steam comes from the Celt.

The circumstances under which the present writer was
led to look into the philological peculiarities of the Gaelic
tongue were as follows. Like others of my countrymen,
I had been brought up under the traditions of the classical
schoolmasters, who directed all our youthful ambition to
things far distant in time and space, and never dreamt
of hinting that the wild primrose at our feet, peeping up
modestly from the base of some oozy slope, might be
worth looking at scientifically, as well as the Victoria regia
spreading forth its huge broad leaves and unfolding the
fragrance of its rich white petals on the sunny breast of
some Peruvian lagoon. Our native Scottish music and
lyric poetry, second to none in literary history, was never
once mentioned as a subject worthy of scholastic recognition; both these things, as nothing conducive to a man's
" advancement in the world," were left to the vulgar influences of the street and the fireside. Gaelic, of course,
though existing quite in a vivid state a few miles up the
country, in the estimation of those nice quoters of Horace
and Virgil was a barbarism as little imagined as the Um-
brian and Oscan dialects might be to a polished literary
gentleman of the Augustan age in Rome. Well, I grew
up in ignorance and apathy, like other young men who
had received the benefit of a classical education, and made
the usual tour through the Highland glens, from Ballater
to Blair-Athole and Loch Tay, without taking note that
there was any such language as Gaelic in the world. ·
Some ten or fifteen years ago, however, having arrived at
man's estate, and learnt better how to use my eyes and
ears, upon one of my frequent vagabond flights through the
Highland hills, I took up my quarters for some weeks at
Kinloch-Ewe, and then and there I picked up my first
mustard-seed of the rare old language, somewhat as follows. It seemed only a human thing to speak occasionally

to the men who hang about inns and give tendance to men and horses, and as the weather cannot always be talked about, and even dogs, grouse, and salmon will occasionally fail, I fell upon the device of trying a little philology. So I inquired of the lad who was tightening the belly-band of the Rosinante that was to lend us a cast towards Loch Torridon what was the Gaelic for a horse. "*Each*," he replied. Here, of course, I recognised one of my oldest acquaintances in the grammar-school—*equus*, with the tail lopped off, and the original Indo-European *k* softened down after the favourite fashion of the Caledonian Celts into a *ch*. So far successful, I then asked what was the Gaelic for a *mare*, and got for answer *capull*. Here again was an old college friend, whom I remembered having first seen in the company of that pleasant little pudgy lyrist (*lepidus homunculus*) of the Augustan age, from whom to quote fluently was considered a valid certificate for the degree of D.D. in the then extant Marischal College of Aberdeen. Encouraged by this first essay, I went on to ask what was the name of that high hill there, pointing to a huge jagged Ben a little to the south, with two sharp points united by a long ridge or spine, indented all along as it were with canine teeth. "That," said the lad, "is Ben Eigh." "And what does *Eigh* mean?" "A file." Here my Latin was at fault, though I found afterwards that this word also signified *ice;* and that both the English and the Gaelic could be scientifically deduced from the Greek πήγ—νυμι. Anon, however, the Latin cropped up again; for taking part in the local worship, according to the Presbyterian form, next Sunday, in the school-house (there being no church in that quarter), I determined to notice specially what word would be repeated oftenest in the course of the service: this turned out to be AGUS; in which, of course, I immediately recognised the Latin *ac*, the German *auch*, and the Scotch *eik*, all, I have no doubt, connected with the verb *aug-eo*, to increase. Proceeding on the same track, I found that nothing was easier than to cull a small collection of Gaelic words from the mere names of the places through which I travelled, aided by accidental incidents. The very name of the broad sloping Ben which I saw before me every morning on the north side of Loch Maree, Ben *Sliabh*, was manifestly the Latin *clivus*, and that from the Greek κλίνω, the original form of the English *lean*. One other circumstance I will mention in connection with these peripatetic studies in Gaelic philology. As most of the country people whom I catechised had received no school drill in grammar, partly from the general misfortune of their position, partly from a superstitious idea—say rather lazy prejudice—entertained by certain school authorities, that the study of the mother tongue is prejudicial to the acquirement of any other language, I was often baffled in my pursuit of Gaelic by the answer, " *There's no Gaelic on 't, sir*," and this in cases where I soon learnt to find from my pocket dictionary[1] that my informant was altogether wrong. There was Gaelic on 't ; but the lad or lass to whom I put the question, though exercising a bilingual faculty, had never been trained to leap dexterously from the one form of speech to the other ; and as a confused attorney often fumbles in vain about his tables for papers which are nevertheless there, so the Celt who knows only a little shallow currency of colloquial English seems to have forgot his Gaelic also, and in all likelihood can read neither his Gaelic nor his English Bible without labour and sorrow. This is the natural result of the stupid system of neglecting the mother tongue, and forcing English down the throat

---

[1] *A Pronouncing Gaelic Dictionary, to which is prefixed a concise Gaelic Grammar*, by Neil MacAlpine. Edinburgh : Maclachlan & Stewart.

of innocent children who can no more be changed into
Saxons by a mere stroke of pedagogy than the heather on
the hills can blush itself into roses from hearing a lecture
by the Professor of Botany.

I have set down these small personal experiences of
first lessons in Gaelic, principally because I have found a
notion pretty generally prevalent that it is an extremely
difficult language, and not to be overcome by any ordinary
resolution. Here, as in more grave matters, ignorance
proves herself the mother of imagination, which makes
cowards of us all. For the sake of those who may be
disposed to follow my track through these unfrequented
ways, I will jot down here the remaining steps of my procedure in the acquisition of the venerable old tongue. I
first took the Gaelic Bible, which from my previous familiarity with the English I soon learnt to read.[1] Monro's
Grammar helped me over the principal difficulties of
flexion; and for the pronunciation—like the French, somewhat peculiar—MacAlpine's Dictionary, before mentioned,
did admirable service. In order to ascertain how far my
original impressions of a strong affinity with Latin were
correct, I took the occasion offered by rainy days—not
unfrequent at certain seasons of the year in the Highlands—to run over the dictionary, and make a classifica-
tion of the radical words according to their apparent affinity

---

[1] Southey, I remember, somewhere in his diary says that it was his
fashion always to commence the study of a new language with a version
of the New Testament; and there can be no doubt that to those who
know their Bibles a better method can scarcely be proposed. In fact, if
any Highland mother, anxious to give her son a good Christian education,
were to ask me how best to proceed, I should say, without a moment's
hesitation, let him read the Gaelic Bible daily along with the English,
and translate the one back into the other alternately, and this will be a
way to work the Gospel into his head and his heart, a hundred times more
efficient than any amount of Greek he is likely to carry off from a ten
years' classical training in Eton and Oxford.

with Latin, Greek, or German. I was thus enabled to start with some hundreds of roots already familiar to me under a slightly altered form. While pursuing this book-ish method, I had, of course, at the same time, being resident among the hills some three or four months every summer, ample opportunity to pick up various current vocables from the mouth of the people. After some years of altogether fitful and broken study in this fashion (for I never dreamt at first of making a serious business of the language), I began to be annoyed by that disagreeable sensation of incompleteness which so often accompanies fragmentary and superficial knowledge; so, without aban-doning altogether the easy beaten track of the Gaelic Testa-ment, I plunged for a bold variety into the bright streams and dark lochs of lyric poetry in the Highlands, and began to rejoice in the sweet melody of *Màiri laghach* and other popular Celtic airs. But as a man cannot be singing always, any more than he can make a dinner upon honey, I looked about for prose in various directions; and as I happened to be living not far from the district where Prince Charlie landed in 1745, I found the life of this brilliant adventurer by Mackenzie (Edinburgh, 1844) most suitable for my purpose. Anon I stumbled on the *History of Scotland* by Mackenzie, and the *History of the Reformation* by Mackay, with a translation of Fox's *Book of Martyrs* by Dr. MacGillivray; not to mention various entertaining scraps of biography, history, and fictitious narrative, which I found in the Gaelic periodical called *The Gàel.* This style of reading furnished me by degrees with a pretty large vocabulary, but gave me no help in the ready use of those colloquial terms which are most neces-sary for intercourse with the people. To remedy this defect, my studies sought their natural complement in the *Highland Tales* by John Campbell of Islay, and the *High-*

land Dialogues by the Reverend Norman Macleod, the father of the late distinguished genial evangelist and apostle of that name, in the *Teachdaire,* an account of which will be given in Chapter v. below. After this there remained nothing for me to do but to keep steadily reading on, an hour or two a day, till by frequent repetition the dictionary should become superfluous. This, of course, was merely a matter of resolution : the road was plain; the only remaining difficulty was to go on step by step, and not to flag; as indeed it will be found generally that it is weakness of will, and not lack of capacity, that is the great bar to intellectual progress among those who have any wish to know.[1]

The objections which are generally urged to the study of the Gaelic language are of that description which it is always easy for ignorance to invent, but which are so utterly false and flimsy that they seem scarce worthy of answer to a person who knows anything. A large number, indeed, of current fallacies sported on all public questions might be conveniently ticketed under the category—apologies for doing nothing. It is so comfortable to sit on your easy chair after dinner, with a bottle of orthodox old port before you, and your pipe in your mouth, and to think that every man is "a d——d fool" who wishes you to do anything beyond the customary routine of your shop, or your church, or your paternal estate. It may be useful, however, occasionally to press logic into the service against this tremendous power of inertness, if not with the hope to move it, at least with the satisfaction of making certain very clever people look stupid for a

---

[1] After writing this, I found that for acquiring a knowledge of colloquial Gaelic, there are few books preferable to the Gaelic translation of Bunyan's *Pilgrim's Progress* (Edinburgh, 1840). There is also a large quarto edition, more recent, which I have seen, but do not possess.

moment.   Well, in the first place we are asked, Why maintain an uncouth language, which keeps people in barbarism, and builds up an impenetrable wall of partition between the Celt and the rest of the civilised world ? To which I have several answers : *first*, the language is not barbarous, but a very fine and polished dialect, rather too polished, somewhat like French, and specially adapted for music, as we shall prove by and by ; *secondly*, it is not so much the possession of their own language, their own traditions, and their own sentiments, that separates the Gael from the rest of the world, but the remoteness of his geographical position, and the remissness of the British Government in not having long ago organised an efficient school-system in those remote regions, of which the teaching of English should have formed an integral part.   And as for the mother tongue, in the parallel case of Lowland boys we know that it is not the knowledge of English at school that prevents a boy from learning Latin, but it is either the bad method of his master, who does not know how to teach him, or it is the indifference of the boy, who does not care to learn.   But this latter element, however active in a classical school, certainly does not show itself in the Highlands ; rather the contrary : every poor Highlander is, above all things, eager to learn English ; and if he does not see his aspirations always crowned with success, it is the fault of his superiors, who do not send · schoolmasters into the glens, properly equipped with the two-edged sword of the " Beurla " and the native Gaelic, as every Highland teacher ought unquestionably to be. The idea that a knowledge of the mother tongue, under such circumstances, acts as a hindrance to the acquisition of English is entirely unfounded.   The mother tongue is *there;* and, instead of building up a wall against the Saxon, which the young Gael cannot overleap, it is just the natural stepping-stone which you must use to bring the sturdy mountaineer into the domain of your more smooth civilisation. The policy of stamping out the characteristics of a noble race, by carrying on a war against the language, is essentially barbarous ; it can be excused only, if excusable at all, by the existence of such a political mis-alliance as that between Russia and Poland ; and, in fact, I fear there is to be found, in this quarter of the world, a certain not altogether inconsiderable section or party who hold, if not in theory, yet practically, by this Russian principle. The sooner—I have heard them say as much—the Saxon, who is God's peculiar elect vessel, can swallow up the Celt, so that there shall be no more Irishmen in Ireland, and no more Highlandmen in the Highlands, so much the better. This is a doctrine altogether in harmony with the teaching of a distinguished master of physical science, which, transferred to the moral world, simply means that the stronger are always right when they leap upon the back of the weaker, and use them for their own purposes ; but it is a doctrine directly in the teeth of all gospel, and which allows a man to play the wolf or the fox whenever he can against his brethren, and baptise himself, with all cheapness, a hero for the achievement. Are the men who advocate such inhuman measures not sometimes touched with shame when they find themselves identified with the old Roman robbers, who civilised the world with the sword of rude invasion, and of the march of whose legions it was justly said by their own wise historian,—*Ubi solitudinem faciunt pacem adpellant?* St. Paul, of course, inculcates the exact contrary doctrine ; for he tells us to " condescend to men of low estate," and to " weep with them that weep," and to " rejoice with them that do rejoice." How any Highland proprietor can reconcile his belief in these texts with the principle of forcibly stamping out the Gaelic language I cannot comprehend. But I will put down here what the noble son of a good Gaelic laird has printed with regard to the position of landed proprietors in this matter. "I find," says John Campbell of Islay, "that lectures are delivered to Sunday-school children to prove that Gaelic is part of the Divine curse, and Highland proprietors tell me that it is 'a bar to the advancement of the people.' But if there is any truth in this assertion, it is equally true, on the other hand, that English is a bar to the advancement of proprietors if they cannot speak to those who pay their rents; and it is the want of English, not the possession of Gaelic, which retards the advancement of those who seek employment where English is spoken. So Highland proprietors should learn Gaelic, and teach English."[1] This is sense and justice. The Gaelic people, while they do not forget their Gaelic, should study English; and the Highland proprietors, retaining their English, should study Gaelic.

So much for the middle wall of partition. But, in the second place, it is often said, Why should a man go out of his way to study a language which has no literature? The answer to this is twofold,—*first*, that the language has a literature, and a very valuable one; *second*, that we are not arguing here with persons who are expected to go out of their way to learn a foreign language, but with those who, having a native language at their fireside, go out of their way . to neglect, to disown, and to forget it. As to the literature, we shall show particularly what it is worth by and by. Meanwhile, the existence of such a book as M'Kenzie's *Beauties of Gaelic Poetry* (which would make a score of volumes as poetry is printed), with the simple mention of the names of Alastair M'Donald, Duncan Ban M'Intyre,

---

[1] A Plea for Gaelic, in *Highland Tales*, vol. iv. p. 358.

Dugald Buchanan, and, for prose, the late Dr. Norman Macleod and the other writers in the *Teachdaire*, not to mention Ossian, may be sufficient to expose the ignorance of the persons who say that Gaelic has no literature. But let it be so ; let Zeuss, and Apel, and Ebrard, and Windisch, and all the other learned Germans, who " go out of their way" to study Celtic, be declared fools; the question still remains, why intelligent persons, living in the midst of a Gaelic-speaking population, should not pick up the beautiful wild flowers of popular utterance that gem the glens with beauty as they pass. And then, what do we mean by *literature ?* Is the mere printed book the valuable thing ? or is it not rather the living heart and soul and impassioned utterance of a people, wherein the true value of a literature dwells ? To a man with open eyes and a warm heart, living a Highlander in the Highlands, the language of the people is valuable simply because it is the language of the people, and, as such, contains at once the oldest signature and the newest expression of their best memories and their loftiest aspirations. Whoso wishes to live with the people from within, and not merely from without, will wish to know their language. Whoso is indifferent to the people, and all that marks them out in history as a distinct and noticeable type of humanity, will be indifferent to their language.

Again, it is asked, Why should any support be given to a language which is dying, and will be dead in a very few years if not artificially supported ? To which I answer, Why should we act violently and contrary to nature by endeavouring to stamp out a language which, as a social fact, is obstinately alive, not only here, but in America, and not rather, so long as it is alive, treat it kindly and use it wisely ? It is by no means an easy thing to root out a language twined, as every mother-tongue is, round the deepest fibres of the popular heart; but let it be that the Gaelic language is destined to die out in a hundred years at the most, is that any reason why, being there, it should not meet with a kindly recognition from wise and good Christian men? Philologers will tell you that the spoken language of the people to hearing ears often reveals more secrets of the beautiful framework of human speech than all the dead treasures of the library; and supposing the language dead, like other departed things will it not acquire a peculiar new interest by this very fact that it is no more? and shall we not then begin to blame ourselves, as foolish mortals so often must, that we made so little use of it when alive? Our wisdom certainly here, as in all other matters, is to avoid extremes. While we do not put into operation any artificial machinery for exciting a galvanic life in a language that is flickering to its natural close, we abstain, on the other hand, from refusing to nourish the mountain child with his natural food, and to check the spontaneous outflow of Celtic sentiment and Celtic song by an artificial cram of Saxon grammars and dictionaries. To teach English to all the children of the British empire is an imperial duty; to smother Gaelic where it naturally exists is a local tyranny.

Lastly, the Gaelic language, we are told by those who are eager for its extermination, is so peculiar, so difficult, and so remote from all the ordinary capacities of persons who use civilised speech, that it cannot be learned without an expenditure of time far beyond the value of any attainable result. Now those who make this objection always confound two things of the most opposite nature—the difficulty of a language when acquired by a stranger, and its difficulty to a native. The former is often a very formidable affair; the latter sinks to a negative quantity, and may be practically disregarded. It may be said generally, indeed, that no language is difficult to the person who speaks it, and who draws it in, he knows not how, as he sucked the milk from his mother's breast. The only difficulty with the mother tongue, to a mother's son, is in learning to read it; but this also in some languages is much easier than in others, and in Gaelic is much easier than in English. For all that the little Highland boy who has been taught to read English requires in order to manipulate his Gaelic Bible, is simply to transfer some of the simplest habits of English spelling to the familiar spoken tongue, and all is learned. The letters, in the first place, are the same—not, as in Irish, foreign to English eyes;[1] and the habit of softening or slurring an aspirate consonant, as in *might, light, fight,* has merely to be extended to a larger family of such cases, and the reading of Gaelic becomes as easy as the reading of Latin to an English boy in a classical school. Thus, in the middle of *saoghal* and *sabhal,* the two medial consonants are omitted, and the spoken words, *saol* and *sawl,* remain; and in the same way *b, m, g, c,* at the commencement of a word, are softened into *bh, mh, gh,* and *ch,* whose pronunciation is as uniform to the ear as to the eye. It is not, therefore, the difficulty to the learner, but the ignorance, indifference, laziness, and prejudice of the teacher, that makes the reading of Gaelic so shamefully neglected in many Gaelic schools. It is an act of intellectual suicide of which an intelligent people should be ashamed. As to strangers, no doubt Gaelic is considerably more difficult to an Englishman than either

---

[1] I believe that the use of the old character in Ireland, combined with the less active habit of Bible-reading natural to a Roman Catholic population, are the two principal causes which have made Irish at the present moment little better than a dead language, as compared with the vitality of Welsh and Gaelic. The Welsh, however, from certain social causes, is much more vital than the Gaelic.

French or German, for the plain and obvious reason that English is a composite language, which already contains French and German as its two principal ingredients; while the peculiar phenomenon of the change of the initial consonant by aspiration—of which anon—naturally adds another difficulty with which the Englishman and the classical scholar must specially grapple. But there is nothing here to shake a man of common pluck out of his composure, any more than in the formidable array of irregular verbs in Greek, or in Hebrew the mystery of the roots. It is imagination here, as in most other cases, that either creates or magnifies the difficulty; and the mother of imagination, as we had before to remark, is ignorance.

The cumulative impression made on an impartial mind by the statement of these objections is, that they are all alike unfounded, proceeding as they do either from the ignorance which assumes where it has never taken the trouble to inquire; or from the insolence of the many delighting in an unkindly way to lord it over the few; or from the prevalence of the vulgar fallacy that things near our feet are unworthy of being looked at, simply because they are near our feet, while things far away ought to be run after and searched into, chiefly because they are far away; or again, from the short-sighted notion common among self-styled practical men, that nothing is worthy of being done or known in the world which does not bring money directly into a man's pocket; or, finally, from that meagreness of soul which delights in the constant repetition of some bald monotony, and to which that rich variety of type in which nature luxuriates, acts as a fretful irritant rather than an elevating stimulus. With such considerations —it is scarcely necessary to observe—neither philosophy nor science, nor poetry nor good policy, has anything in common. Neither in any way is it the character of society, as it has grown up in Britain, to rejoice in centralised monotony rather than in local diversity of type. And in respect of the general attitude to be maintained towards the unifying advances of so-called modern civilisation, a large-hearted policy would seek rather kindly to cherish what inherited varieties of type we still retain than violently to exterminate them.

Having cleared the ground of this rubbish, let us now proceed to some real business. The Gaelic language is one of the oldest and least mongrel types of the great Aryan family of speech, which has entered so largely into history as the organ of the highest forms of human civilisation, both in the East and West. With the exception, indeed, of the two famous branches of the Semitic family—the Hebrew and the Arabic—the Aryan family contains within itself everything that has notably contributed to human progress from the earliest historical tradition down to the present hour. The people who in prehistoric times used the great mother tongue, at present known only by its various-faced offspring, seem to have swarmed off from the great central tableland of Persia, one half eastward, forming fruitful settlements on the banks of the Indus and the Ganges, known in the book-world as the creators of the great Sanscrit literature—and the other half westward in various streams, the fountain-heads of all European culture, under forms far more rich and various than the less mobile type of society rendered possible in the East. Of these Western streams, the most notable, by far, were the Greek and Roman, to the former of which we trace back the main features of the intellec-tual, and to the latter the grand outlines of the political and juridical physiognomy of the existing states of Europe. In philological character the languages spoken by the Greeks and Romans bear a strong family likeness; but their fates since the breaking up of the classical world have been singularly different. While the Greek, by the weight of its rich intellectual traditions, has preserved itself, with a few insignificant changes, as a perfectly pure and indefinitely luxuriant form of living speech, the language of the Romans, crumbling down with the great political fabric which it supported, afforded materials of which new languages of a specifically modern character were created,—French, Italian, Portuguese, Spanish, and a few others of minor note, all of which, to borrow a geological phrase, may be fitly designated as Metamorphic Latin. Next in importance to the Greco-Roman branch must be reckoned the Teutonic, raised in the shape of modern German to a grand position in the front rank both of speculation and action. The language spoken by the Germans, though in colloquial usage liberally sprinkled with fragments of Latin, Greek, and French, is in its structure essentially homogeneous, and in its most classical forms borrows none of its beauties from any other variety of human speech. The language spoken by the English, originally, like the German, a pure and uncorrupted Teutonic dialect, in the course of time, by frequent rude shocks of political change, had its natural growth altogether maimed; and instead of growing up into the likeness of a luxuriant and wide-spreading tree, presented—after a long course of simmering in the pot of Latin, French, and Greek ingredients, mingled in the strangest and most arbitrary fashion—the appearance as of a mottled cake or a porphyritic flag-stone, . in which a hasty huddlement of unsymmetrical fragments had produced a sort of motley beauty which the most cunning design would have been inadequate to produce. Less fortunate hitherto in their outward development, though certainly not composed of less capable elements, are the other members of the great Aryan family that are now playing, or have in times not far distant played, a

prominent part in the great drama of public life in Europe.
The Russians, with their Slavonian dependants under
German dominion, in Bohemia, and other parts of the
Austrian empire, have only in the present century dared
to throw off that dependence on foreign languages and
literatures which marked an imported civilisation; but
there can be no doubt that with the reign of the late
Emperor Nicholas, the seed was sown of a luxuriant growth
of purely national culture, which may at no distant period
open to the great Slavonic language a field of successful
operation, as wide as ever was spread before the ambition
of imperial Rome.   For the Celtic languages, on the other
hand, it is difficult even for the most sanguine to predict a
brilliant future.   Untoward political circumstances have
combined with remote geographical position to force what
remains of the great Celtic stock into the position of mere
adjuncts of an essentially Teutonic civilisation.   No doubt
in France the Celtic genius remains, and has sent out from
time to time flashes of vivifying social electricity to which
every country in Europe owes much of its present progressive impulses; but France, though inspired with a Celtic soul,
speaks a Latin language, and in a philological aspect is at
the present moment as much a part of Rome as Cornwall
is a part of England.   As master of his own peculiar type
of Aryan speech, the Celt has maintained himself, and that
in rather a sorry fashion, only in Ireland, the north-western
half of Scotland, in Brittany, and in Wales; and the
literature which he has handed down, whether in the
Hibernian, the Gaelic, or the Cymric form, though naturally
dear to those who speak it, and of no common significance
in reference to the early history of the British Isles, with
certain specific attractions also for the eye of the philologer,
is neither of sufficient extent nor of intrinsic value enough
to exert any sensible influence on the great tidal currents

of European culture. No doubt, it is still on the cards, as one may say, that Wales, or Ireland, or the Scottish Highlands, shall produce a poet of a truly popular character, who may deserve the honours of a world-wide renown, no less than the great Ayrshire ploughman; but the neglect with which the exuberant poetical productions of Alastair M'Donald, Duncan Ban M'Intyre, Rob Donn, and other Celtic bards, have been treated by the general British public, encourages only the faintest hope that even a Celtic Burns, were he to appear to-morrow, would be able to achieve for his works the celebrity which they might deserve. It was the good fortune of Burns that he lived in a district close under the eye of the most progressive and prosperous part of Scotland, while the language which he used, though at first no small obstruction to his fame, was so little different from classical English, that a scholarly Oxonian or Cantab might delight to study it for recreation, just as a learned Greek of Alexandria, in the classical days, might make a philological excursion amongst the boors of Doric Thebes or Syracuse. Had Robert Burns sung in Gaelic instead of Scotch, his works at the present day might have been as little known in Europe, or even in Edinburgh, as the satires of Rob Donn.

In attempting a scientific anatomy of the materials of which any language is composed, the first thing to be done is to discount the foreign or loan words. These words, no doubt, in one sense, and so far as general currency is concerned, form part of the language, and it may be not the least prominent part; but to the eye of the philologer they present the appearance of a foreigner, who may have adopted the dress and assumed the manner of the country where he sojourns, but about whom there is always something that, to the practised eye, indicates the want of native blood. But the external marks by which these words are recognised do not always indicate with equal clearness the source from which they sprang. In the words *prestige, éclat,* and *rendezvous,* for instance, as they are used in current English, the French character of the utterance shines out so manifestly as to be evident to a mere schoolboy; but in the great stock of Latin words which come to us through the French, and which in the days of Chaucer perhaps were scarcely distinguishable from pure French, are now so thoroughly Anglicised, whether by some slight alteration or curtailment, or by the mere backward shifting of the accent, that no one thinks of their origin except historically, as when one says that the Queen of England and Empress of the Indies is by legitimate descent the Electress of Hanover. It will thus be a matter of considerable difficulty sometimes, and of a delicate historical sense, to determine whether any given word substantially identical with the same word in a cognate language forms part of the original stock of both languages, or is a later importation. And in settling this point the conclusions of pure science are apt to be strangely disturbed by a wrong-headed patriotism, a virtue which has as little to do here as mathematics has with mint sauce. Most Celtic writers on etymology, indeed, seem to have proceeded on a principle exactly the reverse of what Aristotle lays down as the guiding motive of great political reformers—ζητοῦσιν οὐ τὸ πάτριον ἀλλὰ τἀγαθόν, " *They seek not what is patriotic, but what is good.*"[1] And so far has this sacred rage for absolute Celtism proceeded, that they not only contend for the Celtic origin of many words manifestly borrowed from the Latin in historical times, but they will employ themselves in spinning the most transcendental theories from the supposed Celtic anatomy of words whose real Latin or Greek etymology lies patent to a

[1] *Pol.* ii. 8.

mere schoolboy. As an example of this sort of patriotic etymology take the following from a book otherwise full of most excellent matter, and inspired by a spirit of manhood and independence far from universal even among those who boast the purest Celtic blood in their veins :—

"The Culdees were in spirit evangelical, and, like the evangelical clergy of the present day, not attached to, or perhaps even tolerant of, natural theology. Hence, probably, their hostility to the Druid priesthood. But they were incapable of misrepresenting them either in their lives or doctrines. The statement that the Druids offered human sacrifices may have been believed by, but did not originate with, the Culdees. The report may have arisen from the circumstance that the Druids were the criminal judges among the Celtic clans, and that the criminals sentenced to capital punishment were executed by phlebotomy within the Druid circle. The corrupt Roman theologist who could not comprehend a worship without a sacrifice may have believed that these criminals were innocent victims sacrificed to superstition, and the basin-like hollow to be found in all the Druid altar-stones to receive the blood of the executed criminals may have confirmed, if it did not give rise to, that belief. Had the Culdees been capable of misrepresenting the religion of the Druids, they would not have preserved their name for God, the soul, the good, the bad, etc., since these names are descriptive, and refute every falsity circulated in reference to their religion and morality. They had three names for God: *deo*, from the roots *ti*, a great being, and *eol*, knowledge; *dia*, from *ti* and *agh*, pronounced *á*, good; and *bith-uile*, abbreviated *bel*, from *bith*, life, and *uile*, all. It is thus seen that the Druid represented God as the great, the good Being, the life of all. He had two names also for the soul,—*deo*, from his regarding the soul as an emanation of

God. Hence when a person dies the Highlander does not say, 'thuair (huayr) e'm bas,' as he would say of a beast; but, 'chai an deo as,' the soul has gone out of him. The other name of the soul is still more striking, *anam*, from *an*, antagonism, defiance, and *am*, time,—that is, the antagonist or defier of time, or, in other words, the immortal."[1]

This is mere Bedlam. With *am*, however, and *anama* and ἄνεμος we have nothing in the meantime to do; our first business being, as we said, to cast out all words of foreign origin, partly that we may get a clear result, partly with a practical view, that, in learning the language, we may start with so much material already known. On what principles then are we to determine the pedigree of a word in doubtful cases? Plainly by a historical method in the first place, just as we determine the pedigree of a family; for mere guessing only indicates where knowledge may be found, never finds it; as, for example, one man may derive the name of Campbell from the Norman *Campo-bello*, and another from the Gaelic *Cam-beul* (wry-mouth), both with equal probability and with an equal lack of scientific certainty. To attain this certainty the first step is to settle how the presumptions lie. Is it likely that under known historical conditions such and such a word should be adopted from such and such a source? Now the circumstances which determine the people who speak any one language to adopt words from any other language are so obvious that there can, in the general case, be little difficulty in perceiving from what presumptions we ought to start. It is the simple Darwinian law that with mathematical certainty solves this, as so many other matters: in the struggle for existence, the stronger conquers and the

---

[1] *Language, Poetry, and Music of the Highland Clans*, by Donald Campbell (Edinburgh, 1862), p. 16.

weaker goes to the wall. The only further question here is, In what does the strength consist, that peculiar strength which conquers in the matter of language? And the answer is plain : It is political dominance or intellectual strength, or both together, that enable one language to conquer another, and by conquest either to produce absolute extermination (not at all an easy matter, however, in any case) or to establish that sort of dependency which marks the relation of the borrower to the lender. By intellectual superiority Greek conquered Latin; by political ascendency Latin conquered Gaul and Spain; by preponderance in both kinds the Mediæval Roman and the Romanesque languages of more modern times conquered the Armoric, Cymric, and Gaelic Celts of the extreme west. To a man who knows the commonest processes of international influence it were simply a miracle if the present dwellers beyond "the rough boundaries" in the Scottish Highlands were found using a language altogether unadulterated by mediæval Latinisms and Anglicisms of later adoption. Even the Greek, with all its wealth and force of inherited intelligence and religious cohesion, during the period of its subjection to the Turks and Italians, did not find its panoply proof at all points against the temporary settlement of a Tartar and Italic phraseology; much less was it to be expected that the mountain-dwellers beyond the Severn and the Tay should have preserved their language intact from the elevating contagion of the Latin forces, which for long centuries were both above them and amid them. No doubt a race of mountaineers driven into remote regions by a political power like that of the Romans in Britain master of all the plains, and preserving a rude independence behind their granite fastnesses, might have little temptation to borrow political or military phraseology from their declared enemies ; but we must remember that as Greece conquered

Rome by her literature, so Rome conquered Celtism by her
Church; and the Churchmen who ruled in those days were
men who wielded in the most important matters a secular
as well as a spiritual power, and were in fact not only the
priests, but the statesmen, the men of business, the land-
improvers, and the literary organs of their age. We are
therefore justly entitled to presume that under their powerful influence the Gaelic language would adopt terms borrowed from classical or low Latin, in the same manner
that Rome adopted her philosophical and scientific terminology from Athens. To what an extent this took place
the following list, which makes not the slightest pretence
to completeness, will abundantly testify:—

1.	Abhlan,	Oblatum.
2.	Abstol,	Apostolus.
3.	Achd,	Actum.
4.	Agair,	Agere.
5.	Altair,	Altare.
6.	Aor,	Oro,
7.	Bachull,	Baculus.
8.	Baist,	Baptizare.
9.	Balladh,	Vallum.
10.	Beist,	Bestia.
11.	Long,	Navis longa.
12.	Bonneid,	Bonnet.
13.	Buideal,	Bottle.
14.	Caisdeal,	Castellum.
15.	Cäs,	Casus.
16.	Cathair,	Cathedra.
17.	Cill,	Cella.
18.	Cleir,	Clerus.
19.	Coisrig,	Consecrare.
20.	Sòlas,	Solatium.
21.	Coirbte,	Corruptus.
22.	Comhfortaich,	Confortare.
23.	Companach,	Companion.
24.	Comunn,	Communis.

25. Connspoid,   .   Consputare.
26. Sagart, .   .   .   Sacerdos.
27. Fabhor, .   .   .   Favor.
28. Feill,   .   .   .   Vigiliae—or—Festalis.
29. Creid,   .   .   .   Credo.
30. Creutair,   .   .   Creatura.
31. Crois,   .   .   .   Crux.
32. Crun,   .   .   .   Corona.
33. Cuairt, .   .   .   Court.
34. Cubaid,   .   .   Cubeta (Spanish).
35. Cabar, .   .   .   Capreolus (see Littre in *Chevron*).
36. Curam, .   .   .   Cura.
37. Damhsa,   .   .   Dance.
38. Deacamh, .   .   Decuma.
39. Deblidh,   .   .   Debilis.
40. Diseart,   .   .   Desertum.
41. Pris,   .   .   .   Pretium.
42. Cognis, .   .   .   Conscientia.
43. Dubailt,   .   .   Duplex.
44. Eaglais,   .   .   Ecclesia.
45. Easbuig,   .   .   Episcopus.
46. Eisimplar, .   .   Exemplare.
47. Faidhir,   .   .   Fair, feriæ.
48. Falluinn,   .   .   Pallium.
59. Ifrinn, .   .   .   Infernus.
50. Diabhol,   .   .   Diabolus.
51. Deamhan, .   .   Dæmon.
52. Deisciobuil,   .   Discipulus.
53. Onair,   .   .   .   Honor.
54. Maduinn, .   .   Matutinus.
55. Feasgar,   .   .   Vesper.
56. Nollaig,   .   .   Natalis.
57. Collainn,   .   .   Calendæ.
58. Luireach, .   .   Lorica.

On some of these words, as *luireach* for instance, a doubt
might be raised whether it did not rather form part of
the original stock of both languages; but with regard to
the great body of them, no person accustomed to deal

with such questions can for a moment doubt. In fact, considering the extremely curtailed form in which Latin words often appear in Gaelic, as when *pater* becomes *athair*, pronounced *aar*, and *plenus* becomes *lan*, there can be little doubt that not a few Gaelic words whose origin is not written on their forehead nevertheless stand where they stand in the family, not by birth but by adoption; or, to use the expressive phraseology of the Gaels themselves, they are not sons of the womb but of the breast. So much for Latin. If we ask now what further influences, social, political, or intellectual, exercised a contagious dominance over the Gaelic tongue, the answer is at hand. The maritime dominion of the Scandinavians for four hundred years, up to the battle of Largs, in 1263, and the adoption of the English language by the Scottish Court from the days of Malcolm Canmore, erected the platforms from which this influence was exercised. Of the Scandinavian influence, prominent marks meet the tourist everywhere in the topography and terminology of the west and north-west Highlands.[1] Every *nish*, for example, so common in Mull and Skye, and even on the east coast, sometimes near Tain, is the ear-mark of the Norwegian sailor, which has blotted out the original *Ruadh* or *Ross*, just as St. Andrews has supplanted the old names of Mucross (Swine's Cape) and Kilribhan (Kingsmoor), by which that celebrated academical seat was anciently known. And under the same influence it will always seem rather probable that the Gaelic words *bata, stuirm, seol*, and some others, are borrowed from the cognate forms of the German *boot, sturm*, and *segel*. With regard to English,

---

[1] Captain Thomas read an interesting paper before the Antiquarian Society of Edinburgh, to the effect that two-thirds of the topographical names of places and farms in the Western Islands are, to this day, not Gaelic but Norse. See *Transactions* for 1876.

whether in the general sense of that term, or in the specific form of Lowland Scotch, there can be little doubt that its operation in corrupting the Gaelic tongue has been very powerful, and is increasing in potency every day. Of this there is no need to bring forward special examples. If even in a language of such lofty intellectual independence and such rich linguistic resources as the German, we can scarcely light upon a paragraph of a newspaper in which French and Latin phrases are not found hopping about quite at their ease, much less in a language like Gaelic, whose literary culture has been scanted, and whose social front is constantly retreating, can it be expected that the language of daily life should be able to keep itself free from constant accessions of half-assimilated or altogether unassimilated Saxonisms. There is perhaps nothing that a traveller from the Lowlands associates more closely with life in the Highlands than a plate of " ham and eggs ;" and yet I remember well one day when, being wet to the skin, in a little inn not far from Arisaig, I marched from the cold discomfort of the parlour into the reeky warmth of the kitchen, and immediately began holding some philological discourse with a little dirty boy, who was performing certain culinary ministrations about the fireside. " What is the Gaelic for *ham and eggs* ?" said I. " There is no Gaelic on't," said the lad, after a little stupid consideration. " No Gaelic on't!" said I ; " nonsense ! I know the Gaelic for *eggs* myself ; there must of course be Gaelic for *ham :* surely you know the Gaelic for *ham and eggs ?*" But the boy only looked more profoundly stupid ; and all that I could get out of him was, " *There pe no Gaelic on't, sir !*" This is a sample of how the mother tongue dies out, as inch by inch the speech of the dominant majority makes its irrepressible inroads : just as we find in Ireland, when you ask a peasant the name of some old conical Ben, expecting to hear some Irish appellation, you are bluntly told that it is " SUGAR-LOAF," and nothing more does he know of it. Let this therefore pass without more formal illustration. More instructive for philological purposes it may prove to inquire how far, from the manner in which the Latin words in the above lists are modified so as to meet the habit of the Gaelic ear, conclusions can be drawn as to the general genius and character of the borrowing language; for that such conclusions may be drawn is evident, inasmuch as the ear of no people acts in an arbitrary and capricious way, but always according to a certain fixed norm and favourite habitude. Thus the English language, left to its own instinct in using French words borrowed from Greek or Latin, regularly flung back the accent on the antepenultimate, as in *theólogy*; while the German, in the same class of words, retained the original Greek accent, as *theologíe*, from θεολογία. Exactly the same accentual phenomenon presents itself in Gaelic. Not one of the polysyllabic Latin words in the above list, on receiving the Celtic denizenship, retains its original accent, where that accent, as in *sacérdos*, would stand upon the last syllable of the curtailed Gaelic form—*sagart :* from which perhaps it may appear that the English habit of throwing the accent back on the antepenultimate is of Celtic origin, or at least must condescend to accept a Celtic cousinship. So much for the accent. But in all such words as *ságart*, from *sacérdos*, *peacach*, from *peccatum*, *péarsa*, from *persona*, the reader will remark that the Latin word is regularly curtailed of the final syllable, just as in *velocidad*, Spanish for *velocitatem*, *podestá*, Italian for *potestatem*. Another noticeable thing is that scarce one of these adopted words ends in a vowel; from which circumstance the conclusion is plain, that the Gaelic language is

averse to a vocalic ending, and, in fact, except in the case
of monosyllables, such as *cnu, mo, la*, and in cases where
the final consonant has been softened away by the breathing, as *righ, lagh, gath, gaoth*, very seldom has one. Further,
it will be noticed that the change, in not a few cases, proceeds further than the mere apocope, to use strictly grammatical language, of the termination. Four syllables are
contracted into two, as in *easbuig* from ἐπίσκοπος, *coisrig*
from *consecrare*, and so forth. Sometimes whole syllables
being unaccented in Latin, fall off from the beginning, as
faosad from *confessio*. Very often also a trisyllable, after
throwing off its termination, has the middle consonant
softened away by the breathing, and the word, though
written as two, is pronounced as one syllable ; so *saoghal*
(*sæculum*), pronounced *saol*. Sometimes one or two consonants in the middle of a word are simply ejected
without any help from the breathing, as in *feill* from
festalis or *vigiliae*, like the French *noailles* from *natalis*.
This is exactly the same phenomenon in vocal effect,
though to the reading eye the impression is different,
which has changed the German *magen, sagen, hagel, nagel*
into the English *maw, say, hail, nail*, and a whole family of
such syncopated dissyllables. Furthermore, it will strike
the student that in the above list of words the sharp or
surd consonants of the Latin are regularly changed into
the corresponding *blunts* or sonants ; thus *b* for *p*, in the
case of *episcopus*, and *g* for *c* in the case of *sacerdos*,—a
change, however, which, in modern spoken Gaelic, has little
practical significance, and often means the reverse of what
it seems to mean ; for, to my hearing, in the Gaelic of
Argyllshire at least, a *g* in many cases is regularly pronounced like a hard *c*, and a *b* like a sharp *p*.
Having got thus far into the genius of the Gaelic
language by an intelligent glance cast on the loan words,

the next step to make, when we proceed on the wise principle of associating the unknown with the known, is to
note systematically the broad lines of similarity or agreement with the other more generally known Aryan languages
which the Gaelic grammar presents. And here every
student of philology at once turns to the numerals, as from
their nature a set of conventional signs less liable to be
changed by the play of imagination than any other part
of the language. A glance at these will be sufficient to
show their identity with their Latin prototypes :—

1. Aon, ...	Unus.
2. Dha, ...	Duo.
3. Tri, ...	Tres.
4. Ceithir, ...	Quater.
5. Coig, ...	Quinque.
6. Se, ...	Sex.
7. Seachd, ...	Septem.
8. Ochd, ...	Octo.
9. Naoi, ...	Novem.
10. Deich, ...	Decem.
20. Fichead, ...	Viginti.
100. Ceud, ...	Centum.
1000. Mile, ...	Mille.

Some important laws of interlingual mutation which
might be illustrated from these forms will be more fitly
referred to afterwards; meanwhile the reader acquainted
with Greek will observe that where the two classical
languages present any noticeable difference the Gaelic
regularly approximates to the Latin rather than to the
Greek. Another very stable element in the structure of
all the Aryan languages we find in the pronouns. The
reason of this seems to be, just as in the case of the
numerals, that the signs for the three persons, *I, thou, he,*
being once settled, are used just like the mathematical +
and —, beyond the range of any play of fancy or caprice of

fashion which might eject them from their place in the realm of conventional utterance. So the *m* for the first person, the *s* for the second, and the *t* for the third appear with slight alterations in the flexion of the verb from the Sanscrit in the extreme East to the Gaelic in the extreme West. Among other things it is interesting to observe how the agglutinated pronoun *mi* of the Greek τίθημι and τίθεμαι, in the Gaelic asserts its original independence, as in *tha mi ag radh, am I a-saying*, that is, *I say*, where the position of the personal pronoun in the Gaelic as an affix is much more natural, and certainly more primitive, than its place as a prefix in English; for the natural order of words in sentences is not, as commonly in English, the order of cool logic, but the order of impassioned imagination. In the Gaelic as in the Latin, the substantive verb (which we may take here incidentally) is compounded of fragments of more verbs than one,—in Latin of two, in Gaelic of three. In the *am bheil thu ?*—are you ?—so often heard in the mouth of a Highlander, we distinctly recognise the Greek πέλομαι, in the *bha* the Latin *fui* (Greek ἔφυ), and in the *is* the Sanscrit *as*. As for the *tha*, so constantly heard in Celtic colloquy, I am inclined to think that it comes from the Sanscrit *asti*, by syncopation and a stress laid on the final vowel, which is at the same time broadened, in the same way that the Greek οὗτος, through the Attic οὑτοσί, might become τοσί, and finally τοσά. But let that drop. The pronoun of the third person in the Greek verb, except in the middle voice, τίθεται has been altogether rubbed away, as in φιλεῖ; while in Latin it stands out boldly, *Amat*, and in English takes the form of the allied sibilant *loves*, by intermediation of the aspirate in *loveth*, while in Gaelic it has dwindled down to *e* and *i*, which are only the unaspirated forms of our *he* and *she*. After pronouns, the character of formulised signs, not easily ousted by fashionable mutations, is most strongly asserted by prepositions and conjunctions and other particles, especially when used for modifying verbal roots : for that a very considerable scope for change and enlargement has been left open in the sphere of independent conjunctions and prepositions, any one may see from the existing French and Italian as compared with the Latin, from English as compared with German, and the vulgar Romaic set side by side with the classical Greek.   Of prepositions and other particles common to the Gaelic with the classical languages the most prominent are—

Comh, ...	Cum.
Eadar, ...	Inter.
Inbhir, ...	Infra.
Fo, ...	ὑπό.
Ath, ...	αὖθις.
So, ...	εὖ.
Do, ...	δυς.
Gun, ...	ἄνευ, *ohne* German, English *un*.
Agus, ...	Ac, καὶ, English *eke*, German *auch*.
An?	An ?
Na, ...	νη.
Ann, ...	εν, in.

Besides numerals, pronouns, and particles the whole array of prefixes and affixes, which constitute what grammarians call the formative element in language, seem to fall under the head of formulised signs, independent and significant words originally, beyond doubt, but gradually assuming the conventional character of a mere mathematical + and — standing apart from the contagious atmosphere of shifting fancy and capricious association.   Let us therefore cast an eye over this ground, and see what relics of the old Aryan machinery of suffix and prefix have been here preserved.   And here it is only natural to expect that of the rich array of flexional terminations as exhibited in the Sanscrit noun and the Greek verb, only small fragments should have remained in the drifted ruin of the Gaelic. I use a phrase here accidentally at which I hope the quick sensibilities of trans-Grampian philologers will not take offence. Most of the languages now spoken in Europe have emphatically the character of a drift, and none more characteristically than the English. In the Gaelic noun we find, in the first place, the dative plural is *ibh*, corresponding manifestly to the Sanscrit *ibhya*, the Latin *ibus*, and the old Homeric $\phi\iota\nu$; this with the nominative plural of feminines in *n* is the only trace of flexion by suffix which appears in the first of the five declensions as given by Monro. This plural *n*, of course, which does not belong to the classical languages, is a link connecting the Celtic declension of a certain class of nouns with the Teutonic, as in German, *Der Knabe, Die Knaben*, and in English such fragments saved from a general shipwreck as *ox, oxen ; brother, brethren*. The same plural nasal appears in the other declensions pretty largely ; but beyond this in the declension of the nouns in modern Gaelic I find no trace of the ancient classical suffixes, unless it be perhaps in the *e* of the genitive of feminines, as *creag, creige*, which however in practice is often dropt. The Gaelic article *an*, which may be regarded as a demonstrative proclitic to the noun, is perhaps a relic of the Greek *ἐ-κεῖν-ος*, German *jen-er*, Scotch *yon*. Adjectives present the same *e* in the genitive feminine that distinguishes feminine nouns of the first declension, and monosyllables add *a* or *e* for the plural. The suffixes for the comparative and superlative degrees of the adjective, so easily recognisable in Sanscrit, Greek, and Latin, have either dropt away from the Gaelic, or were never possessed. Almost a total wreck also, even more so than in English, is the scheme of the Gaelic verb ; for we find no terminational difference for the persons ; as in the case of *paisg*, to wrap (the etymon of the English *basket*), the past tense of which is declined through all the persons unchanged, as follows :—

1. *Phaisg mi,*
2. *Phaisg thu,* } Singular,
3. *Phaisg e or i,*

4. *Phaisg sinn,*
5. *Phaisg sibh,* } Plural,
6. *Phaisg iad,*

—a phenomenon, however, which suggests the question, whether the Gaelic language, in using unagglutinated terminations to express the persons does not rather preserve the original form of the flexion in which the terminations were pronouns in an independent attitude, and recognisable as such ; for the *mi* in *Phaisg mi* is plainly the same to the ear as the $\mu\iota$ in $\tau\iota\theta\eta\mu\iota$, only capable of disjunction from the verb to which it is enclitically attached. The imperative of the same verb in the form—

1. *Paisgeam,*
2. *Paisg,*
3. *Paisgeadh e or i,*
4. *Paisgeamaid,*
5. *Paisgibh,*
6. *Paisgeadh iad,*

exhibits a more complete approximation to the fulness of the Greek and Latin personal endings; but as this mood is naturally less used in practice than either the past or the present, its terminational suffixes contribute little or nothing to the vocal character of the verb. Among the other parts of the active voice we notice the termination *inn* of the conditional mood as perhaps identical with the $\eta\nu$ of the Greek optative in the oldest conjugation, while the *s*, which appears in the future as *ma phaisgeas mi*, seems to claim equal relationship with the Greek σ in $\check{\epsilon}\sigma o\mu a\iota$. The present participle active presents an aspirated *d* as in *phasgadh*, which is plainly the τ that appears in the genitive or full form of the Greek participle $\tau\acute{v}\pi\tau o\nu\tau o\varsigma$, with the ν dropt before the dental, according to a well-known law of comparative philology, and the aspiration added to the sonant dental. In the passive voice, the future often used for a present, discovers at once the *r* so characteristic of the Latin as compared with the Greek verb, thus *ma phaisgear*, if I shall be wrapped. The past tense shows again *ad* for the Latin *t*, as *phaisgeadh mi*, I was wrapped ; but the pure *t* appears in the participle, as in the Greek $\gamma\rho a\pi\tau\acute{o}\varsigma$, Latin *scriptus*, Gaelic *sgriobta*, and also in Sanscrit. So much for the element of flexional termination in verbs. But in fact a great part of the business of the verb in Gaelic is done by prepositive auxiliary verbs, as in other modern languages ; so in *tha mi ag ràdh*, I am a-saying, *i.e.* I say ; *Am bheil mi pasgadh ?* am I wrapping ? *Am bi mi pasgadh ?* shall I be wrapping ? *An robh mi pasgadh ?* and so on. In verbs beginning with a vowel or *f* pure, *d*, or *dh*, like our *did* or the German *that*, serves to indicate the past tense. Let us now cast a glance on the principal suffixes used to turn roots into nouns, adjectives and verbs, and see how far they agree with familiar Latin or Greek terminations of the same class. To form the adjective, in the first place, we find the Greek suffix $\rho\acute{o}\varsigma$, in the form of *rach*, as in *dos*, a tuft, *dosrach*, tufty ; then the κ in $\iota\kappa\acute{o}\varsigma$ (English *ish*, Danish *isk*, German *isch*) is softened into *ch*, as in *toileach*, willing, from *toil*, $\theta\acute{\epsilon}\lambda\omega$, *cnapach*, knobby, from *cnap*, a knob (German *knopf*). The Latin adjectival termination *alis*, as in *provincialis*, so common in English, appears frequently in Gaelic under the form *eil*, as *ainmeil*, famous, from *ainm*, a name, *cionail*, kind, from *cion*, love, favour. In personal designations to express agency the old *r* asserts itself strongly in the form *air*, identical with the Latin *arius ;* as from *breab*, to kick, *breabadair*, a weaver, because of the use of his feet in the practice of his trade ; *brocair*, a badger or fox-hunter, from *broc*, a badger. Whether this *air* is a corrupted form of *fear*, as Armstrong indicates, matters little, the question still remains whence the *r* came in the Latin *vir*, and the German *er*, he. Abstract substantives appear in the form *inn*, Greek *aίva*, as in *bochd*, poor, *bochdainn*, poverty ; *fior*, true, *firinn*, truth ; also in *chd* and *adh*, as in *naomhachd*, holiness, from *naomh*, holy, and *fireannachadh*, justification, from *fireannach*, just, which all point to the dental in the Latin substantives *sanctital*, *justificatio*, *claritudo*, etc. Diminutives are expressed by two terminations which are both found in the Teutonic languages, viz. *an* and *ag*, as in *loch*, a lake, *lochan*, a little lake ; *slat*, a rod, *slatag*, a little rod or twig, like the German *Magd*, *Mädchen*, and the Scotch *bit*, *bittock*, and the English *hill*, *hillock*. Finally, in verbs, the old Greek *ίζω*, so potent in modern English under the forms of *ise* and *ize*, and so rich in a progeny of *isms*, takes a prominent position in Gaelic under the favourite aspirated form of *ich*, as from *bog*, soft, *bogaich*, to make soft, or boggy; from *cruaidh*, hard, *cruadhaich*, to make hard. Such are the principal points of flexional agreement between the modern Gaelic and the other languages of the Aryan family more familiar to the general scholar. Into more minute and curious details my ignorance of the most ancient Irish and the purpose of the present work alike forbid me to enter.

Before proceeding to examine the roots or raw material of the language, and to attempt a tabulation of them according to their classical and Teutonic affinities, it will be convenient to discuss here what remains of the formative or flexional element of the Gaelic—that part of it, namely, which does not consist in prefixes or suffixes, and which presents few or no points of agreement with the non-Celtic members of the Aryan family. The first thing that strikes us here is the habitual use, for the purposes of nominal and verbal flexious, of that modification of the internal vowel, which appears in the Greek φεύγω, as compared with ἔφυγον, in ἔμεινα as compared with μένω, and in a large class of nouns, substantive and adjective, derived from verbs whose characteristic consonant is *l*, *r*, *m*, and *n*. Thus from στέλλω we have στολή and στόλος, from σπείρω σπόρος, from βρέμω βρόμος and βρόμιος, from τείνω τόνος, and from στένω στόνος. The same phenomenon is more common in German, where in a certain class of nouns it distinguishes the plural from the singular, as *Brüder* from *Bruder*, *Hände* from *Hand*, and many others. In English isolated wrecks of this once general vowel modification still remain, as in *man, men, mouse, mice*, and the causative verbs *fell, graze*, and *glaze*, from *fall, grass*, and *glass*. But in Gaelic this change appears most prominently in the cases of nouns, of which, I think, there is no example in the classical languages; for the ε in πατέρα from πατήρ, and such like cases, does not affect the root, and the prolongation of the ō in *bŏs*, from *bŏv-is*, is merely a matter of contraction. Besides, changes of this kind in Latin and Greek often affect only the quantity of the vowel, as in *vĕnio, vēni, lĕgo, lēgi*, whereas in Gaelic another vowel is inserted, and the flexion is made by changing the vowel into a diphthong, or two vowels that flow so sweetly into one another as almost to become a diphthong. Thus in the first declension, containing a numerous class of nouns, the genitive singular and nominative plural are formed by changing *a* into *ai*, as *dùn*, a song, *dùin*, of a song, *dùin*, songs. So *brog*, a shoe, becomes in the genitive singular *broige—carn*, a heap, becomes *cuirn—long*, a ship, *luinge—dall*, blind, *doill—clunn*, a child, *cloinne*—*clach*, a stone, *cloiche*—*ceòl*, music, *ciùil*—*beul*, a mouth, *beòil*—*fiadh*, a deer, *féidh*. In a few cases, contrariwise, the double vowel or diphthong of the nominative becomes a single vowel in the genitive ; as in *ceann*, a head, *cinn*—*lion*, a net, *lìn*—*athair*, a father, *athar ; mathair*, a mother, and *brathair*, a brother, follow the same rule.

In the comparison of adjectives the same principle reigns, as *bàn*, fair, *baine*, more fair—*borb*, fierce, *buirbe*, fiercer, and so on ; and a considerable class of verbs change *ai* into *a : caidil*, sleep, *cadal*—*caill*, lose, *call*, etc. But the most characteristic device for nominal and verbal flexion in the Celtic, of which not a trace exists in the classical languages, is what goes by the name of *aspiration*. This, as the name imports, is simply a breathing, represented by the letter *h*, which modifies the letter into a softer form, and sometimes smooths it away altogether. Thus in masculine nouns of the first declension the vocative singular is always like the genitive, except that the former is aspirated. Thus *bard*, a poet, *baird*, of a poet, *a bhaird*, O poet, where the effect of the *h* is to soften the *bh* into a *v*. The same device is used to turn the root of a verb into the past tense, as *saoil*, to think, but *shaoil mi*, I thought, in which case, as regularly after *s*, the effect of the added aspirate is to obliterate the preceding sibilant altogether. This obliteration is carried still further in the case of F, as in *fios*, German *wissen*, English *wit*, where an added *h* produces *fhios*, pronounced *ios = ees*. After the nasal *m* the aspirate also produces *v*, only with a slight nasal touch, easily learned by practice. Whether from accident, or from a peculiar delicacy of phonic refinement, the Highlanders use this softening of the initial *b*, *f*, *m*, *p*, *c*, *g*, to bring out the feeling of gender ; thus, a big man would be *fear mor*, but a big woman, *bean mhor*. But this favourite aspiration has extended far beyond the form of the individual words, and asserts itself even more powerfully in the contact of word with word in regularly piled sentences. With changes of this sort, produced by various kinds of assimilation, the Sanscrit scholar is familiar; and as in that language it is the fashion, when two words exercise this sort of contagious influence on one another, to unite them, as if they were one word—it being in fact impossible in many cases to disentangle them,—a peculiar difficulty presents itself to the student of Sanscrit, of which Greek presents only a very few and easily mastered examples. In Gaelic the difficulty is much less than in Sanscrit, but still it is sensibly felt. The final letter of the preceding word indeed never, as in Sanscrit, annihilates or makes insensible the initial letter of the following word; but when certain words precede, the following consonant must always be aspirated; as *mo*, mine, *gaol*, love; these when combined produce *mo ghaol*, where the *h* softens the *g* down into something like *y*. The principle of this curious change is evidently euphonic, for it takes place principally after *vowels* and *liquids*, as *mo, do, bhu, mar, mu, fo, de, tre, troi*, and the effect produced is plainly to transform the consonant into the quality which is most agreeable to the sweetness of the vowel. How deeply this soft vocalic influence has worked its way into the structure of the Gaelic language, appears from the fact that in all cases where a single consonant flanked by a vowel on each side appears in Latin, this consonant is first aspirated in Gaelic, and then drops out altogether; thus *pater, mater, sæculum, caper*, become *athair, mathair, saoghal, gobhar*, in which words, as now pronounced, the medial consonant is altogether swamped, and the aspiration scarcely heard.

Let us now examine the roots, and endeavour to ascertain both the linguistic forms with which they seem to claim closest kinship, and the marks by which, as Celtic denizens, they are distinguished from their nearest cousins in the cognate languages.

I have gone through Armstrong's Gaelic Dictionary very carefully twice, arranging all the roots alphabetically in columns, and placing in a line parallel to each column of Gaelic roots, the real or probable corresponding roots in Greek, Latin, German, English, and Scotch. My list includes about eight hundred words, and from a rough comparison with another list which I made, I should say it leaves two-thirds of the simple vocabulary of the language unconnected with any known form of Aryan speech. I am perfectly aware, however, that an estimate of this kind can yield only an approximate result; for, to give the investigation a really scientific value, I should require to ransack Danish, Swedish, Icelandic, Anglo-Saxon, and the Sclavonic languages, not to mention Sanscrit,—in fact, devote my life to the investigation of Celtic roots, which it is neither my inclination nor my duty to do. It is evident also that doubtful cases in modern Gaelic etymology can be settled only by a knowledge of the history of the language from the earliest Irish records up to the most recent phase of modern Irish; and from this region also I feel myself excluded by prudential considerations. Nevertheless a reasoned analysis of Armstrong's dictionary has its value; and in a rough way will indicate the general character of the materials of which the living language is made up. Now the general result which my analysis affords is this, that of the four Aryan languages, with which I compare it, the Gaelic presents the strongest affinity with the Latin, after that with the German and the Teutonic element of the English, including Scotch, —least of all with the Greek. How far there may be any real connection with Hebrew, apart from the slippery manipulation of bilateral roots, in which personally I am not much inclined to believe, I shall leave it to others to determine.[1] That pear, I fancy, is not yet ripe. How much of the material of the present English language may be a direct inheritance from our Celtic-speaking ancestors, I shall also leave undetermined; my studies lead me to suspect that it is much less in quantity than Dr. Charles Mackay, and other diligent diggers into English foundations from the Celtic side, are fond to believe. Not a few of the words, which in the first plunge of my Celtic ardour I suspected to be primeval British, turned out, on consulting the Anglo-Saxon dictionary, to be good Teutonic, so that the fatherhood of the vocable at least remains doubtful, and the presumption is certainly in favour of the Saxon rather than the Celtic original. For however influential the Hibernian culture was in the early stages of Christian civilisation, there cannot be the slightest doubt that, as the middle ages culminated, it was completely overshadowed by the Teutonic, or absorbed generally, I imagine, pretty much in the same way that Albanian is at present being absorbed by the Neo-Hellenic. The strongest proof of this, to my mind, is in the vocabulary of Burns's Poems, a vocabulary belonging to that very locality where the Celtic language long maintained its ground against the Danes, Saxons, and Norman-English, who pressed forward from the east and south-east. Let any moderately informed Gaelic scholar cast a glance over the glossaries appended to the common editions of the Ayrshire bard, and he will be astonished to find how few of the peculiarly Scottish words are Celtic. Our Scottish language, so far as I can see, is a mere variety of English, pretty much as Doric is of Greek; and the peculiar words

---

[1] My friend Dr. Macpherson of Lairg has, at my request, furnished me with a note of some of the most striking Hebrew roots which he considers identical with the Gaelic; but I feel that I am not in a condition at present to do justice to that part of the subject.

in its vocabulary which are not Saxon will, in most cases, I apprehend, be of French rather than of Gaelic origin. In the dialect of "Aberdeen awa'," with which my boyhood made me familiar, I have observed several Celtic words which have no currency in the south; that district having naturally warded off the invading Teut by the cold ridge of the Grampians, which falls down to the sea beyond Stonehaven and Fettercairn. So much for the general character of the lexicographical material. Let us now inquire under what special form the Aryan roots present themselves.

Starting, after the example of the Sanscrit grammarians, with the guttural consonants, we find that the hard *c* of the Romans, and *k* of the Greeks, which the Teutonic languages soften into *h*, retains its place firmly in Gaelic; in fact, though the sound of *h*, and its cognate *ch*, is one of the most common in Gaelic words, there is not a single word in the language which commences with that letter. The Highlander therefore can no more say *haggis* or *hall*, than the Englishman can say *loch* or *fraoch*; neither does he omit it altogether, or change it into a *c*, but it becomes a *t*, as *taigis* and *talla*, this *t* being a euphonic product common in the declension of Gaelic nouns commencing with a vowel, as *an-t-uisge*—the water. For the same reason, $\chi\epsilon\iota\mu\acute{\omega}\nu$ in Greek, and *hiems* in Latin, become *geamradh*. Here follow a few of the principal Gaelic roots with initial hard *c* :—

Capull, ...	Caballus.
Cac, ...	Caco.
Caile, ...	Calx.
Caraid, ...	Car-us.
Cairt, ...	Cortex.
Cam, ...	Cam-urus.
Can, ...	Cano.
Ceaird, ...	Cerdo, $\kappa\acute{\epsilon}\rho\delta o\varsigma$?
Ceart, ...	Certus.

Ceil,	Celo.
Cead,	Cedo.
Claoidh,	Clades.
Claoin,	κλίνω.
Cleith,	Crat-es.
Cliabh,	Clivus.
Cliar,	Clar-us.
Cliu,	κλέος.
Cluinn,	κλύω.
Cobhan,	Covinus.
Coir,	κῦρος.
Coire,	κοῖλος.
Colbh,	Clava.
Coluinn,	κῶλον.
Comh,	Cum.
Corn,	Cornu.
Cre,	Creta.
Croch,	Crux.
Cruaidh,	Crudus.
Cu,	κύων.
Cuileag,	Culex.
Cuil,	Cule-us.

In some cases, however, the Latin *c* becomes a *g*, as—

Gabh,	Capio.
Gabhar,	Caper.
Gaineamh,	κόνις ?
Gearr,	κείρω.
Geinn,	Cuneus.
Glas,	Clavis.
Gearan,	Quer-or.

In the majority of cases *g* remains from Latin *g*, as in—

Geum,	Gemo.
Gin,	Gigno.
Gloc,	Gloc-ire.
Gluc,	Glut-io.
Gne,	Genus.
Gnuis,	Genæ ?
Grabh,	γράφω.

Gradh, ...	Grat-us.
Greigh, ...	Grex.

But though the Gaelic has retained both the gutturals, surd and sonant, in the initial of the roots, in declension and otherwise there is a strong tendency to soften them into the *ch*, perhaps the most favourite sound of the Gaelic language. Of this we have examples in *ach* for *ager*, *each* for *equus*, and many others. We must not omit to notice, also, a peculiar transition of hard *c* into *s*, and then into the cognate *t*, from the infection of the following slender vowel, as in *scinn* from *cano*, *Tearlach* from *Carolus*, *teine* from *cand-eo* and *in-cend-o*, *deas* from *dexter*, *sith* from *quiet-is*.

Proceeding to the dentals we find that both in the sonant and surd form they present the front of their classical sisterhood unaltered:—

Da, ...	δύο.
Damh, ...	Dama.
Dan, ...	δεινὸς.
Darach, ...	δόρυ.
Deich, ...	Decem.
Deas, ...	δέξιος.
Deud, ...	Dent-is.
Dia, ...	Deus.
Doilich, ...	Doleo.
Doire, ...	δόρυ.
Dorrach, ...	Durus.
Druim, ...	Dorsum.
Doth, ...	δαίω.
Druchd, ...	δρόσος.

In the same manner the *t* group presents itself—

Tachair, ...	τυγχάνω,
Tairnneanach, . .	Tonitru,
Talamh, ...	Tellus,
Tana, ...	Tenuis,
Tar, ...	Trans,
Tarbh, ...	Taurus,

Tarruing,	.	.	.	.	Traho,
Teach,	.	.	.	.	Tignum,
Teas,	.	.	.	.	Tæda,
Teirig,		.	.	.	Tero,
Tiom,	.	.	.	.	Timeo,
Tir,	.	.	.	.	Terra,
Toirm,		.	.	.	Turma,
Tom,	.	.	.	.	Tumulus,
Torr,	.	.	.	.	Turris,
Traigh,		.	.	.	Tergeo,
Trealbh,		.	.	.	Tribus,
Treas,	.	.	.	.	Tres,—

with a few exceptions, where the Gaelic surd represents
a Greek or Latin sonant, as in *teagaisg* for *doceo*, *tuireadh* for
ὀ-δύρο-μαι, and some others. And, of course, as the Gaelic
has no *th*, this combination being always self-obliterative in
a Highland mouth, the Greek θ, as in θύρα, will be represented by *d*, as in *dorus*, or by *t*, as in *toil*=θέλω.

With regard to the labials, in the sonant *b* I find considerable variety, though the unchanged Greek and Latin
form is perhaps entitled to claim the greater proportion of
the roots :—

Bo,	.	.	.	.	Bos.
Bach,	.	.	.	.	Bacchari.
Bad,	.	.	.	.	βάτος.
Balbh,		.	.	.	Balbus.
Beann,		.	.	.	βουνός.
Beith,		.	.	.	Betula.
Blad,	.	.	.	.	Blaterare.
Bochd,		.	.	.	Bucca.
Bram,		.	.	.	βρέμω.
Breun,		.	.	.	βρωμάω.
Buail,		.	.	.	βάλλω.
Beul,	.	.	.	.	βῆλος.

On the other hand *f* comes in for a share :—

Ban,	.	.	.	.	Fem-ina, Æolic βαν.
Bi,	.	.	.	.	Fui, φύω.
Bileach,		.	.	.	Folium.

Bonn, ... Fundus.
Bram, ... Fremo.
Bris, ... Frango.
Brathair, . . . Frater.

And *v* for some :

Baille, ... Villa.
Bior, ... Veru.
Beatha, ... Vita.

p also will not be without a claim, as in—

Baile, ... πόλις.
Beag, ... Pauc-us.
Beann, ... Pinna.
Beir, ... Pario.
Bochd, ... πτῶχος.

Even *m* shows front, as—

Bainidh, ... μαίνομαι.
Beus, ... Mos ?
Bleoghainn, . . . Mulgeo ?
Buan, ... Moneo.

With regard to all these cases, however, it must be
borne in mind, as before remarked, that though, in the
original pronunciation of the Gaelic, there must have been
a very marked difference between the blunt *b* and the sharp
p (otherwise ἀπόστολος could never have been changed
into *abstol*), yet, as the Highlanders generally now speak,
b appears much more akin to *p* than to our broad *b* ; and
in the same way a written *g* is very often practically a
sharp *k*. With regard to the written Gaelic *p*, it has the
peculiarity of being the least common initial letter in the
alphabet, except *o*, the whole number of roots that I could
collect under it being twenty-five. Closely connected
with this peculiarity is the fact that in a well-known class
of cases initial *p* in Latin or Greek has been changed into
c, while in another equally familiar group the initial *p* has
vanished altogether. The first group, which finds its

Hellenic prototype in the Herodotean κότε for πότε, contains the following common words :—

Caraich, . . .	Par-o.
Càraid, ...	Par.
Cas, ...	Pes ?
Cloimh, . . .	Pluma.
Corcur, . . .	Purpura.
Cog, ...	Pugno.
Cuaille, . . .	Pal-us.
Caisg, ...	Pascha.

The most familiar examples of the second group are—

Athar, . . .	Pater.
Agh, ...	Pec-us.
Iasg, ...	Pisc-is.
Iol, ...	πολύ.
Uchd, ...	Pect-us.
Uircean, . . .	P-orc-us; Ital. *orca*; E. *urchin*.

The principle on which this curtailment depends is sufficiently obvious, viz., laziness and feebleness; a principle which, in other departments of human energy, produces only evil, in language sometimes contributes to harmony. Accordingly in Greek we find

αἶα alongside of γαῖα.		
εἴβω	„	λείβω.
αἰνός	,,	δεινός.

And in Gaelic we find the *p* is not the only initial consonant that falls off, but the other labials also sometimes, as in

Iteag, ...	German *fittich.*
Aodach, . . .	Vestis.
Ath, ...	Val-um.
Eearrach, . . .	Ver.
Ibh, ...	Bibo.
Iarunn, . . .	Ferrum.
Aill, ...	φελλ-εύς, Germ. *fels.*

And other letters too—

Ait, ...	Læt-us.
Iarr, ...	Quæro.

Of the labial family, there remain now for consideration only *f* and *m*. In a considerable number of familiar instances Gaelic *f* is Latin *v* :—

Faidh,	Vat-es.
Failtich,	Valeo.
Folaich,	Velo.
Fannan,	Vannus.
Faol,	Vulpes.
Farsuing,	Porro.
Fear,	Vir.
Fearrsaidh,	Verto.
Feart,	Virtus.
Feasgar,	Vesper.
Fcur,	Vir-eo.
Ficheat,	Viginti.
Fion,	Vinum.
Fior,	Verus.

But there are other cases in which *f* stands for *p ;* and in a few cases—as in the instance of the Greek ἵππος, compared with the Latin *equus*—we find a Gaelic *f* evolved from a *qu*, as in

Fois, } Fcith, }	Quiet-um.
Feoraich,	Quæro.

The naso-labial letter *m* is notable for the large number of Latin roots it contains in proportion to the whole number of words commencing with that letter ; thus,

Mag,	μωκᾶσθαι.
Mairg,	Mæreo.
Mall,	Moll-is.
Mam,	μάμμη.
Maoth, } Math, }	Mit-is.
Marbh,	Mort-uus.
Mathair,	Mater.
Meadhon,	Med-ius.
Meall,	Mol-es.

Meamna, ...	μένος.
Meas, ...	Messis.
Meas, ...	Metior.
Meil, ...	Molere.
Miann, ...	μένος.
Meur, ...	μέρος.
Mil, ...	μέλι.
Mile, ...	Mille.
Min, ...	Min-uo.
Mios, ...	Mensis.
Mo, ...	Meus.
Moch, ...	Mox.
Monadh, ...	Mons.
Mor, ...	Major.
Mùin, ...	Mingo.
Muineal, ...	Monile.
Muir, ...	Mare.
Mulachan, . . .	Mulgeo.
Muth, ...	Muto.
Mniu, ...	Moneo.

That is very nearly the half of the whole roots in my list
commencing with *m*. The same phenomenon is displayed
in the roots commencing with the dento-nasal *n*, which, in
Gaelic, are very few, and more than the half plain Latin, as

Na and Ne, . . .	Ne and νη.
Naoi, ...	Novem.
Nead, ...	Nidus.
Neamh, ...	Nimb-us.
Neul, ...	Nebula.
Nochd, ...	Nud-us.
Nochd, ...	Noct-em.
Nodaich, ...	Nod-us.
Nuadh, ...	Nov-us.

With regard to this letter, it is worthy of notice that,
when followed by another consonant, it has a great tendency to fall out, as in

Fichead	*for*	Viginti.
Mios	„	Mensis.

The liquid *l*, to which, in certain cases, the Highlanders give a beautiful vocalic trill, presents a fair array of Latin roots, which need not be quoted at length here. In two of these words, an initial *p* has manifestly fallen off before the liquid, as above we saw it vanish before the vowel—

Lan, ... Plen-us.
Leac, ... πλάκ-α.

I imagine also that *lus* and *loisg*, words signifying *flame* and *fire*, are only curtailed forms of the Greek φλέγω and the English *flash*, while the Latin agrees with the Gaelic, dropping the initial *p* in *luc-eo ;* though perhaps this word and the Greek λεύσσω are more properly connected with the Greek γλαυκός and the Scottish *glaik.*

One phenomenon with regard to the *l* deserves special notice. It sometimes seems to slide in softly after the initial consonant of the root, just as the Italians insinuate a *u* in *buono* from *bon-us.* Hence we have *slan* for *san-us*, *glunn* for γόνυ. In the same way the Latin *plecto* stands connected with the Welsh *basg*, from which we derive the word *basket* (*bascauda*), whose Celtic origin was long ago celebrated by the Roman epigrammatist Martial.

The snarling or canine liquid *r* is no favourite with the Celt, at least as the initial of words, and most of them are easily recognised in Latin, Greek, or German. In three of these, the Greek and Latin present a prefixed vowel, evidently not belonging to the root :—

Reitha, ... Ariet-em.
Ruadh, ... ἐρυθ-ρός.
Ruig, ... ὀρέγ-ομαι.

In others an initial labial appears to have fallen off. As in Æolic Greek we have βρόδον for ῥόδον, so *reo* is evidently a fragment of φρίσσω, *frig-eo* and *rigeo ;* and *roimh* comes as indubitably from some old form of *prim-us.*

Along with the hard *c*, the sibilant *s* has the honour of carrying off the greatest number of Celtic roots ; and we are not to wonder at this, for *ch*, *sh*, and *s* are the three cognate forms naturally dominant in all languages which incline to aspiration. This we see in the Greek, where sigmas are often accumulated in an offensive manner, and joined with ψ, χ, ϕ, and θ in a combination which only to Greek ears can seem agreeable. The sibilant, in fact, is only a variation of the simple aspirate, as we see in the word *hiss*, which unites them both to their cognate vowel with that dramatic effect which is one of the most striking beauties of the English language. In my list I have nearly two hundred roots commencing with the sibilant *s* ; and their equivalents, in the majority of cases, seem found rather in the Teutonic than in the classical languages. One peculiarity with regard to this letter deserves special notice. As in Greek we have σμικρός and μικρός, so in Gaelic some old roots present an initial *s* not found in the sister languages ; thus—

Smachd, ...	Macht.
Smaointeach, . .	Ment-em.
Smeur, ...	Mor-um.
Smior, ...	μυελ-ός.
Snath, ...	νήθω.
Snamh, ...	Nav-is.
Sniomh, ...	νήθω.
Sneachd, ...	Niv-em.
Srian, ...	Ren-um.
Sruth, ...	ῥύω.
Stain, ...	Stannum ; E. *tin*.
Speal, ...	Falc.
Sliob, ...	Læv-is.
Sluagh, ...	λαός.

Sometimes the *s* is retained and the following consonant thrown out, as in

Scas	*for*	Sist-o.
Sil and siol,	,,	Stillo.

The combination *str*, so full of rough vigour, seems to have been peculiarly distasteful to the musically cultivated ear of the Celt, so he generally toned it down to *sr ;* thus :

Sraid   *for*   Stratum.

Sreang   „   στράγγω.

That *s* is evolved from *c* when a slender vowel follows, we have already noticed. Thus *searb* comes from a-*cerb*-us, and with an interposed liquid as in *sliabh* from *clivus*.

After this detailed dissection of the parts, let me conclude by piecing the structure together again, that we may know how it looks as a whole. As an organ of intellectual expression, therefore, and as a means of producing an æsthetical effect, what sort of language have we got ? As an organ of intellectual expression, the Gaelic, in common with Greek, German, Sanscrit, and all self-evolved languages, has the advantage of being able on all occasions to fling out new branches from the native stem, and grow to exuberant enlargement as occasion may require. What a patchwork, on the other hand, has been made of our old Saxon, by the bitter frost which nipped its early budding, and the constant habit of borrowing thence resulting, the learned among us, as well as the unlearned, though in very different ways, are made constantly to feel. The English language, as we have it now, is not so much a coherent growth as a disturbed organism. Our words, accordingly, are not coins with an intelligible sign and superscription, but mere counters. How different is Gaelic, where every word tells the story of its own composition to the unlettered peasant as vividly as to the most learned etymologist. A whale, for instance, is *muc-mhara*, literally, a sow of the sea ; an adopted son is *uchd-mhac*, literally, a son of the bosom, as contrasted with a son of the womb ; a swallow is *gobhlan-gaoithe*, *i.e.* a bird that oars the breeze with its forky tail ; while the word *cruthachadh*, to create, used in the first verse of the first chapter of Genesis, to a Highland laddie, under a competent teacher, will at once suggest the fundamental notion of the Platonic philosophy, viz., that *cruth* or form, μόρφη, is the necessary and legitimate product of the action of Divine reason upon matter. Now every one knows that the English language, without a long process of root-digging in Greek and Roman soil, cannot be made to yield such significant results; and therefore the Gaelic language for the education of the Highland peasantry has an advantage which English to the English peasant has not, and can never be made to have. But from this great advantage the poor Highlander has got very little benefit, partly from the neglect of his language by schoolmasters and people in the middle and upper classes, who ought to know better; partly from the fact that beyond the sphere of the Scriptures and popular theology the language has received very scanty culture, and so, instead of developing its own native powers, as Greek and German are continually doing, it has fallen into a general habit of pilfering from the English,—so far no doubt from a strong social necessity, but much more from the vulgar contempt of what is native, and the silly affectation of what is foreign. When the soul of a nation has been lost, and people have begun to be ashamed of themselves, there is no hope that the language, which is a living expression of their nationality, shall be true to its capabilities. We find, therefore, that, notwithstanding the noble effort made by the father of the late · Dr. Norman Macleod to give Gaelic prose its natural position in the intellectual training of Highlanders, beyond the domain of the pulpit, the language still practically remains confined, like Scotch, to the region of popular song; the precious pearls of his *Gaelic Courier* having, to speak the honest truth, been flung before swine. The consequence is that though the English half of the most recent Gaelic dictionaries contains pure Celtic equivalents for such modern scientific terms as Chemistry, *feallsanachd-brighe*, yet, as they have obtained no currency among a people who in ninety-nine cases of a hundred cannot spell the tongue which they speak, they are not to be regarded as forming part of the language ; and even in talking of objects which move in the familiar sphere of common life, for one Highlander that asks for his *biadh-maidne* nine hundred and ninety-nine will ask for their breakfast. We shall say, therefore, that, as an organ of intellectual expression, the Gaelic is a language of grand capabilities, but of very stunted attainment. It is like a healthy boy, whose education was altogether neglected, and now at the age of sixty, the man who has grown out of the boy finds himself too old to learn ; or, to use another simile, it is like a lusty vegetation which, in the months of April and May, sent forth largely the green and golden promise of a weighty harvest, but all through June and July and August, instead of sunshine and warmth, there came only a succession of biting frosts, battering hailstones, tearing blasts, and sweeping floods—and now, what says the reaper?

As a means of producing an æsthetical effect there is much more to be said for the Gaelic; and the vulgar notions on this subject, vented by ignorant Englishmen and Lowlanders, will be found in most cases to be the reverse of the truth. It is commonly said, for instance, that Gaelic is a harsh and barbarous and unpronounceable language. It is, on the contrary, a soft, vocalic, and mellifluous language. The notion of its harshness arose, no doubt, partly from the fact that English-speaking tourists scarcely ever hear it spoken except by uneducated and unlettered people, partly also from the acquired defects of the English organs of utterance, which make *ch* for *k* appear a harsh and difficult sound, whereas to well-developed organs it is one of the most soft and fluent. *Boidheach*, for instance, is a more melodious word than the English *lovely*, though it ends in the *ch*, the original termination of adjectives in the Teutonic as well as the Celtic languages, but which the English have attenuated into a feeble *y*, as in *mighty*, for the German *mächtig*. But though *ch* is not a harsh, but a soft sound, I think there can be no doubt that it occurs so frequently in Gaelic as to amount to a mannerism ; at the same time there are few if any languages that have not slid, by the indulgence of a favourite habit, into some orthoepic one-sidedness, as the sibilation above noted in the Greek, the cloying monotony of *o* and *a* in Italian, and the overwhelming breadth of the first vowel of the alphabet in Sanscrit. We shall, therefore, allow the final *ch* of the Highlander to pass with a very slight reprobation, remembering our own *which* and *such*, and *stitch* and *crutch*, and not a few other dental sibilant and palatal combinations, in no wise pleasant to an ear studious of euphony. But, in order to take a true measure of the melody of the Gaelic language, we must take specially into account the liquids, or continuous letters, *l*, *r*, and *n*, and the vowels, of which latter we have hitherto said nothing. In the enunciation of the liquids the Gaelic possesses a peculiar virtue unknown to the English, in a sort of continued trill or roll given to these letters in certain cases, as in *lamh, lan, ruadh*, after the fashion of *gn* in the Italian *regno*. The gamut of the vowel sounds indeed presents a variety and richness against which Sanscrit, Latin, and Italian compare as an instrument of seven strings with one of ten. For the Gaelic has not only its fair proportion of the deep and broad *o* and *a*, the most musical of the vowels, but, like German, it has the deep, rich, hollow diphthongal sounds of which Sanscrit and Latin, two of the oldest types of the Aryan family, are altogether devoid. The vowel sounds in Italian I should compare to those stripes of bright colour, broadly distinguished, which we sometimes see in a flaring draper's window; whereas the deep and hollow sounds of the *oe* in German and *ao* in Gaelic, and the fine delicate *ue*, suggest rather the beautiful blending of green, yellow, and orange in those lovely sunsets so marvellously displayed, when it pleases God, over the seas of the Western Highlands. Again, I have often thought that those deep hollow diphthongal sounds, which are so prominent in Gaelic, possess some mysterious affinity with the murmur of the ocean-waves beneath deeply scooped cliffs, or the moaning of mournful winds through the crannies of the tempest-rifted rocks. Be that as it may, no man with an ear will deny vocalic depth and musical sweetness to the following lines. I write them phonetically in order that the English reader may not be impeded by the necessary discounting of the mute consonants :—

> *Hooi Coooolin aik balla Hoora*
> *Fo yoora craoiv yuille na fooaim ;*
> *Y 'aom a hlcay ri carraig nan coas*
> *A skia vore r'a haov air an air.*
> *Vaw smaiontean an eer air Cüirbre,*
> *Laoch a huit leis an garv-choarag,*
> *N'uair hawinig ferr cöid a hooain*
> *Looa vac Feeil nan caim ard.*

Observe here that the diphthong *ao* is pronounced with a hollow sound, pretty much like the *oe* in the German *Goethe.*

Now take these same lines, according to their printed spelling, and see how they look :—

> *Shuidh Cuchullin aig balla Thura*
> *Fo dubhra craoibh dhuille na fuaim ;*

Dh'aom a shleagh ri carraig nan chs
A sgiath mhor r'a thaob air an fheur.
Bha smaointean an fhir air Cairbre,
Laoch a thuit leis an garb chomrag,
N'uair thainig fear coimhead a' chuain
Luath mhac Fhithil nan ceum àrd.

FINGAL, i. 1-8.

Well, is not this a very absurd exhibition, you will say,
or at least a very strange, untoward, and unhappy affair?
and does it not make the language extremely difficult, and
almost impossible for a stranger to master? Untoward
and unhappy in one view it certainly is; but neither
strange, nor absurd, nor involving any special difficulty.
The same phenomenon occurs in French; and in our own
English, if not in a wider range, at least in a much more
wayward and wanton fashion. In French, no doubt, when
the *s* of *estre* ceased to be pronounced, the word became
être, just as in the English the German *magen* became *maw*,
and the German *legen, lay;* but in another large family of
words, such as *might, light, sigh, high*, we followed the Gaelic
fashion of retaining in print the mute consonants which
had been obliterated in speech; a procedure which has at
least the valuable advantage of exhibiting the history and
pedigree of the word bodily before the eye, which otherwise could only be recovered by a laborious process of
etymological research. Who, for instance, could have
divined the identity of the French *épée* with the Greek
σπάθη, if he had not been led lexicographically through
the various intermediate forms which the same word presents during the long stages of its transformation? Contrasted with this French word, the Gaelic *gabhar*, pronounced
goar, a goat, has the great virtue, that the moment a philologer sees it in a book, he recognises its identity, through

a course of normal transformations, with the Greek καπρός. And let it be noted in favour of the mute letters in Gaelic, as compared with the respectable supernumeraries in English, that they are much more subject to laws, and therefore in practice much more manageable. A *dh* or *gh* at the end or in the middle of a Gaelic word, between two vowels, will simply be silent; I know that in the case of *righ*, a king, for instance, and the same rule holds in the case of *lagh*, and a hundred similar words; whereas in English, if I drop the final *gh* in *plough*, I have no guarantee that I shall not be forced to resume it in *rough*, and give it the value of *f*. In this case, therefore, living as we do in a glass house, we were wise to fling no stones.

So much for the unfounded objections made to the language of the Caledonian Celts by persons who have not only not taken the trouble to study it, but who are utterly incapable of forming a scientific estimate of the comparative physiology and pathology of any language. But I am not here as a dishonest merchant, to magnify the virtues of my wares, while I conceal their faults. I will therefore not disguise my opinion, with regard to Gaelic, as to French, that they are both over-refinements, and therefore corruptions and degradations, of the Latin language. What the French has gained in epigrammatic concinnity, and the Gaelic in vocalic sweetness, they both have lost in masculine vigour and equestrian tramp. As in a face where there is too much fat, the bones which mark the features disappear, or at least lose their emphasis, so in a language which both systematically drops terminations and smooths over medial consonants, a deficiency in force and in majesty must necessarily be the result. For though the effect of dropping the final consonant will be to leave a vowel-termination, as in *stua* for *stuadh*, *bua* for *buaidh*, *cro* for *crodh*, *la* for *lagh*, *ree* for *righ*, and so forth, it is evident that the word so mutilated into a broad vocalic monosyllable, could never take its place in the grand cavalcade of high-mounted speech which we admire in the well-compacted periods of Greek, Roman, Italian, and Spanish eloquence. I consider therefore that Gaelic, like Scotch, must be content with having achieved a high excellence in popular song, as the French has in the *chansons* of Béranger and the witticisms and fine point of conversational repartee ; still all the three must for ever remain strangers to the majestic architecture of Miltonic rhythm (an excellence which he owed to his Latin element), the deep-bosomed undulation of a Platonic period, and the magnificent massiveness of a Ciceronian sentence.

One only point with regard to the physiognomy of the language remains ; but that may be despatched in a single word. It is well known that the Celts, both in the Scottish Highlands and in the fields of beautiful France, delight in a peculiar use of the nasal organ, unknown to the Teut, whether in Saxony or in the British low countries. If this be a fault, I have no wish to conceal it; if it be a beauty, it is my business to laud it. And to my ear it is a beauty ; not that nasalism, as fully developed in some quarters of America, is not one of the most hideous distortions of human articulated speech ; but a mere touch of a vice is sometimes a virtue, or rather certain vices are only virtues run to seed. Arsenic, as we all know from the criminal reports, in sufficient quantity is a deadly poison ; but the·same mineral salt, moderately administered, purifies the blood and adds a gloss to the skin. So let it be with the delicate nasal twang of the educated Highland lady. I should as soon think of removing it as of robbing the Highland birches of their peculiar fragrance or the Highland whisky of its flavour.

CHAPTER II.

PRE-CHRISTIAN AND MEDIÆVAL.

" Mar ghath soluis do m' anam fein
Tha sgeula na h-aimsir' a dh'fhalbh."—OSSIAN.

THERE is no fact in history more certain than that poetry, in the development of literature, precedes prose; and the reason of this is obvious. To a people living under the simple natural conditions and requirements of human life, the idea of making a formal record in books, or in any other way, for the purpose of plain prosaic perusal, never occurs; reading has no place in the exercise of their functions; and books, of course, do not exist. But that which does exist among human beings, and always must exist where blockish insensibility does not prevail, is the capacity of emotional elevation above the common level of daily life; and this elevation is found in poetry,—lyrical poetry, or narrative poetry inspired by a lyrical enthusiasm. Such moments, of course, do not occur every day; they seize a whole people only on great and striking occasions, when some obstructive difficulty has been removed, or some joyful liberation has been achieved; and so by the stimulus of their novelty, no less than by their inherent grandeur, they create a popular expression of the potentiated national feeling in the shape of song, and a popular record of that feeling in the faithful memory of the people and the professional minstrels who are their spokesmen. We shall therefore justly expect to find, as a normal fact in the history of all peoples, that so soon as an enslaved race shall have escaped from a hated bondage, the expression of triumphant gratitude to God for that deliverance will burst out in some such exordium as the well-known one—"I WILL SING UNTO THE LORD; FOR HE HATH TRIUMPHED GLORIOUSLY: THE HORSE AND HIS RIDER HATH HE THROWN INTO THE SEA!" Or that other one no less familiar—"AWAKE, AWAKE, DEBORAH; AWAKE, AWAKE; UTTER A SONG: ARISE, BARAK, AND LEAD THY CAPTIVITY CAPTIVE, THOU SON OF ABINOAM." In such utterances, where cymbal and guitar, and the tramp of exultant feet, accompany the full outstreaming of the substantial joy of a mighty people, we behold with a healthy admiration that natural union of poetry, piety, and history with music, which in these days of sundered energies and curious specialties is too often sought for in vain. It was not so in the earliest times. It was not then possible to find knowledge without love, poetry without piety, piety without music, or facts of any kind sung or memorised without significance; whereas in these days of widespread prose and wonderful bookmongery, every trifle is recorded, and it requires a special faculty of discrimination to pick the nutritive grains out of the heaps of sand and gravel with which it is served up. It is easy from this to see how in all lands popular poetry possesses a value far superior to many imaginative creations of a later age, however richer in fancy or more finished in execution. The production of your modern poet in a literary age may often be the mere manifestation of some individual peculiarity; a floating bubble iridescent with all beautiful pictures; or an airy architecture, radiant from base to battlement with an imaginative masonry of gold, and silver, and precious stones; but with all this it may remain only the ingenious whim or the baseless speculation of a single idle gentleman, not the harmonised record of the struggles and the achievements of a whole people. Early popular poetry is always history inspired by passion and embellished by fancy. It is an unsifted chronicle certainly, but it is not chronicle without soul; it is the romance of history if you will, but it is not therefore false; it is history without dust and dry bones, and therefore more attractive. It is like the heather on the breezy mountains, which is only so much the more pleasant that it was never forced by artificial appliances from the gardener, nor exhibited for the admiration of a fashionable assembly in West End gatherings.

That the infancy of literature is sung history or sung biography we have a striking example in the well-known passage of the *Iliad* (Book IX.), where the ambassadors sent by Agamemnon to soothe the moody wrath of the son of Peleus, find him solacing his soul with singing old heroic ballads to the accompaniment of the lyre :—

> "And soon to the tents and dark-hulled ships of the
>   Myrmidons they came,
>   And found the chief, where, with his clear-toned lyre,
>   he did delight
>   His soul—a lyre with silver bridge, and made with
>   mickle sleight
>   Beautiful, which from spoils he chose of sacked Eëtion's
>   town ;
>   With this his soul he soothed, and sang old gests of
>   high renown."

And in accordance with this we find that the greatest production of Greek poetical genius is, when analysed, but a collection of popular heroic ballads, fused and organised into that form of finely rounded unity, which we call an Epic poem. Homer certainly was a singer, not a writer; an ἀοιδός not a φιλόλογος or a σοφιστής; and, though writing was in all probability known in Greece before his time, it was used mainly as a record for preservation, not at all as a literary medium. From beginning to end, indeed, the poetry of the Greeks in its most perfect form was only a part of music, and was composed to be heard, not read; their so-called tragedies were sacred operas; and their poetical feet, about which modern metricians delight to discourse so minutely, are in fact musical bars, and have no significance divorced from sweet song. So universal was the wedlock of poetry and music in ancient times, that even the harsh material of law was fused into this form. Strabo tells us that the Iberians who inhabited the part of Spain which is watered by the Guadalquivir were accounted the most learned of their tribe, that they possessed a grammatical language, containing, among other records of past time, laws written in verse to the extent of six thousand lines.[1] Tacitus gives a similar report of the ancient Germans.[2] And with regard to the inhabitants of ancient Gaul generally, Marcellinus, who lived in the middle of the fourth century P.C., has the following interesting passage :—" In these parts of Gaul, spreading northward from Marseilles, no mean amount of intellectual culture prevailed, of which the germ is to be sought in the Bards, the Euhages, and the Druids. Of these three orders, the Bards composed heroic verses in praise of the achievements of illustrious men, accompanying their words with the sweet notes of the lyre; the Euhages devoted themselves to the study of the sublime aspects of nature and the regulated order of its phenomena; while the Druids, of a more lofty genius, bound themselves, after the example of Pythagoras, by the bond of social brotherhood, and soaring into transcendental regions, began to

[1] *Geog.* iii. 139, c.   [2] *German.* i. 2, 3.

despise human affairs, and to inculcate the immortality of the soul."[1] About the Druids, as they are described in this passage, much may have been talked without much foundation, and many things disputed with a plausible scepticism; but about the Bards no man doubts; they are a fact as certain as the episcopal succession in the Church, or the consulate in the Roman Fasti. Bards were in fact as necessary to the completeness of Celtic society, from Julius Cæsar downwards, as newspapers are to the political nutriment of the modern Englishman. In regard to this matter the author of *Fingal* is as true to the genius of the times which he describes in the stormy north, as Homer is to the temper of the sunny south. Without a tale from Demodocus, the feast of the luxurious Phæacians in the Eighth Book of the *Odyssey* would have wanted its chief attraction; and in the same way, a day of battle and blood in *Fingal* is incomplete without the lay of Carol to season the sorrow of the evening meal, where so many dear familiar faces were missed.

> *Fhreagair mac Sheuma, an triath,*
> *Charuill tog do ghuth gu h-àrd*
> *Air gach linn a bh'ann nach beò ;*
> *Caithear oidhche ann am mìn-dhan,*
> *Faighear gairdeachas 's a' bhròn*
> *S iomadh saoi is òigh bu chaoin*
> *Ghluais o thùs' àn Innis-fàil*
> *Is taitneach dàin air na laoich*
> *O thaobh Alba nam fuaim àrd*
> *N'uair dh'aomas farum na séilg*
> *Fo ghuth Oisein nan caomh-rann*
> *'S a fhreagras aonach an deirg*
> *Sruth Chona nan toirm mall.*—FINGAL, i. 565.

[1] Ammianus Marcellinus, xv. 9.

> "Then out spake Semo's noble son :
>   ' Carol, raise thy voice on high ;
>   Of the times gone by let the minstrel sing,
>   Let the night be spent in soothing song,
>   That joy from sorrow may sweetly spring.
>   Many the youths and maidens fair
>   That moved in Innisfail of yore ;
>   Pleasant to hear the song of their praise
>   Echoed on Alba's sounding shore,
>   When the din of the chase has died away,
>   And Ossian stirs the tuneful theme,
>   And the haunt of the deer on the hill replies
>   To Cona's gently-murmuring stream.' "

And when the bard has finished his tale, the blue-eyed chief of Erin pours over him the fulness of his satisfaction, and requests a second strain :—

> " Pleasant, O bard, is thy song on the hill,
>   The words that rise from the days of renown,
>   Soft and sweet as the gentle rain,
>   When the sun on the flowery lea looks down,
>   When the thin grey shade flits o'er the Ben,
>   And the breeze floats lazy and light in the glen ;
>   Strike, son of Phena, thy harp again !
>   Right pleasant to me is thy song on the hill."

These observations will prepare us for what we are to expect in the earliest surviving literature of the Celtic Muse in the Highlands of Scotland. It is not so much what we call a literature that we have to do with as a minstrelsy, and that minstrelsy not consisting, as poetry now does, in the occasional imaginative outbursts of brilliantly endowed individuals, but rather inherent as an essential element in the fixed organism of society. The minstrelsy was an institution as necessary to the Celtic life of the middle ages as Christian preachers now are to the working of the Christian Church; an institution which survives even to the present day, partly in the important personality of the piper who performs his resonant parade at certain hours before the halls of our Highland magnates, partly in the hereditary love of the Highland people for the lyrical expression of their thoughts, and their comparatively meagre expatiation in the current modern form of prose. The Celt in the Highlands is not yet a reading animal; and when books and reading, with all the cumbrous apparatus of modern schools, shall have finally displaced all that remains of the social minstrelsy of the Scottish Celt, an element of popular culture will have been lost, of the importance of which the men who frame our Education Reform Bills and manage our School Boards do not always seem to be aware.

In making a survey of the intellectual productions of the Caledonian Celts, the matter before us naturally falls into four great divisions :—I. The Bardic or Minstrel literature of the mediæval period, commencing at some indefinite period in the border land betwixt Heathenism and Christianity, and stretching out to the era of the Reformation, or a century or so beyond it. II. The succession of Celtic poets of more or less notable originality who flourished between the end of the sixteenth and the end of the eighteenth century. III. The remarkable epiphany of the Celtic Muse on the great European stage, under the auspices of James Macpherson, in the year 1762. IV. The condition of Celtic literature in the Highlands from the subsidence of the great Ossianic excitement produced by Macpherson down to the present hour. Of these four periods I shall now give a sketch in their order, not meaning in any wise to exhaust a fertile theme, but only to call attention to a subject which, from an unhappy combination of influences, has been either unduly subordinated, unworthily neglected, or altogether ignored.

Amid the immense mass of traditional materials moulded and remoulded into popular song, and floating about as a stimulating element in the atmosphere of mediæval life, it is extremely difficult to lay the finger certainly upon this or that fragment and say to what particular century or epoch it belongs. But this much we may unquestionably say, that the reverence for the past, which is inherent in all healthy-minded peoples, and was specially potent in the Celts, will not willingly allow the monuments of its earliest lyrical inspiration to be buried under the rank growth of the present. If the glittering novelty of to-day is strong to attract the popular gaze, because of its glitter mainly, and because of its novelty, the hoary sign-post that points through centuries will often claim a veneration from its age that it could not earn by its virtue; and so, among the collections of popular Celtic poetry that have been made at various times in Scotland and Ireland, we are justly entitled to look for much whose origin extends further back than any date that strict evidence would entitle us to assign to it. Of the old Celtic traditional poetry common to Ireland and Scotland—for the intimate connection of Hibernian and Caledonian culture shines like a golden thread through the lyrical literature of both countries—the most notable collection is that made by Mr. Campbell of Islay, and published under the title of the *Book of the Finn.*[1] The greater part of this collection,

---

[1] *Leabhar na Feinne.* London, Spottiswoode, 1872. Printed for the Author. Gaelic only. Mr. Campbell surely means to add a volume with au English and, if possible, an elegant Latin translation. Such a work belongs to the world.

taken down by the patriotic zeal of the distinguished author from popular recitation, presents of course no literary landmark by which the date of its composition could be determined. Nevertheless we have here the sort of stuff on which the patriotic spirit and the imaginative capacity of the common people was fed for centuries before the Reformation, and even prior to the Christian era. One certain date only, and a date which enables us to exclude all productions of the Celtic Muse more recent than the Reformation, is afforded by the Book of the Dean of Lismore, which, to the non-Gaelic scholar, presents the best materials for judging of the state of professional bardic minstrelsy during the lustiest epoch of the middle ages. Of this book and its contents, therefore, we shall now proceed to give a short account.

In the beautiful village of Fortingall, situated at the extreme east end of the picturesque winding Glen-Lyon, which extends westwards behind Schihallion towards Ben Doran and the hills of Tyndrum, there lived, at the era of the Reformation, a Churchman belonging to a sept of the great clan M‘Gregor, who, to the vicarage of his Perthshire clachan, added the dignity of the Deanery of Lismore, at that time the Episcopal seat of the Bishops of Argyll. This gentleman, with a largeness of sympathy which contrasts favourably with the narrowness of certain modern Presbyterian divines in the north, who will hear of nothing but sermons, employed his leisure hours in collecting into a commonplace-book a number of those historical and other ballads which formed the staple of intellectual recreation in all parts of the country inhabited by the Celtic race. This collection of course contained nothing but what had received the stamp of popular acceptance and general currency. Its contents may therefore justly be considered as being generally several centuries older than the Reformation ; so that its genuine character, as containing the most authentic remains of early Caledonian poetry, cannot be disputed, and its value to the literary and civil historian of mediæval Scotland is altogether unique.   The worthy collector of these interesting remnants died in the year 1551, going piously and quietly to his rest just when John Knox was beginning to shake the foundations of all comfortable old Church life in Scotland by the rumbling earthquake of a necessary reformation. After his decease, his collection of ballads wandered, as is the course of such things, through various old family shelves, desks, and presses, till, in the last century, it came into the possession of the Highland Society of London, by whom it was handed over to the custody of the sister Society of Scotland ; thence it sought and found a fitting place of refuge in one of the learned vaults of the Advocates' Library, principally through the agency of Mr. William Skene, whose labours in the field of early British history are largely known and universally appreciated. Considering the character and position of the custodiers, it may appear strange to some that such a book was not given to the public a hundred years ago, at the time when the publication of alleged Ossianic poems by Macpherson excited such a wide ferment of opinion in the British literary world.   But it was easier to battle about Celtic poems than to take the trouble to study them.   In the midst of all that bandying of sharp words about Celtic matters, Celtic books were not read and the Celtic language not studied ; but there was a peculiarity of the Dean M'Gregor's collection which made it a sealed book even to the most expert scholars of the day.   This peculiarity consisted in the circumstance that the learned Churchman, by a curious anticipation of Pitman and the modern phonetic orthoepists, had written down his popular songs, not according to the character and spelling long sanctioned by the authority of Irish scholars—the spelling at present used in Irish books, and originally used in the Gaelic Bible,—but by the simple application of the Roman letters to express phonetically the spoken Gaelic of the then Scottish Gaels. Of course it required a man not only of learning, but of purpose and decision, to attempt such a decipherment; and accordingly the book had to wait for a half-century after the Ossianic inquisitions of the Highland Society of Edinburgh, before it found a worthy translator in the person of the Reverend Dr. Thomas M'Lauchlan of the Gaelic Free Church, Edinburgh. To the interpretation of the old Gaelic by this learned Presbyterian Churchman Mr. Skene added a valuable introduction, containing, besides an account of the Dean's book, a philological estimate of the Irish and Scottish varieties, for they are scarcely dialects, of the Gaelic, and a critical verdict on the famous Ossianic question, which we shall have occasion to discuss afterwards.

I have said that the Book of the Dean of Lismore is unique in its way, and must be regarded as containing a most valuable treasure of old Celtic material; but I must now warn the reader not for that reason to expect to find in it the highest flights of the Celtic Muse. Quite the contrary. It is no very easy task, from the high strain and hot spur of lyric poetry, as we find it in the lofty flights of Shelley, Coleridge, and other notable English singers of the last generation, to tone readers down to the simplicity and sobriety which like a fundamental key-note lies at the bottom of all genuine poetry of the people. But apart from this, the great body of the poetry in the Dean's collection will certainly not rank high when compared with the popular ballads of Scotland, of Germany, of Servia, or even of the modern Greeks. For

vividness of portraiture, fervour of feeling, truth of character, rich flow of humour, and great wisdom of life, unless
my patriotic sentiment deceive me, I think there are no
compositions of purely popular growth anywhere that surpass the Scottish songs and ballads, compared with which
not a few of the poems in the Dean's collection are scarce
worthy to be called poetry at all; indeed, I have little
doubt that the bards who wrote them, in many cases, were
a sort of necessary professional appendage to a great
family, functionaries who composed verses on important
occasions, pretending as little to any real poetic inspiration
as a family chaplain drawling out his tame weekly discourse in the family chapel may boast of the glowing
apostleship of St. Paul. No doubt those bards were no
hirelings; they were quite honest and loyal so far as they
went. But if a poet be, as Plato will have it, a winged
animal, these Macnabs and Macdougalls and Macrories
show rather like ducks in a village pond than like eagles
ministering to the thunderbolt of Jove. In fact, if these
old professional bards were only well skilled in family
genealogy, which it was their business to be, and had been
decently indoctrinated in the tricks of Celtic versification,
which was a simple matter of drill, like learning to write
Greek iambics in Oxford, they might play their part at a
great local gathering with much more effect and applause
than if they had possessed the ethereal glow of Shelley,
the eagle swoop of Byron, or the rich quaint pregnancy of
Browning; just as a Parliamentary orator, well versed in the
Whig and Tory traditions of the House, will make a more
telling speech on some great party occasion than a man of
ten times his ability, who has not lived in the atmosphere
of Parliamentary manœuvre nor been studious to wield
the Parliamentary war-weapons. But if these poems have
not often a high poetical value, they have always a genuine

historical interest, which interest may often be then greatest when the poetical contents are at zero ; as in the familiar case of the catalogue of the ships in the *Iliad*, and the village calendar in the *Works and Days* of the old Bœotian theologer. We must remember also, in forming a judgment on the poetic genius of the mediæval Celts from the Dean's book, that the compiler of such a collection was not in the position of a modern editor requested by Murray or Macmillan to publish a volume of elegant extracts. The Dean of Lismore had no doubt personal reasons for not a few of his preferences ; and an old scrap of curious family record was often of more interest to him than the most beautifully conceived poem.

The contents of the book generally bear the stamp and character which we have just indicated as characteristic of all early national poetry,—not allegoric struggles between the two primeval elemental powers of light and darkness, as Max Müller would have it, but simply the glowing memories of the great heroic achievements of mighty men in the days that are past. Exactly the same sort of materials, I imagine, as those out of which Homer constructed the heroic architecture of the *Iliad ;* or under which, in more recent times, a pent Greek patriotism slumbered for centuries, till it blazed out grandly in the Liberation War of 1821-5. In the background of all historical vistas there is generally seen looming out from amid the clouds an imposing march of men of large proportions and stout achievements, before whom the present generation stands in wonder and in awe, as feeling themselves the dwarfed production of a less lusty nature. Men were not only bigger in those days, in respect of bony frame—like the body of Orestes, seven cubits long, which the smith of Tegea found in a stone coffin, according to the story in Herodotus,—but they were real demigods, with a high-strung vitality, so that even the gods, as we see in Homer, were not always a match for their prowess. The men who occupy this position in these old Celtic poems are called the Feinne, and as such are naturally the most prominent figures in the most ancient part of the Dean's book. These are the same Titanic personages whose warlike brawn, when strongly moved, in Macpherson's *Fingal*, shakes the rocks from the sides of the Ben, tears the trees up by their roots, and hurls the red ruin down into the foamy-flooded torrent of the glen. And of this race of awful Celtic patriarchs, not the least impressive in the sad solemnity of his presence is the blind old bard himself, Ossian the son of Fionn, who sings the immortal achievements of his mighty kindred. All who have looked into Macpherson's book know how the blind old bard stands there in the vestibule of the Fenian temple of fame, bearing the weight of years with a certain calm dignity of hoary feebleness, and looking back with sad admiration on exploits of youthful lustihood which could be enacted no more. It was only natural, if this was a genuine flesh and blood minstrel of old Celtic tradition, and not a mere lay figure put up for artistic effect by the modern man of Badenoch, that we should expect to find him occupying the same position, and exhibiting the same features in the Dean's book. And so it is. The collection divides itself naturally into two distinct parts, one part more ancient, and bearing no trace of Christian sentiment, and the other more modern, and showing distinct signs of sacerdotal preponderance. The poems of the first class generally bear the words—

The author of this is Ossian, the son of Finn,

as a superscription, which we may take for good evidence of the popular feeling that there was a flavour of the most hoary antiquity about these poems which was not found in the others. We shall take the second in order as a favourable specimen,—the English version in M'Lauchlan, —to which, if I have in some cases added rhyme, it was because it seemed only fair to these old songs of the Celtic Muse not to deprive them of that luxury of recurrent sound, which is one of the principal charms of their art.[1]

Is fad an nochd na neula faim.

"Long are the clouds this night above me;
The last was a long night to me.
This day that drags its weary way
Came from a wearier yesterday.
Each day that comes is long to me:
Such was not my wont to be.
Now there is no fine delight
In battle-field, and fence of fight:
No training now to feats of arms,
Nor song, nor harp, nor maiden's charms,
Nor blazing hearth, nor well-heaped board,
Nor banquet spread by liberal lord,
Nor stag pursuing, nor gentle wooing,
The dearest of dear trades to me.
Alas ! that I should live to see
Days without mirth in hut or hall,
Without the hunter's wakeful call,
Or bay of hounds, or hounds at all,
Without light jest, or sportive whim
Or lads with mounting breast to swim
Across the long arms of the sea.—

---

[1] The Gaelic poetry generally rhymes only the vowel, but no good purpose could be served by imitating this vocalic assonance here. In poetical translations it is always wise to humour the habit of the ear which belongs to the language of the translator.

> Long are the clouds this night above me.
> In the big world there lives no wight
> More sad than I this night.
> A poor old man with no pith in my bones,
> Fit for nothing but gathering stones.
> The last of the Finn, the noble race,
> Ossian, the son of Finn am I,
> Standing beneath the cold grey sky,
> Listening to the sound of bells.—
> Long are the clouds this night above me!"

The following looks like a monkish addition in some later age :—

> "Gain, O Patrick, from thy God,
> When we are laid beneath the sod,
> That He may keep us free from harm.—
> Long are the clouds this night above me!"

It is curious to observe how the sombre nationality of this old Fenian bard has propagated itself even into the most recent life of the Caledonian Celts, exhibiting a diverse phase in the sentimental monotone of Macpherson's Ossian and the solemn sepulchral piety of certain North-western Gospellers. A historical theorist of the stamp of the late Mr. Buckle might find it worthy of inquiry whether ancient heathen bards and modern Calvinistic preachers were equally the products of the dark clouds that roll their volumes round the grim crags of Glencoe; and then the question would arise, how under similar influences of the west coast of uttermost Kerry and Galway, such freakish sportiveness and grotesque humour should have blossomed out.

Persons who are strongly infected with the modern sentimental abhorrence of WAR, and who do not, with Aristotle,

recognise in the stern phenomena of international antagonism a grand training-school for a great part of virtue,
will find little pleasure in the perusal of some of the most
prominent of those ballads, which refer to the frequent
early encounters between the Celts of the west of Scotland
and the east of Ireland with the sea-rovers of Scandi-
navia. Of the historical reality of the facts out of which
these ballads grew there cannot be the slightest doubt.
Behind all the mist of the Bens and the floating
wraiths that hang on by the silver skirts of the black
clouds, there is certainly something much more solid and
substantial than the darkness and the dawn into which
it is the fashion of the German school of mythologists to
resolve the early epic traditions of all peoples without discrimination. But more interesting to the student of history than the firmly based reality of these old songs is the
ideal of the chivalrous Fenian warrior which they present;
an ideal which in a wealthy commercial country like Great
Britain may even now be held up to the youth in British
schools with a more elevating moral effect than some
things that are most carefully set before them. It is
only a Quaker that sees in a great warrior nothing but a
sublime butcher; the true heroic type of a Celtic warrior
adds to his courage and his self-sacrifice a generosity and a
gentleness which make him one of the most finely-tempered
specimens of humanity. Of poems holding forth to admiration this high type of character there are two in the
collection: one, attributed to Ossian himself, in praise of
his illustrious father, the chief of the Boisgne branch of the
Fein, and the other to Fergus the Bard, in praise of "high-
minded Gaul," the head of the other branch of the Fenian
called Clan Morn. We shall be content with the first—

> " 'Twas yesterday week
> I last saw Finn;

Ne'er did I see
A braver man;
Teige's daughter's son,
A powerful king;
My fortune, my light,
My mind's whole might,
Both poet and chief.
Braver than kings,
Firm chief of the Feinn.
Lord of all lands,
Leviathan at sea,
As great on land,
Hawk of the air,
Foremost always.
Generous, just,
Despised a lie.
Of vigorous deeds,
First in song.
A righteous judge,
Firm his rule.
Polished his mien,
Who knew but victory.
Who is like him
In fight or song?
Resists the foe,
In house or field.
Marble his skin,
The rose his cheek,
Blue was his eye,
His hair like gold.
All men's trust,
Of noble mind.
Of ready deeds,
To women mild,

A giant he,
The field's delight.
Best polished spears,
No wood like their shafts.
Rich was the King.
His great green bottle,
Full of sharp wine,
Of substance rich.
Excellent he.
Of noble form,
His people's head,
His step so firm,
Who often warred.
In beauteous Banva,
Three hundred battles
He bravely fought.
With miser's mind
From none withheld.
Anything false
His lips ne'er spoke.
He never grudged,
No, never Finn;
The sun ne'er saw King
Who him excelled.
The monsters in lakes,
The serpent by land,
In Erin of saints,
The hero slew.
Ne'er could I tell,
Though always I lived,
Ne'er could I tell
The third of his praise.
But sad am I now,
After Finn of the Feinn!

Away with the chief,
My joy is all fled.
No friends 'mong the great,
No courtesy.
No gold, no queen,
No princes and chiefs.
Sad am I now,
Our head ta'en away !
I'm a shaking tree,
My leaves all gone.
An empty nut,
A reinless horse,
Sad, sad am I,
A feeble kern.
Ossian I, the son of Finn,
Strengthless in deed.
When Finn did live
All things were mine.
Seven sides had the house
Of Cumhal's son.
Seven score shields
On every side.
Fifty robes of wool
Around the King.
Fifty warriors
Filled the robes.
Ten bright cups
For drink in his hall.
Ten blue flagons,
Ten horns of gold.
A noble house
Was that of Finn.
No grudge nor lust,
Babbling nor sham ;

> No man despised
> Among the Feinn.
> The first himself,
> All else like him.
> Finn was our chief,
> Easy his praise,
> Noblest of Kings.
> Finn ne'er refused
> To any man,
> Howe'er unknown;
> Ne'er from his house
> Sent those who came.
> Good man was Finn,
> Good man was he.
> No gifts e'er given
> Like his so free.
>   'Twas yesterday week."

The ideal here set forth is perfectly Homeric. Achilles in his best moments and his most favourable aspect might have stood for it.

In the second part of the Dean's collection, where a distinctly more modern element speaks out, in addition to the two ballads of real and mimic war—for hunting is always the best school of soldiership—we have moral and aphoristic poems; quite in the natural order of things, just as Hesiod with his metric fragments of rustic wisdom accompanies or follows very shortly after Homer with the pomp of his military processions and his flash of hostile encounters between Greek and Trojan. In Homer himself, as the well-furnished repertory of all the life and all the wisdom of his age, we find not a few of those sagacious, curt sentences, into which men unacquainted with books are fond of compressing their experience of human life. Closely allied to the sententious is the element of popular satire, the same that in Hesiod created the story of Pandora, in which all the ills of humanity are charged by the bearded half of the community to the unsanctified curiosity of the un-bearded. In this department, from the satirical versifiers of the Dean's book down to Rob Donn, the favourite bard of the Mackay country, and the sour-blooded creature who heaped his rhymed maledictions on Glen Nevis and Glen-coe,[1] Gaelic literature never wanted emphatic spokesmen. Indeed, where there is no leading article in the *Times* or the *Scotsman*, some authoritative individual must wield the lash, and in such society as that of the Highlands the local bard was the only person who could effectively per-form the function. The pulpit might condemn great sins, but it was too dignified to laugh at small follies, and not seldom lacked courage to meddle with strong offenders. Among the didactic bards in the Dean's Book, one Phelim M'Dougall is particularly prominent, from whom we extract a string of aphorisms each of which might form the text of a most profitable sermon :—

> " 'Tis not good to travel on Sunday,
>   Whoever the Sabbath would keep ;
>   Not good to be of ill-famed race ;
>   Not good is a dirty woman ;
>   Not good to write without learning ;
>   Not good are grapes when sour ;

---

[1] I forget the fellow's name, but I have seen some notice of him some-where in the *Gaidheal*. The verses about Glen Nevis—a vile slander—I amused myself translating as follows :—

> " Glen Nevis, cold and bleak, barren and bare,
>   Grey stones the only crop that prospers there.
>   A glen so long and dreary, wild and waste,
>   Thieves found the den exactly to their taste ;
>   On such a glen, so crowned and cursed with evil
>   God turned his back, and left it to the devil !"

The lines on Glencoe are equally severe, but perhaps better merited.

Not good is an Earl without English;
Not good is a sailor, if old;
Not good is a bishop without warrant;
Not good is a blemish on an elder;
Not good a priest with but one eye;
Not good a parson, if a beggar;
Not good is a palace without play;
Not good is a handmaid if she's slow;
Not good is a lord without a dwelling;
Not good is a temple without a burying-ground;
Not good is a woman without shame;
Not good is a harper without a string;
Not good is fighting without courage;
Not good is entering a port without a pilot;
Not good is a maiden who backbites;
Not good is the poverty of a debtor;
Not good is a castle without an heir;
Not good is neglecting the household dogs;
Not good is disrespect to a father;
Not good is the talk of the drunken;
Not good is a knife without an edge;
Not good is injustice in judging;
Not good is the friendship of devils;
And thy Son, oh Virgin most honoured,
Though he has saved the seed of Adam,
Not good for himself was the cross.
Not good is a reader without understanding;
Not good for a man to want a friend;
Not good is a poet without a subject;
Not good is a tower without a hall;
Not good is a web without fulling;
Not good is sport without laughter;
Not good are misdeeds when prosperous;
Not good is marriage without consent;

> Not good is a crown without supremacy;
> Not good is ploughing by night;
> Not good is learning without courtesy;
> Not good is religion without knowledge.
>
> > Not good."

These maxims are not adduced as evidence of any unusually keen practical sagacity in the people who made them, but in so far only as they serve to throw light on the fashionable virtues and vices of the age. The very first one shows us clearly that the objection to Sunday travelling, which some people represent as the offspring of Presbyterian Calvinism, was expressed in the Catholic Church before the bold Saxon had blown the first blast of his trumpet. The sixth maxim is noteworthy, as showing the general prevalence of Gaelic through all classes of society at the time when it was written. For taking a part in the business of the kingdom, the local thane, however mighty in Gaelic at home, would require a familiarity with the English tongue. In the present day one might invert the maxim, and say, *Not good is a lord of the soil who has no sympathy with the language, the traditions, and the poetry of the people from whom he draws his rents.* Another maxim, " Not good is a crown without supremacy," shows an admirable insight into the weak point of aristocratic government in the Highlands, when every thane was a king, and every king might be a despot. The same rhyming moralist, or some brother bard of the same kidney, sets forth his special dislikings in an aphoristic shape, and ends very naturally by telling us that it is impossible for him to exhaust the bead-roll of the things which he dislikes. Earl Gerald, the fourth Earl of Desmond, known in Ireland as Earl Desmond the Poet, indulges largely in satirical effusions against the fair sex; a very cheap thing

to do, as there were no literary ladies in those days strong
enough with the pen to fling back the ill-natured badinage.
An anonymous writer indicates his estimate of monks and
monasteries in a sufficiently intelligible way by saying,

> " I, Robert, went yesterday
>   A monastery for to see ;
> But to my wishing they said nay,
>   Because my wife was not with me !"

But, while the bards performed the function of public
censors with sharp incision when required, their main duty
consisted in the celebration of the great deeds of the brave
heads of their clan, especially of those who showed a
princely liberality in the remuneration of bards.   Thus
Finlay MacNab, the red-haired bard, sings the praises of his
patron, Ian Dubh MacGregor of Glenstrae, who was buried
at Dysart in Glenorchy, 26th May 1519, in the following
strain :—

> " I've been a stranger long
>   To pleasant-flowing matter ;
> I'm tired of lashing fools
>   With unproductive satire.
> I've dwarfed my Muse for nought,
>   But now she shall grow bigger
> By chant of lofty theme,
>   The praise of the MacGregor.
> A prince indeed is he,
>   Who knows the craft of ruling,
> Well taught in each degree
>   Of proper princely schooling.
> No lies there needs to coin ;
>   The duty of the poet
> Commands to know the truth,
>   And when he knows to show it.

His courage in his breast
Is one long breath of daring;
Bold, but when mercy calls,
Not deaf to gentle sparing.
MacGregor of the Blows
They call my prince most rightly,
For when his arm comes down,
In sooth it comes not lightly.
You never wait in vain
For him to make a quorum,
When forth they ride to drive
The flocks and herds before them.
Myself will sing his praise,
The first in breast of battle,
Or over Lowland braes
To drive the lifted cattle."

It is worthy of notice in these verses, that the proper
princely schooling here talked of does not in any wise
mean reading and writing, but rather knowledge of family
history and dexterity in all such knightly accomplishments,
musical or gymnastic, as were fashionable in those days.
The well-known right of the Gael to harry the lands of the
Saxon, is asserted likewise without disguise in the same
bard's eulogium of his master's war-steed :—

"The horse that I praise is MacGregor's,
The prince of good riders is he;
The lord of a house that was ever
To bards open-handed and free.
From Erin they came for to praise him,
To Albyn the man to behold,
The MacGregor who plunders the Saxons,
And fattens the Gael with their gold."

Nor is there anything strange in this. The Greeks and

the Romans held exactly the same doctrine with regard to
all barbarians; and modern Americans, I imagine, with
regard to their neighbours, are nothing more righteously
inclined. In politics neighbours are always enemies; and
a big neighbour like Rome was the natural enemy of the
whole world.

The ferocity of human beings who live in a habitual
state of warfare shines forth clearly enough in Homer,
where even the queenly Hecuba wishes that with her close-
infixed teeth she may eat through the liver of the stout
Greek man who slew her son; and we naturally expect to
find strong demonstrations of the same kind in the war-
songs of the Celtic bards. In a *Brosnachadh-Catha*, or in-
citement to battle, which bears internal evidence of having
been written on the eve of the invasion of England which
terminated so fatally at Flodden field, the following lines
occur :—

> " Burn their women, lean and ugly!
> Burn their children, great and small!
> In the hut and in the palace,
> Prince and peasant, burn them all!
> Plunge them in the swelling rivers,
> With their gear, and with their goods;
> Spare, while breath remains, no Saxon,
> Drown them in the roaring floods!"

One truth that stands out clearly in these curious poems
is the well-known Highland pride of family, a pride that
with much that is good and elevating, has done not a little
harm to our old Highland lairds, who found in the day of
need that pedigree was a very pretty thing to boast of, but
a very sorry thing to feed on. Some of the poems are
mere rhymed genealogies and family histories, which have

no interest except to the professed genealogist. In one singular poem, half in joke we imagine, the writer washes himself free from the stain of bastardy by the detailed enumeration of all the noble races whose blood had mingled in the rich veins of his ancestry :—

> " Men make boast of noble blood :
>   Though money has its praises,
> I'd much liefer be well born
>   Than count the wealth of Crœsus.
> Hear me, gentles and commons all,
>   Cease your blame and banter;
> When I my pedigree rehearse,
>   You'll find I am no vaunter.
> From great Clan Dougall I descend ;
>   No better blood is flowing,
> But richer made in me from founts
>   That I will soon be showing.
> From the Mac Chailein a good part
>   Of my life's blood I borrow,
> Mac Chailein, bountiful to bards,
>   Then how should I find sorrow ?
> In Earla I was born and bred,
>   I tell you true the story,
> A very noble place it is
>   'Twixt Aros and Tobermory.
> Macdonald lies off to the west ;
>   I dwell with good Clan Gillean,
> Brave men who stood in battle's breast
>   A hundred 'gainst a million.
> MacNeil of Barra, too, most sure,
>   Gives gentle blood to me, sir;
> And Colonsay doth make her boast
>   I'm kin to the MacFie, sir.

The mighty masterful MacSween,
  Clan Ranald and Macleod, sir,
The stoutest chiefs e'er tramped on green,
  Give substance to my blood, sir.
The Cattanachs and the MacIntoshes
  Both make a goodly figure
In my proud line; and linked with them,
  Clan Cameron and Macgregor:
And Stewart's seed, though sown on earth
  More wide than any other,
The tale is true that one of them
  Was my grandsire's grandmother;
And if you will to do me harm,
  I rede you well consider
That I have cousins stout of arm
  In Breadalbane and Balquhidder.
Clan Lauchlan and Clan Lamond, too,
  Are numbered with my kin, sir;
I really see no end in view
  When once that I begin, sir;
For in my veins of noble blood
  Dame Nature was so lavish,
She added some drops from the flood
  Of thy pure fount, Clan Tavish,
Lads that do plenish our green hills
  With virtue and with vigour,
Tight little men, but with more pith
  Than many who are bigger.
I visit MacDougall of Craignish,
  And from the good MacIvor
I get my dinner full and free,
  And never pay a stiver.
And now my race and lineage rare
  When you have bravely mastered,

> You'll find the best of all your bloods
> Flows in my veins—the bastard!"

So much for the professional Celtic bards of the middle ages; ages full of rich gleaming veins of stout humanity, profitable to the wise digger, but which in their totality no wise man would wish to recall.

CHAPTER III.

FROM THE REFORMATION TO MACPHERSON.

'Αναξιφόρμιγγες ὕμνοι,
Τίνα θεὸν, τίν' ἥρωα,
Τίνα δ' ἄνδρα κελαδήσομεν ;—PINDAR.

BETWEEN the poetry of the Dean of Lismore's Book and that which we are now about to consider there is a wide gap. I cannot tell how it is,—perhaps it is not wise always to demand reasons for the sudden rise of poetical or artistic schools,—but somehow or other, even in the furthest west and most thoroughly Popish of the Western Highlands, the spirit of intellectual individualism seems to have infected the atmosphere; and an army of Celtic poets comes into view, in whom the elements of family-genealogy and clan-eulogy, though in no wise extinct, are subordinated to the personal character and genius of the bard. This is a thoroughly modern element; an element, however, which in the Highland poets never thrusts the workman with undue prominence—as in the case of Lord Byron—into the foreground of his work. The Celtic bard of this epoch, though no longer the mere spokesman of the clans, is thoroughly popular not only in the character of his environment and in the tone of his treatment, but generally in the choice of his subject. He does not compass heaven and earth, like some of our modern poets, to find a subject, and find a bad one after all. If he does not find it in his own

bosom, he will certainly find it among his own hills.
Among the most ancient of these poems—no person seems
to know the date exactly—is one made known to the
general British public three-quarters of a century ago by
the accomplished Highland lady, Mrs. Grant of Laggan.[1]
The name in Gaelic is, *Miann 'a 'bhaird aosda*, that is, "The
Aged Bard's Wish."   It is the third in Mackenzie's collection, and starts thus :—

> *O chiraibh mi ri taobh nan allt*
> *A shiubhlas mall le ceumaibh ciùin*
> *Fo sgàil a bharraich leag mo cheann,*
> *'S bithus' a ghrian ro-chàirdeil rium.*

> " O place me by the purling brook,
>   That wimples gently down the lea,
>   Under the old trees' branchy shade,
>   And thou, bright sun, be kind to me !"

And again :—

> *O cuir mo chluas ri fuaim Eas-mòr*
> *Le 'chrònan a' tearnadh o'n chreig.*
> *Bi'dh cruit agus slige ri 'm thaobh*
> *'S an sgiath a dhiòn mo shinnsir 's a' chath.*

> "Where I may hear the waterfall,
>   And the hum of its falling wave,
>   And give me the harp, and the shell, and the shield
>   Of my sires in the strife of the brave ! "

This poem, by whomsoever written, is extremely beautiful,
melodious in language, polished and graceful in execution,
so as not undeservedly to claim a place in the great echo
chamber of Highland poetry, very similar to that occupied
by Gray's *Elegy* among ourselves.   But more noteworthy,   .

---

[1] Poems by Mrs. Grant of Laggan.   Edinburgh, 1803.

perhaps, than its internal excellence is the evidence which it affords of a poetry of high literary culture existing in the Highlands long before the time of Macpherson. It is quite modern in its sentiment and tone; a tone, if I may venture to guess, perhaps caught from the pastoral poetry of the Italians about the time of Milton fashionable in England, with a reminiscence of the old Ossianic times, but without the slightest flavour of Christianity. In these respects it seems to belong to the same school as Macpherson's *Ossian;* and as a significant precursor of *Fingal*, though in a much less ambitious style, it seems to me to deserve much more attention from Lowland critics than it has hitherto received.

The two other poems in Mackenzie's collection which precede "The Aged Bard's Wish" are entitled *Mordubh* and *Collath*. They are in the style and manner of Macpherson; and, though assumed by Mackenzie to be ancient, do in all likelihood belong to that same school of modern literary Gaelic to which we have referred "The Aged Bard." Of the first poem, *Mordubh*, an English prose translation appeared in Clark's *Caledonian Bards*, published in 1778, and a poetical version by Mrs. Grant of Laggan in her poems. About this book a mystery hangs, which it seems impossible to clear up. Mrs. Grant declares her perfect faith in the honesty of the translator, who, according to a MS. note in my copy, was by birth a Badenoch man, afterwards bred as an engraver in Edinburgh, and finally settled as a land-surveyor in South Wales; but in an age where, from the success of Macpherson, the temptation was great to trump up Caledonian poems, one cannot feel warranted to take stand upon it as on any very sure foundation. Of the second poem, *Collath*, the authorship is spoken of by Mackenzie as a matter of literary fact, when he says that Fonar, the author of this poem, belonged to the illustrious and once powerful family of Collath. But Mr. Campbell, in his *Highland Tales* (iv. p. 224), asserts that the author of this piece was the Rev. Mr. Maccallum, minister of Arisaig in Inverness-shire, who published it as an ancient poem in the first edition of his old Gaelic poems in 1820; and when he found his pious fraud passing current, was seized with a twitch of conscience, and in the preface to the third edition of the poems in 1842 confessed to the authorship. And this witness is true: for, though I have not been able to lay my hands on this edition, on account of its extreme rarity, I saw a complete copy of the preface with the confession in the possession of a gentleman well known for his curious collection of Gaelic books.[1] These two poems, therefore, both in their style and in the ambiguity or admitted disingenuousness of their authorship, may be regarded as coming fitly under the rubric of the famous Ossianic controversy, and may have some not unimportant indirect bearing on its critical treatment. In the meantime we shall behave wisely by simply dismissing them from our view.

The well-marked figure who leads the van of the goodly company of post-Reformation lyrical bards, is MAIRI NIGHEAN ALASTAIR RUAIDH, that is, Mary the daughter of Red Alexander; for the Highlanders, like the Homeric heroes, with the strong feeling of clanship which possessed Greeks and Celts alike, generally add the patronymic to the personal name, just as the botanists mark at once the common and the peculiar in any plant by a double name, of which one characterises the genus and the other the species. Mary was a Macleod, born at Rowdil, at the south-east corner of Harris,[2] in the year 1569, and her father was

---

[1] Mr. James Macpherson of the Union Bank, Edinburgh.

[2] At this place there is an interesting old monument of the Macleods, belonging to the year 1428. See *Murray's Handbook of Scotland:* Inver-

son of *Alastair Ruadh* or Roy, as Lowlanders call it,[1] a descendant of the chief of the Macleods. Mary, like many of the authors of our best Scottish songs, was not professionally a poet; she merely had the fountain of human sympathy deep within her, which, fed from the old lyrical habit of her race, gushed out as occasion might call in the fresh and natural way which it is the highest glory of professional poets like Goethe to imitate with success, as it is, on the other hand, a most perilous seduction for a popular poet like Burns, to prink the unadorned simplicity of his ploughman's Muse with the glittering spangles and curious lace-work of a highly polished literary style. Her function in life seems to have been that highly respectable one which figures so largely in the *Odyssey* and the Attic drama: she was τρόφος, or nurse, to five lairds of the Macleods, and two of the lairds of Applecross. As such, her headquarters were at Dunvegan, the castled seat of the Macleods, on one of those picturesque tongues of sea that fork themselves far inland on the west coast of the isle of Skye. Here she was often seen sitting alone in a brooding humour on the cliffs looking seaward, or oftener, no doubt, especially in her later years, going from house to house with her tartan *tonnag* fastened in front with a large brooch, and a silver-headed cane in her hand, in search of that easy gossip on all subjects of local interest in which poets of a healthy tone find the natural fuel for their human sympathies. She is reported also to have been signally addicted to snuff—a most unpoetical practice—and whisky,

ness-shire, Harris. The large and commodious steamboats which now visit those parts will generally, at the request of intelligent travellers, stop here long enough to allow a hasty inspection of the monument, which is within the church, close to the shore of the snug little bay of Rowdil.

[1] *Roy* of course is an approach to the phonetic spelling of the Gaelic. The real spelling, *ruadh*, shows at once its linguistic identity with the Greek ἐ-ρυθ-ρός, the German *roth*, and our own *red*.

which, of course, in those cold regions, was the natural surrogate of that wine which maketh glad the heart of man, and from which few persons of a poetical temperament are averse. Mary's attachment to the bottle seems, however, never to have transgressed the limits of that salutary stimulus which Nature, under depressing climatic influences, wisely allows; for she lived even longer than the longest-lived of those healthy Greek sages whose longevity the great Greek humorist in a special treatise has commemorated.[1] Mary died at the patriarchal age of 105, and lies buried in Harris.

Of her merits as a poetess the Highlanders speak in very glowing terms. Mackenzie in his introduction to her Poems says :—

"Mary Macleod, the inimitable poetess of the Isles, is the most original of all our poets. She borrows nothing. Her thoughts, her verses, her rhymes, are all equally her own. Her language is simple and elegant; her diction easy, natural, and unaffected. Her thoughts flow freely and unconstrained. There is no straining to produce effect; no search after unintelligible words to conceal the poverty of ideas. Her versification runs like a mountain stream over a smooth bed of polished granite. Her rhymes are often repeated, but yet we do not feel them tiresome or disagreeable. Her poems are mostly eulogistic; yet they are not the effusions of a mean and mercenary spirit, but the spontaneous and heartfelt tribute of a faithful and devoted dependant."

How far this is strictly true my senses are not yet sufficiently exercised in the æsthetical appreciation of Celtic literature to enable me to decide; but there is certainly a very peculiar charm in the verses generally called *Luinneag Mhic Leod*, which appear in almost all collections of Gaelic

---

[1] Lucian, περὶ μακροβίων.

songs, and of which I have ventured a translation. The circumstances connected with the composition of this poem are characteristic. The then chief of the Macleods, to whose dependency she belonged, seems to have been of the opinion of the Pope, that it is dangerous for a person exercising absolute power to be freely handled by his subjects, even in the way of eulogy; for the man who has exercised the right to praise may not unnaturally suppose that he has the corresponding right to blame; at all events, to be dragged before the public frequently, either in the verses of a popular rhymer or the columns of a newspaper may not often be the best means of commanding popular respect. It is a point of policy with those who wish to loom large in the public eye not to make themselves cheap. So the laird of Dunvegan, whom Mary served, seems on some occasions to have been more annoyed than flattered with the effusions in which, after the fashion of Bœotian Pindar, she paraded the details of his personal and family history before the gossip-loving Hebrideans; he took offence hugely at her freedom (which, as a poetess, she was certainly entitled to), and banished her as a punishment to the island of Mull, or, as some say, the lonely and inhospitable Scarba.[1] Of course Mary could not relish this any more than Madame de Stael could feel comfortable out of the atmosphere of the Parisian saloons; so she seized the first opportunity, which the recurrence of family birthdays presented, of writing a Pindarico-Alcaic ode to the young laird. In consideration of this the savage breast of the chief smoothed its shaggy bristles down, and Mary was allowed to return to her beloved isle of mist and mountain, on condition that she should make no more songs. To this condition she

---

[1] The high island north of Jura, which rises up before the tourist as he steams westward through the Crinan Canal, and sees the horizon of the Atlantic opening in bold outline before him.

willingly consented; making songs with her was only an accident—to be in Skye was the very soul of her existence. But Mary is not the first rhymer who has made promises of this kind which she found it impossible to keep. A bird is a bird, and will sing. So Mary, after having given proof of her loyalty to her chief by a long-studied abstinence from rhymed eulogy of the family, was at length betrayed into the forbidden luxury of an ode. One of the laird's sons had been ill, and, after a severe struggle, recovered. This was too much for Mary's womanly nature and poetical tendencies. She must make a poem on the recovery; and of course the laird heard of it; and of course also Mary was called to answer for her contumacy. *Why did she commence writing poems about the family again? Did she not know that it was forbidden? Was she not brought back from Mull on the express condition that she should never again bring the name of Macleod into any rhyme?* To which thundering charge Mary replied quite coolly, *Cha'n oran a th'ann: cha'n 'eil ach cronan:* "This is not a song; it is only a crooning."[1] So much for the story; the verses written in Mull before her recall are as follows :—

LUINNEAG MHIC LEOD.

I.

I sit on a knoll,
All sorrowful and sad,
And I look on the grey sea
In mistiness clad,
And I brood on strange chances
That drifted me here,
Where Scarba and Jura
And Islay are near.

---

[1] The word "*cronan*" is both Gaelic and Scotch. I do not know that it is found in the Teutonic languages.

II.

Where Scarba and Jura
And Islay are near ;
Grand land of rough mountains,
I wish thee good cheer.
I wish young Sir Norman
On mainland and islands
To be named with proud honour,
First chief of the Highlands !

III.

To be praised with proud honour,
First chief of the Highlands,
For wisdom and valour,
In far and in nigh lands ;
For mettle and manhood
There's none may compare
With the handsome Macleod
Of the princeliest air.

IV.

And the blood through his veins,
That so proudly doth fare,
From the old kings of Lochlinn
Flows richly and rare.
Each proud earl in Alba
Is knit with his line,
And Erin shakes hands with him
Over the brine.

V.

And Erin shakes hands with him
Over the brine;
Brave son of brave father,
The pride of his line,

In camp and in council,
Whose virtue was seen,
And his purse was as free
As his claymore was keen.

VI.

And his purse was as free
As his claymore was keen ;
From such stem what wonder
Such sapling hath been !
Large-souled and free-handed ;
And who died of thee,
Clan Rory of banners
Brought dying to me.

VII.

Clan Rory of banners,
O never from thee
May another death-message
Be wafted to me !
Rare jewel of mortals,
Though banned from my sight,
With my heart I thee worship,
Thou shapeliest knight !

VIII.

With my heart I thee worship,
Thou shapeliest knight,
Well girt in the grace
Of the red and the white ;
With an eye like the blaeberry
Blue on the brae,
And cheeks like the haws.
On the hedge by the way.

IX.

With a cheek like the haws
On the hedge by the way,
'Neath the rarest of locks
In rich curly display ;
And the guest in thy hall
With glad cheer shall behold
Rich choice of rare armour
In brass and in gold.

X.

Rich choice of rare armour
In brass and in gold,
With sharp swords, thin-bladed,
The tools of the bold,
With rifles and carbines,
Well-aiming and true,
And strings of stout hemp,
To long bows of good yew.

XL.

And strings of stout hemp
To long bows of good yew,
And big guns for which gold
In big payment was due ;
And arrows, smooth-polished
And feathered full fair,
From the plume of the eagle,
With silk rich and rare.

XII.

O dear Son of Mary,
To thee is my prayer,
From danger preserve him,
Whate'er he may dare,

When he tracks the wild deer
The lone mountains among,
And climbs the steep corrie,
With foot firm and strong.

XIII.

And climbs the steep corrie,
With foot firm and strong,
And pets the old dogs,
And gives law to the young,
Where from touch of his prowess
The blood soon shall flow
Of the deer white behind,
And the red-hided roe.

XIV.

Of the stag and the red deer,
Where ranged in a row,
Thyself and thy comrades
Shall gallantly show,
Well-trained in the chase,
And well-tried in the weather,
And never at fault
With their chief on the heather !

From Mary Macleod we advance to IAIN LOM, who performed a prominent part in the warlike struggles and political combinations of Charles I. and II. Iain Lom, or Bare John (how he got that name is not clear), belonged to the Keppoch family, who inhabit the country on the Spean behind Ben Nevis, a branch of the great clan of the Macdonalds. His connection with the best blood of the country brought him, by a plain path, into public importance,—an importance which was naturally greatly increased by his poetical talents, combined with great vigour and decision of character. His manliness and independence, and determination not to be beaten, were signally displayed in the case of the trustees of the young heir of Keppoch, who had been sent abroad for his education. These trustees, not perhaps formally such in law, but cousins of the same blood, had assumed, or had been intrusted with, the management of the young laird's property during his absence. Such long leases of delegated power have never been without a strong temptation to the greed and the ambition of a certain class of men in lawless times; so the well-beloved cousins in this case took advantage of their position to deprive their ward first of his property and then of his life. This faithless massacre took place about the year 1663. In cases of this kind, when the party about to perpetrate a villany is in full possession of the advantages arising from the personal influence exercised on a large population through a considerable series of years, it is extremely difficult to get the people to unite in protesting publicly, by bold word and brave deed, against what they feel to be a villany. Under such circumstances, man is too surely discovered to be by nature a cowardly animal; and moral courage shines out as the most rare and the most noble of the virtues. The hero of the hour in this case was Iain Lom. He stood up in the glen on the braes of Lochaber, in the attitude of Plato's just man, alone against the blood-stained usurpers; and when unaided at home, he fled from the land, but not from his purpose, to find a powerful and efficient ally in Sir Alexander Macdonald, the lord of Sleat, in Skye. The murderers were seized and beheaded; and the just retribution which overtook them was made more emphatic by the hot denunciation from the bard, who, like Achilles in the *Iliad*, was as fierce in his revenge as fervid in his affection.

In the movements which immediately preceded the battle of Inverlochy, Bare John had kept his eyes wide open, and from his local knowledge had been in a condition to give the commander of the Royal troops exact information as to the approach of the Campbells from the east. All poets are not, like King David and Byron, also soldiers; and an anecdote is told of John's conduct just when the battle was going to commence, which shows how little ambition the Keppoch bard had to rival the immortal feat of Æschylus in singing the victory which he had helped to gain. "Make ready now," said the general-in-chief to the bard; "you guided us to the enemy, we shall guide you to the fight." The poet was not in the habit of smelling gunpowder; he had no notion of being shot in a stupid way which he did not professionally understand; yet, of course, of all imputations in his Celtic heart he could the least stand the reproach of cowardice; he stood dumb for a moment; till in the despair of necessity his ready wit flashed out the reply, "Fight? of course, Sir Alasdair, that's only natural; but, if I go along with thee to-day, and fall in battle, who will sing thy victory to-morrow?" "Thou art in the right, John," said the chief; "let the shoemaker stick to his last; I will fight the battle to-day, and you will celebrate my prowess to-morrow."

This anecdote, contrasted with the affair of the trustees, certainly shows that physical courage is one thing and moral courage another. But perhaps the bard was not so far in the wrong as he may appear to persons of the temper of Lord Byron, who was half mad from the beginning, and being precociously weary both of life and poetry, could be satisfied with no stimulant less potent than a plunge into the cannon's mouth. Homer certainly, had he been professional bard to Agamemnon, when the Atridan was going on some special day to perform his *ἀριστεία* before the

admiring Argives, would not have been invited personally
to join in the fray. He might have said without shame,
had he been so invited, "I am a singer;" as Demosthenes
afterwards said, "I am a ῥήτωρ," and Thomas Carlyle, in our
day, when asked for a special measure to set the joints of
the dislocated age—"*I am a writer of books ; I am not a politician !*" That Bare John could risk his life as well as other
people when such a sacrifice lay plainly in the way his
conduct with regard to the faithless cousins sufficiently
shows. He also, on a notable occasion, flung himself into
the power of his grand enemy the Marquis of Argyll,
though on this occasion, perhaps, he thought himself safe
with the shield of that sacredness which belonged among
the Celts to the profession of a bard. So severe and so
stinging had been the satires which the royalist poet had
fulminated against the hated Campbells, that the chief of
the clan offered a reward for his head. Iain Lom, as if
wishing to act a piece of adventurous drama, went to Inver-
ary, marched into the audience-hall of the Marquis, announced himself as John M'Donald, and demanded his
reward. The Marquis received him with great politeness,
and leading him through a room hung round with heads of
blackcock, inquired "*Am fac thu riamh, Iain, an uiread
sin de choilich dhubha'an aon àite ?*"—"Have you ever seen,
John, so many blackcocks together?" "*Chunnaic,*" said
John—"Yes, I have." "*C'àite ?*" said the Marquis—
"Where?" "At Inverlochy," replied John, meaning the
slaughter of the Campbells there. "*A ! Iain, Iain,*" said
the Marquis, "*cha sguir thu gu brath de chagnadh nan Caim-
beulach ?*"—"Ah! John, will you never cease gnawing at
the Campbells?" "*'Se's duilich leam,*" replied John, "*nach
urradh mi an slugadh.*"—"I am sorry that I cannot swallow
them."

As a specimen of Iain Lom's lyrical powers we can

select nothing better than the verses on the Battle of Inverlochy (1645), which unquestionably possess the merit of genuine lyric fervour, joined to faithful historical portraiture and minute topographical exactness, a combination which makes the poetry of the Celtic bards—who, like Homer, were great realists—often more valuable as historical documents than as flights of impassioned sentiment. For the somewhat ferocious character of the verses, written as they were on a field of blood, amid the bitterness of a prolonged civil war, we need make no apology. In those days the people were not used to use either the sword or the tongue in a mincing fashion; and long after that even the cool and impartial Statute-Book was as bloody as the battle-field.

THE DAY OF INVERLOCHY.

Did you hear from Cille-Cummin
How the tide of war came pouring?
Far and wide the summons travelled,
How they drave the Whigs before them!

From the castle tower I viewed it,
High on Sunday morning early,
Looked and saw the ordered battle
Where Clan Donald triumphed rarely.

Up the green slope of Cuil-Eachaidh,
Came Clan Donald marching stoutly;
Churls who laid my home in ashes,
Now shall pay the fine devoutly!

Though the earldom has been groaning
Seven long years with toil and trouble,
All the loss to plough and harrow
They shall now repay with double!

From thy side, O Laird of Lawers,
Though thy boast was in thy claymore,
Many a youth your father's clansman,
Ne'er shall rise to greet the day more!

Many a bravely mounted rider,
With his back turned to the slaughter,
Where his boots won't keep him dry now,
Learns to swim in Nevis water.

On the wings of eager rumour,
Far and wide the tale is flying,
How the slippery knaves, the Campbells,
With their cloven skulls are lying!

O'er the frosted moor they travelled,
Stoutly, with no thought of dying,
Where now many a whey-faced lubber,
To manure the fields is lying.

From the height of Tom-na-harry,
See them crudely heaped together,
In their eyes no hint of seeing,
Stretched to rot upon the heather!

Warm your welcome was at Lochy,
With blows and buffets thickening round you,
And Clan Donald's groovèd claymore,
Flashing terror to confound you!

Hot and hotter grew the struggle,
Where the trenchant blade assailed them;
Sprawled with nails on ground Clan Duine,
When the parted sinew failed them.

Many a corpse upon the heather,
Naked lay, once big with daring,

From the battle's hurly-burly,
Drifting blindly to Blarchaorainn.

And another tale I 'll tell you,
Never clerk declared more truly,
How the leal and loyal people
Scared the rebel folk unruly.

John of Moydart, dark the day was,
But the sail was bright that bore thee,
When thou kept thy trysting fairly,
And the Barbreac bowed before thee!

Alastair, I praise thy voyage,
Rich in glory, rich in plunder,
Alban greeted thee with joyance,
And Strathbogie's cock knocked under.

If the ill bird dulled his splendours,
When he should have shone most brightly,
With brave birds of ampler pinion,
We can learn to bear it lightly!

Alastair, with sharp-mouthed claymore,
Thou didst vow to work their ruin;
Quick their heels to flee the castle,
Quicker thou their flight pursuing!

Had the men of Mull been with thee,
Thou hadst screwed them down more tightly,
Some who fled had choked the heather,
With their traitor trunks unsightly!

Gallant son of gallant father,
Where thou warrest, thou art winner;
Woe, Saxon, to thy crazy stomach,
When MacCholla sours thy dinner!

By the field of Goirtean-oar,
Who may take his summer ramble,
He will find it fair and fattened
By the best blood of the Campbell !

If I could, I would be weeping,
For your shame and for your sorrow,
Orphans' cry and widows' wailing,
Through the long Argyll to-morrow.[1]

Mackenzie, whose *Beauties of Gaelic Poetry* is unhappily almost my only guide through this much-neglected region, gives next a sequence of about a dozen notable Highland poets, who flourished principally in the seventeenth century, and before the time of the famous Alastair M'Donald of Ardnamurchan, who took part in the rebellion of 1745. Of these I shall only string together a few short notices. The first is ARCHIBALD M'DONALD, or in his own language *Gilleaspuig Ruadh M'Dhomhnuill*, surnamed *An Ciaran Mabach*, who was an illegitimate son of Sir Alexander M'Donald, sixteenth baron of Sleat in Skye.[2] He was contemporary with

[1] Good poetical versions of the bard of Keppoch's poems are not readily to be got. My clansman, Mr. Blackie the publisher, has acted wisely in giving Iain Lom and other Gaelic poets their merited niche in his *Poets and Poetry of Scotland*, 1876 ; but it would require a special edition with historical notes to place the works of this great poet-politician on the pedestal which belongs to them. Mrs. D. Ogilvie, in her book of Highland Minstrelsy (London, 1860), has a poem, " The Vow of Iain Lom," of which the subject is the revenge taken by the poet on the faithless cousins, as narrated in the text. With regard to the battle, I have a note from Dr. Clerk of Kilmallie, informing me that the stone which was erected by the Mac-Donalds to mark the spot where the pursuit ended, a couple of miles above Fort William, has been more than once thrown down by the Campbells, and re-erected by the MacDonalds within the last twenty-five years.

[2] *Gilleasbuig*, or the Bishop's boy, means *Archibald* in Gaelic ; why so, or rather how so, let antiquarians explain. The *Gille* in Highland names implied a position analogous to the $\theta \epsilon \rho \acute{a} \pi \omega \nu$ in Homer, and was a word often used by devotees towards their patron saint, as *Mac-gille-Iain*, contracted *Maclean*, the servant of the Apostle John. *Ciaran* means brown, and *Mabach* a stutterer.

Bare John of Keppoch, and proved himself a most efficient aid in bringing the treacherous murderers of the young laird to condign punishment. For his services in this and other public matters the Ciaran Mabach was amply rewarded by his father, who assigned him an estate in North Uist, where he had the best opportunities of prosecuting those occupations which bring a man of healthy tone and vigorous nerve into connection with real life in a manner the most favourable to the cultivation of the Muse. The next is a lady bearing the designation of DIORBHAIL NIC A BHRIU-THAINN, in English, Dorothy Brown, who belonged to the island of Luing, in the west of Argyll, between Oban and the Crinan Canal. Like the Mabach, she was contemporary with Iain Lom, and shared with both their fervid loyalty to the Stuarts and fierce hate to the Campbells. The power of Highland versifiers in limited Highland districts was something as great as the influence of the *Times* in large political circles ; so their stinging verses, often levelled at known persons, or whole families, not seldom created in particular quarters as violent a hostility as their general talent excited admiration ; and in the Highlands those quick feelings of personal wrong have a deep-seated root in rankling bosoms strongly contrasted with the ephemeral enmities begotten by a smart leader in the *Times*. Long after Dorothy's death, one Colin Campbell, to relieve the fret of his soul against the sarcastic poetess, came to the ground where she was buried, and, trampling on her grave, called down the curse of Heaven on her memory. This ungracious act was witnessed by one Duncan M'Lachlan, belonging to the neighbouring parish of Kilbride, who, without any ceremony, marched up to this rash violator of the decencies of the churchyard, and seizing him by the cuff of the neck, dragged him off the ground ; immediately whereupon he called for a bottle of whisky and in true

Highland fashion drank a *deoch sluinte* to the injured ghost of the poetess on the spot.[1] The third in the list is also a lady; for where passion and music are intimately wedded to song, whether amongst Greeks or Gauls, the female sex, except under some unnatural system of social repression, will always assert a prominent place in the national literature. SÌLIS or Cicely M'DONALD was the daughter of M'Donald, a member of the M'Donalds of Keppoch, flourished in the time of Charles II. and onwards to George I., and married a gentleman of the family of Lovat. Transferred by him to the regions near Inverness, she did not feel that her poetical environment had been improved; and her domestic happiness, whatever it might have been, was suddenly and sadly terminated by the death of her husband in a fit of intoxication. This did not hinder her, however, true woman as she was, from singing his praises in a classical *Marbrann*, or death-song beginning

> *S'i so bliadhna 's faid a chlaoidh mi*
> *Gu'n cheol, gu'n aighear, gun fhaiolteas ;*
> *Mi mar bhàt air tràigh air sgaoileadh*
> *Gun stiùr, gun seol, gun ràmh, gun tuoman.*

> "'Tis a year and a day since I learned to pine,
> Nor music, nor mirth, nor joy is mine ;
> Like a pilotless boat on a lonely shore,
> I drift without rudder, or sail, or oar."

The fourth in Mackenzie's list is a name belonging to a family that figures largely in the Ossianic controversy.

---

[1] Mr. Mackenzie, in the book which I use, says that "a tombstone with a suitable Gaelic inscription is about to be erected to Dorothy Brown," in the place where she is buried, viz., the churchyard of Kilchattan; but I have a letter from the Rev. Duncan Graham, Free Church minister at Kilbrandon, to the effect that no such tombstone has been erected.

NIALL MAC-MHUIRICH, born at the beginning of the seventeenth century, belonged to the celebrated Clan Ronald
branch of the M'Donalds, and as such had his patrimony in
South Uist, under the name, pointed out to this hour, as
Baile-bhùird, the bard's farm.   He was one link in a chain
of family bards, historians, and genealogists, who had been
attached to the Clan Ronald sept through many generations, and in this his capacity as family genealogist, local
historian, and bard of the clan, presents to us in a most
perfect embodiment the social position and dignity of those
ἀοιδοί of ancient Greece from whom Homer drew the rich
materials of his popular epos.   Truly Homeric also was the
manifest carelessness of these men with regard to the per-
petuity of their fame on paper ; they lived in the hearts of
their countrymen, and trusting to this vivid sort of immortality seem seldom to have given themselves any concern
about the dusty niche which they might possibly enjoy some
day in the Advocates' Library, Edinburgh, or possibly even
in the Vatican.   The consequence is, that only a few of
their effusions have been orally preserved, significant, like a
patch of ossified fish in some swathe of pre-Adamite mud,
of a wealth of palæozoic life in some department now altogether blank.   In this respect the lyric poetry of the Celts
presents an exact parallel to that of the Greeks ; it is a
repertory of splendid fragments, and a register of illustrious
wrecks.   The special connection of these Macbhuirich bards
with the Ossianic question we reserve for the next chapter.
The fifth on the roll is IAIN DUBH MACIAIN IC AILEIN—
Black John, the son of John, the son of Allan—likewise
belonging to the Clan Ronald family, and born about
the year 1665.   His headquarters were at a place called
Gulean, in the geologically celebrated island of Eigg.
After him follows the *Aosdana* MAC-MHATHAIN (the old
singer Macmathie), who flourished in the seventeenth century,

lived at Loch Alsh, Ross-shire, was family bard of the Earl of Seaforth, and had free lands from his Lordship in that capacity. Like the whole class of Highland bards, as already stated, he committed nothing to paper, so that only two pieces of his remain, of which one has been imitated in English by Sir Walter Scott.[1] The AOSDANA MAC-ILLEAN, or Maclean, is another bard of the same century, who has had the good fortune to attract the ever-ready sympathies of the great bard of the Border,[2] but who, though family bard to Sir Lachlan Maclean of Dhuart, comes down to posterity, like Sappho, only in the shape of two fragments. Then comes a scion of the famous house of MACKINNONS of Strath in Skye, where they still survive. He was, like most of the Gaelic poets, a good musician ; and by this natural wedlock of sweet words with song, preserved his Muse from running wild into those ingeniously tortuous paths where the dexterity of the performer is a more attractive object of admiration than the grace of the performance. Mackinnon, like some other bards of a fervid temperament, did not always respect the rights of women ; and amorous entanglements of an improper character were the result ; nevertheless, says his biographer, "he died with great demonstrations of respect, in the year 1734, aged 69,[3] and was buried in his native parish, where some of his grandchildren are still living, and much respected." We finish the roll with two notable characters, and a pair of facts illustrating strongly the supposed fiction with regard to "the *blind* old man of Scio's rocky isle." We have

---

[1] In his " FAREWELL TO MACKENZIE, HIGH CHIEF OF KINTAIL." *Scott's Poetical Works*, Globe edition, p. 482.

[2] See the translation or imitation of the elegy on the death of Sir Lachlan Maclean, by Sir Walter Scott. So Mackenzie says ; but I do not find this in the Globe edition where I found the other one.

[3] Besides Mackenzie, I have here an article in the Celtic Magazine for January 1876, signed *Sgiathanach.*

actually got a blind harper and a blind piper, and both apparently, whether from the singularity of their blindness, or, as would rather appear, from its combination with singular genius, the most illustrious of the · brotherhood. RODERICK MORISON, *an clarsair dall*, the blind harper, was born in the island of Lewis, in the year 1646. His father was an Episcopalian clergyman in that part of the world, and of a good position in society. He sent his sons for education to Inverness, young Roderick and two brothers; but scarcely had they settled down there before the town was invaded by that terrible destroyer of beauty, the small-pox; all the three brothers were seized simultaneously, and Roderick had so tough a battle to fight with the enemy that he came out of it only with the loss of his eyesight. His two brothers were more fortunate, and pursuing the studies necessary for their clerical career, were settled in life afterwards, the one in Contin, that beautiful spot behind Strathpeffer, and the other at Poolewe, near the lovely scenery of Loch Maree in Ross-shire. For poor Roderick there was only one course now open. God had enriched him with a grand gift of music; so he cultivated sedulously this divine art, which in the Highlands, as in ancient Greece, was generally coupled with the practice of poetical composition; and being a gentleman by birth, and not without a certain modest competence, he easily found his way into the best circles of society, both at home and in Ireland, where an accomplished harper was always a · welcome guest. While at Edinburgh he made the acquaintance of John Breac Macleod of Harris, one of the last chieftains that, with native Caledonian geniality, scanted ·nothing of the proper family equipment in the personages of bard, harper, piper, and fool, and who was not slow to perceive in blind Rory the very man whose genius would add a charm to his social circle and a lustre to his family history. Macleod at that time was lord of Glenelg, in which beautiful country we find the blind harper settled as a farmer, at a place called Totamor, where, by grace of his profession, he sat rent-free. After the death of his patron, another "king arose who knew not Joseph,"—one of the new style of Highland lairds, who went a-whoring after fashionable English novelties, and instead of bards, pipers, and harpers, peopled their old residences with grooms, gamekeepers, factors, and all sorts of heartless flunkeyism. Ejected from his farm by the ungenial laird of this new school, the blind harper retired to the bleakness of his own native island, where he lived to a good old age, and was buried in the burying-ground of *I*. JOHN MACKAY, piper and poet, who shared with Roderick Morison the loss of outward eyesight, to be compensated by a richer gift of the " vision and the faculty divine," was born in the parish of Gairloch, Ross-shire, in the year 1666. His blindness, however, was congenital, an inheritance from his father. Destined by nature to find his organ of genial utterance in pipe-music, he was sent to the famous college of pipers in Skye, at the head of whom was MacCriummein, a name familiar to the lovers of Celtic music. His arrival in Skye turned the eleven students of pipe-music already studying under that celebrated master into the perfect twelve ; but the moral music which resulted from his arrival was of the nature of a jar rather than of harmonious intervals. The young blind piper soon found that he had more to teach to his fellow-disciples of undimmed vision than to learn from them ; in a very short time he outshone them all ; and against this their unregenerate nature began violently to rebel. MacCriummein, the master piper, did not always act wisely, not interposing himself, as he ought to have done, to soothe down this ignoble but very natural jealousy. On one occasion, it is told, that when John Mackay and another young apprentice were playing before him, he had the imprudence to ask the inferior competitor *"why he did not play as well as the blind boy?"* to which the irritated youth replied, *" By'r Lady, and I could do it; but the skin of that vile glutinous skate that you gave us to dinner is yet sticking to my fingers!"* This was ingenious, but no more. A proverb arose out of the answer, quoted against those who blame the pen, when they ought to mend the writer: *Tha mhebirean as deighe na sgait*—" His fingers are after the skate." But the worst was that the unlucky contrast thus called into prominence by the master, served only to aggravate the already strong jealousy of the other apprentices to such a degree, that they began to plot and conspire against him, like Joseph's brethren against Joseph. An opportunity was not long of being presented for gratifying their spite. One of the MacCriummeins, known by the name of PADRUIG CAOGACH, or Winking Peter, had composed a pipe-tune which achieved a wide popularity. It was, however, defective in one of the parts, that, according to the rules of the art, were essential to a classically rounded pibroch; but somehow or other the author had tried in vain several times to give the composition the requisite finish; the original afflatus would not return, and the pibroch remained a splendid torso. Sometimes, however, it happens in art, that what the author cannot finish, is happily topped by another. So in this case the young blind youth from the Gairloch was visited by an inspiration which enabled him to put the coping-stone on the piece in a manner not unworthy of the master. Not wishing, however, to interpolate his own hand into another man's work, he called the whole complete tune *Lasan Phàdruig chaogaich*, and might naturally have expected thanks for his generosity; but human nature is seldom noble enough for this. The Caogach not only looked on this addition of the lacking top to his work

as an impertinent interference, but took it as a mortal
offence, and went so far as actually to bribe some of the
other apprentices to take away the ambitious young piper's
life. This they did, or rather attempted to do, in a manner
to which the topographical character of the country where
they lived afforded peculiar facilities. They simply asked
him to take a walk with them along the rim of one of the
neighbouring crags, and on coming to a suitable point, they
gave the eyeless young genius a sudden push, and down he
fell a height of twenty-four feet; but, $\theta\epsilon i\alpha$ $\tau\upsilon\chi\eta$, as
Herodotus would have said, " by a divine chance," John
alighted like a cat on his feet, and was not a whit the
worse; and, to witness the truth of the story, the exact
spot of the treacherous precipitation is pointed out at the
present day, under the name of *Leum an doill*, or " The Blind
Man's Leap." After completing the Pythagorean number
of seven years' apprenticeship, Mackay returned to his own
country and had succeeded his father as family piper to
Mackenzie of Gairloch. In this capacity he produced a
rich profusion of pibrochs, strathspeys, reels, jigs, laments,
eulogies, and other such lyrical matter as belonged to the
stock in trade of an old Highland poet and piper. As in
the case of the other Highland bards whom we have mentioned, the practice of his profession in those breezy regions
seems to have been favourable to longevity; for he died
at Gairloch, and was buried in the clachan[1] there, after
having attained the age of a whole century less two years.

After these hasty notices, which, imperfect as they are,
serve to give a vivid glimpse of the truly Homeric life of
those times, we advance by a single step to a name which
wears on its front the distinct kinship at once of the old
family bard and of the modern literary man. This is

[1] *Clachan* in Gaelic does not mean a village, as Lowlanders are apt to
imagine, but a churchyard, or a village where there is a churchyard.

ALEXANDER M'DONALD of Ardnamurchan, commonly called *Alasdair Mac Mhaighstir Alasdair.* His peculiar position, as distinguished from the roll which we have just run over, is most strikingly marked by the fact that he received a regular college education, and that he published a Gaelic Vocabulary, the first thing in the shape of a Lexicon that the records of Caledonian Celtism knew, and therefore well worthy of being noted as a landmark. The date of this work, now very rare, is 1741. Alastair was the son of an Episcopal clergyman in the district of Moidart, where, as is well known, Prince Charles first showed face in his bold but rash attempt to recover the throne which had been forfeited by the despotic policy of his ancestors. His father was a man of might and muscle, and, as the story goes, often earned for himself the evangelical blessing of the peacemakers, by the use both of his strong arm and decisive sentence in the disputes which, inflamed by usque-baugh, would sometimes arise over the grave of the freshly interred clansman. The Clan Ranald, who was dominant in those parts, finding in the son a second edition of the notable brawn and brain of the father, was forward to help his advancement, if he would devote himself to the study of law, while the father rather wished that his son should follow his own sacred calling. Anyhow the vigorous young Highlander prosecuted a course of training at the University fitting him for the practice of an intellectual profession, and was, according to the standard by which learning is measured in Presbyterian Scotland, a fair classical scholar. But he was a poet, and, like a true Pegasus, not at all suited to go quietly into the harness either of the Church or the Bar. Worse than this, he fell in love, as poets are peculiarly apt to do, and married before he had finished his studies ; and, as might have been expected, so far as social position was concerned, this step ruined him. He must do something

for his bread; and all lofty ambitions must stoop to the
drudgery of elementary pedagogic drill. He became parochial schoolmaster at Ardnamurchan, holding with his
school the farm of Cori-vullin, in a delightful situation,
opposite the beautiful little harbour of Tobermory in Mull,
well known to Highland tourists. It does not appear,
however, that M'Donald displayed any peculiar genius
either for pedagogy or farming. If he had the virtues of
a great poet, he had also the vices; he was not strong
enough to follow Shakespeare and Goethe in reconciling
the fitful inspirations of the Muse with the quiet measured
tread of daily life. He could fly, but he would not march.
However, a march of a peculiar kind was preparing for
him. What the Greek revolt of 1821 was to Lord Byron,
that the brilliant adventure of Prince Charlie in 1745 was
to the Ardnamurchan bard. It was not in the blood of
a M'Donald of the true breed in those days to sway a
ferule when the sword was flashing at the school-house
door. M'Donald rose like a giant with the great rising,
and became the Tyrtæus of that dashing but disastrous
affair. He was not a man to do a thing by halves; so he
not only joined the Pretender's army, but embraced the
Popish religion, having been originally an Episcopalian,
and afterwards an elder in the Presbyterian parish where
he officiated as schoolmaster. It is needless to say, that
with the full swelling sails of this new inspiration M'Donald
at a stride became a marked man. His poems were to the
Rebellion of 1745 what the songs of Körner and Arndt were
to the Liberation War of the Germans in 1813. They
belong prominently to the history of the country, however
much, as a consequence of the fashionable neglect of Gaelic,
they may have been generally ignored. After the bloody
finale of that brilliant blunder, the poet and his brother
Angus, like himself a man of great bodily strength, escaping

from the pursuit of their enemies, concealed themselves for a time amid the woods and caves between Kinloch Aylort and Moydart; and, after the rage of the Hanoverians had been somewhat sated, contrived to live in quiet among his friends. He acted for some time as tutor to certain Jacobite families in Edinburgh, and then retired to Moydart, and thence to Knoydart, where he died at Sandaig, near Arisaig. Like other stout Highlanders he lived to a good old age, and was borne to his last rest in the island of *Fionain* in Loch Sheil.

The Highlanders, with one voice, talk of M'Donald as at once the most vigorous and masculine and the most highly accomplished of their poets. They laud specially his large command of the language; while they are forced to admit that, on account of the neglect into which they have allowed their mother tongue to fall, a great many of the words used by him are not now generally understood. From some specimens of his poetry which I have heard read by my Galician friend, Sheriff Nicolson of Kirkcudbright, I should be inclined to doubt whether his taste was always equal to his strength,—whether he did not, in the unchastened consciousness of power, sometimes plant himself critically on the verge where the sublime jerks over into the ridiculous. But be this as it may, he was unquestionably a great poet, as the following version of the first three divisions of his most celebrated poem, the " Launching of the *Biorlinn* " or Barque of Clan Ranald, may, in a fragmentary way, serve to indicate :—

" God bless the good ship of Clan Ranald,
   The first day it leaps on the wave,
   The ship and the sailors that man it,
   The first on the roll of the brave !
   May the Three and the One be their guidance,
   Who tempers the blasts when they bray,

Or tossed mid the war of the billow,
Or lulled in the sleep of the bay!
Great Father, that gathered the waters,
Whose breath is the strength of the storm,
Bless Thou our frail bark and its men,
When the rage of the tempest is warm.
O, Son of the Father, give blessing
To anchor and rudder and mast,
To sail and to sheet and to tackle,
When they stand the rude strain of the blast.
Bless yard and halyard and stay,
All gear both above and below,
Give soundness to rigging and rope,
That no flaw and no fault they may know.
May the Spirit the Holy protect us,
Whose grace we devoutly implore,
Who hath fathomed all depths of the ocean,
And numbered all bays of the shore!

May God bless our weapons, well tempered
With steel of the truest from Spain,
And our mail, in a hundred fights,
That was hacked and dinted in vain!
The shapely curve of the target,
The gleaming edge of the glaive,
All gear that trimly depends
From the shoulder-belt of the brave.
Our bows of the yew well seasoned,
In breast of the battle to win,
Our shafts of the birch, well cased
In the surly badger's skin.
Give poignard and pistol thy blessing,
And tartan that flaps in the fray,
And all the equipment of war,
In the bark of M'Donald to-day.

Let no man be faint or soft-hearted,
Look hard in the face of the storm,
While plank may with plank hang together,
And rib to his rib shall be firm ;
Though the good ship may reel and may stagger,
While a pin or a nail shall be tight,
Though the big wave be bristling around her,
Let him look and not blench at the sight.
In the stormy contention of billows,
Who stands or who wisely shall bend,
Will see the proud crest of the ocean
Lie tame at his feet in the end.
If a wife hath a strife with her lord,
When her fancies are wayward and wild,
Let him budge not an inch from his word,
And she'll sit and not chide like a child.
Even so that wild huge-heaving sea,
When fretful she bristles her quills,
Will yield to the strength of a man,
As the King of the Universe wills.

Now bring the dark boat, deftly-fashioned,
    To the place of sailing ;
Take the poles, the stout, the smooth,
    And push with might prevailing ;
Grasp the shapely oars, smooth-handled,
    Limber oars that lightly
Sweep with venturous van across
    The waters foaming brightly ;
Oars that, when they fall with might,
    Upon the blue sea darkling,
Wake from its bed the sleeping light,
    In liquid beauty sparkling ;
Oars that with their well-poised stroke,
    As the light boat dashes,

Wound the wave, the proudly swelling,
  With a thousand gashes ;
Oars that with well-measured swing
  Bound, all-fearless, leaping
O'er the rough crests and gaping troughs
  Of dark blue depths unsleeping.

Come, stretch your limbs, my lusty callants,
  Lift the oars and bend them,
From your firm palm, strong and sinewy,
  Pith and vigour lend them.
Ye brawny boatmen, stout and stalwart,
  Stretch your length, and readily
Let your hard and knotty muscles
  Rise and sink full steadily,
Making the smooth and polished blades,
  Whose lordship reins the ocean,
Cuff the rough crests of the fretful brine,
  With a well-timed motion.

Come now, thou man of the first oar,
  Thou king of lusty fellows,
Raise the song that makes men strong
  To mount the heaving billows,
Raise the iorram that will drive,
  With shouts of glee the Birlinn
Through the bristling bellowing rout
  Of waters wildly whirling.
Ho ! for the waves, as they hiss and spit,
  To the storm-blast ramping and roaring ;
Huzza for the boat, in its plunging fit,
  Where the foamy streams are pouring !
Ho ! for the blade, so limber, lithe,
  When it twists the writhing billow,

> Huzza for the hand where blisters burn
>   To each hard-pulling fellow,—
> Fellows with shaggy-breasted might,
>   And stout heart never quailing!
> Though oak and iron creak and start,
>   And boom and spar are failing,
> They, in the face of the sea, will steer
>   The slender craft, nor borrow
> Fear from the breath of the cutting blast,
> . Or the gape of the salt-sea furrow.
> This is the crew, o'er the waters blue,
>   With a kingly strength presiding,
> Untired, unflagging, and unspent,
>   On the breast of the rough wave riding!"

Some of the other works of this poet exhibit that love for natural scenery, and that delicate descriptive power in which the Celts seem, by a natural instinct, to have excelled before Thomson and Wordsworth made it part of the fashionable currency of the modern Muse. Of the political pieces of M'Donald, a very effective one for recitation is the following, written under the spur of patriotic and poetic indignation against the pedantry of the Hanoverian Government, after the quashing of the rebellion, in the matter of the Highland dress. The Act of Parliament (19 Geo. II. cap. 39), in which this petty tyranny lies embalmed, contains the following clause :—" And be it enacted, by the authority foresaid, that from and after the 1st day of August 1747, no man or boy, within that part of Great Britain called Scotland, other than such as shall be employed as officers and soldiers in His Majesty's forces, shall, on any pretence whatever, wear and put on the clothes commonly called Highland clothes ; that is to say, the plaid, philibeag, or little kilt, trouse, shoulder-belt, or any part whatsoever of what peculiarly belongs to the Highland garb; and that no tartan or party-coloured plaid or stuff shall be used for great coats or upper coats; and that if any such person shall presume, after the said 1st day of August, to wear or put on the aforesaid garments, or any part of them, every such person so offending being thereof convicted by the oath of one or more credible witness or witnesses, before any Court of Justiciary, or any one or more Justices of the Peace for Shire or Stewartry, or Judge Ordinary of the place where such offence shall be committed, shall suffer imprisonment, without bail, during the space of six calendar months and no longer; and being convicted of a second offence before a Court of Justiciary, or at the circuits, shall be liable to be transported to any of His Majesty's plantations beyond the seas, there to remain for the space of seven years."

Hé an clò dubh,
Hé an clò dubh,
Hé an clò dubh,
B' fearr leam am breacan.

I.

Give me the plaid, the light, the airy,
Round my shoulder, under my arm,
Rather than English wool the choicest
To keep my body tight and warm.

II.

Who is so trim as a kilted laddie?
Tight his gear, and light his adorning,
With only a buckle his belt to fasten
When he leaps to his legs in the morning!

III.

Thou art my joy in the charge of battle,
When bright blades are flashing before me !
When the war-pipe is sounding, sounding,
And the banners are flapping o'er me !

IV.

Good art thou in the stalking of deer,
When peaks are red with the young day dawning;
Mild art thou with sober cheer,
When going to church on Sunday morning.

V.

I with thee would lie on the heather,
Closely wrapt to keep me warm ;
Safe within thy folds defying
Batter of rain and bray of storm.

VI.

Good is the plaid in the day or the night time,
High on the Ben, or low in the glen ;
No king was he but a coward who banned it,
Fearing the look of the plaided men !

VII.

A coward was he, not a king who did it,
Banning with statutes the garb of the brave ;
But the breast that wears the plaidie
Ne'er was a home to the heart of a slave.

VIII.

Let them tear our bleeding bosoms,
Let them drain our latest veins,
In our hearts is Charlie, Charlie,
While a spark of life remains !

So much for the bard of Ardnamurchan, who certainly was a man of big brawn and fervid blood, and quite of a piece with the stout bluff that fronts the Atlantic gales in that part of the world. We must now transport ourselves—though not quite so far as St. Kilda, under Saxon encroachments the destined dying place of the Celt—to the extreme rim of Gaelic life, considerably beyond the familiar ground of the normal Saxon tourist, whether Scotch or English. The west coast of Scotland from the mouth of the Clyde northwards is belted by a long chain of islands, partly of granitic partly of volcanic formation, of which the part farthest to the north-west is popularly called the Long Island. It consists, in fact, of a chain of islands about one hundred and thirty miles in length, hanging so closely together in many places that the sea seems scarcely to be separated from the land, and the land only half redeemed from the sea. The northmost of these isles is called the Lewis, the southmost Barra, while the middle group is composed of North and South Uist and Benbecula. The south part of Lewis, called Harris, is well marked by high mountains, which on a clear day are distinctly visible from the opposite coast of Inverness. In the extreme south, Barra, there are also mountains of considerable height; but the middle region is in the main flat and unpicturesque, except in South Uist, where a mountain that seems to have been baptised by the Icelanders with the name of Hecla rises on the east coast to a height of between two and three thousand feet. Looking down from this height, or from the small elevation of Benbecula, the east side of these islands presents a spectacle of naked bleakness and ragged desolation, which to an Englishman born and bred amid the rich leafy luxuriance of the beautiful midland counties of his fair fatherland, would seem to have been properly set apart as a penal settlement for the most abandoned of human malefactors.

But it is not so. There is a numerous and lusty population in these islands; and in fact it is not always that from a top of a lofty Ben a true idea of the nature of a country can be gained. Along the west coast of these islands stretch long tracts of fragrant grass and natural clover, called in Gaelic technically *machars*, which make the land to flow with milk and honey and all good pastoral things, after a fashion of which even Somersetshire and Holderness might be proud. In the northmost of this remarkable group, North Uist, lived a poet of no small Highland reputation for wit and sarcasm, JOHN MACCODRUM, and whom we have introduced in this topographical way, in order that the reader may vividly be made to understand how good a thing poetry is, which, like the bee, always sucks honey from the flower, and feeds on sweetness where a proser starves. No doubt in England some half a century ago Lord Byron set the keynote to a sort of poetry which rather frets over the barrenness of the human waste than gathers its sweets, and loses the enjoyment of the rose-blossom in fits of sublime indignation at the thorn. But Highland poetry was not such; certainly not MacCodrum's, as the following verses in praise of the beloved island of his birth will abundantly testify :—

THE MAVIS OF CLAN DONALD.

I.

The mavis of Pabal am I; in my nest
I lay long time with my head on my breast,
Dozing away the dreary hour,
In the day that was dark, and the time that was sour.

II.

But now I soar to the mountain's crest,
For the chief is returned whom I love best,

In the face of the sun, on the fringe of the wood,
Feeding myself with wealth of good.

III.

On the tip of the twigs I sit and sing,
And greet the morn on dewy wing,
And fling to the breeze my lusty note,
With no bar to my breath, and no dust in my throat.

IV.

Every bird will praise its own nest,
And why shall not I think mine the best?
Land of strong men and healthy food,
And kindly cheer, and manners good.

V.

A land that faces the ocean wild,
But with summer sweetness, mellow and mild,
Calves, lambs, and kids, full many a score,
Bread, milk, and honey piled in the store.

VI.

A dappled land full sunny and warm,
Secure and sheltered from the storm,
With ducks and geese and ponds not scanted,
And food for all that live to want it.

VII.

A land of oats and bearded barley,
And fields where grass is waving fairly;
Green knolls with yellow sheaves are there,
And snow is shy, and frost is rare.

VIII.

With smiling machars by the sea,
Where marigolds and daisies be,
Bulls, cows, and mares, and stallions stout,
A breed that dies not lightly out.

IX.

A land in all right fair to view,
With well-girt lads of healthy hue;
Moors peopled far with hornèd kine,
And kelp with gold to fringe the brine.

X.

At fair Cladh Chothan I greeted the light,
And Unnair bred me in ways that are right,
In view of the waves of the trenchèd tide,
Where they toss their crests in playful pride.

XI.

The brave Clan Donald I name for mine,
With sail and streamer that rides the brine,
That cuts the foam with steady keel,
And firmly handles the hard grey steel.

XII.

Men they were of might and mettle,
Wise in peace and keen in battle;
Not faint of heart, but ready with glee,
To chase or to stand, as the need might be.

XIII.

Men that were made of no yielding stuff,
That could scowl like the storm when the strife
   was rough,

'Neath the flap of the banner who drew the bright
    sword,
Or flung the bright jest round the banqueting-board.

XIV.

And the slogan of war was their song of delight,
Whose face ever looked to the front of the fight;
Strong were their strokes and hard were their blows,
When in tatters they tore the red coats of their foes.

XV.

O they were manful and mighty of mood,
Nor shrunk, like a woman, from tasting of blood;
They were modest and gentle, but bold in the fray,
And though proud to command, they were prompt to
    obey.

XVI.

They were lofty in spirit, and noble in mien;
A statelier race never trod on green,
And they showed to the foe not the face of a child,
In the breast of the storm, when the war-cry was wild.

XVII.

Then sit round the board, boys, steady and stout,
Take firm grasp of your cups, and drain them all out,
Here's a health to Sir James, and across the blue wave
Be his guidance from God, who is mighty to save!

The man who composed this was unquestionably a great
philosopher, if true philosophy means, as it certainly should
mean, to make the best of everything, and especially of a
bad business. The MacCodrums, to whom our bard belongs,

were a sept of the MacDonalds of Sleat, to one of whom, Sir James, who died at Rome in the year 1766, aged twenty-five years, our poet acted in the capacity of family bard. The occasion of his being elected to this dignity is sufficiently characteristic of the state of kindly mutual interdependence in which Highlanders lived in those days. They were a world within themselves; and what they could not produce at home, no Glasgow steamboat could bring hastily to their need. MacCodrum, like Lord Byron, had a terrible power of satire; and having, like Robert Burns, the habit of picking up his subjects from his immediate environment, happened to have indulged his wanton wit in a humorous escapade against the tailors of the Long Island. The sons of the thread and needle took the matter seriously; and bound themselves by an oath to make no stitch towards covering the nakedness of Mac-Codrum. The consequences were obvious. The poet went about full of rents and patches like a gaberlunzie man. One day when going his usual round in this condition, he was met by the young Laird of Sleat. "What's the matter?" said the thane; "your vestments are leaking all round." "The tailors," replied the bard, "refuse to make my trousers, and I cannot make them myself." "What do the rogues mean?" said the MacDonald. "Revenge, I suppose," replied MacCodrum. "I wrote some verses that seem to have touched them rather sharply, and so—." "Let me hear them," said the Laird. The poet forthwith plucked an old leaf of paper from his pocket, not so tattered as his garments, and straightway read forth the indictment against the tailors. The Laird of Skye was delighted with the humour of the piece, promoted the poet on the spot to the dignity of family bard to the Mac-Donalds, promised him an ample recuperation of his wardrobe from Skye, and made him perpetual tenant of some of the rich machar land in North Uist rent-free. In this position he came before the public prominently as a witness in the great Ossianic question. In a letter from Sir James to Dr. Blair, the æsthetical Aristarchus of those days, dated Skye, 10th October 1763, we find the poet mentioned in the following terms :—" The few bards that are left among us repeat only detached pieces of the Ossianic poems. I have often heard them, and understood them, particularly from one man, called John MacCodrum, who lives on my estate in North Uist. *I have heard him repeat for hours together poems which seemed to me to be the same with Macpherson's translations.*" MacCodrum's name occurs again notably in a well-known incident, often quoted to prove Macpherson's comparative ignorance of the Gaelic tongue. When the editor or author of what are called "The Poems of Ossian" was perambulating the islands in search of remains of the most ancient Celtic poetry, he landed between the grim dogs of Loch Maddy, the most notable place attempting somewhat the attitude of a town, in those grey and barren regions. Thence he struck directly across the black moor, interthreaded with briny waters, towards Benbecula, where he was to be hospitably entertained by the younger Clan Ranald, of whose mansion remains are still shown in those parts. On his way thither the inquisitive ballad-collector met with a man whom at the time he did not know, but who afterwards turned out to be Mac-Codrum, to whom he put the question, as he thought, in perfectly good Gaelic, "*Am bheil dad agad air an Fheinn ?*" intended to mean, "Have you got anything about the Fin in your possession ?" but which to a classical Gaelic ear actually signified, "Have you any claims on the Fin ?" To this the bard gave in Gaelic the appropriate Gaelic answer, "*Cha 'neil: is ged do bitheadh, tha ruiginn a leas iarraidh mis,*" meaning, "No; and even if I had, I could not recover such an old debt, long since prescribed." This sharp exposure of his bad Gaelic from a crude Highlander, as he no doubt thought, was too much for the irritability of an aspiring young literary gentleman; so he trudged on to the castle of Clan-Ranald, and left the deep well of MacCodrum's Ossianic lore unpumped.

MacCodrum was contemporary of Alexander MacDonald, the Ardnamurchan bard, and personally acquainted with him. He had not, however, the literary ambition of the author of the "Biorlinn;" and except the few which he allowed to be published in MacDonald's collection, all his compositions were allowed, after the old Highland fashion, to float about in the living memories of men, from which some of them might, perhaps, even now be recovered. But the memories of Highlanders are—as Plato explained long ago in the Phædrus—every day becoming weaker in proportion as they get into the modern habit of trusting to printed books. For knowledge in this one respect is certainly like money,—the more you have in the bank, the less you carry in your pocket. What a man may put his finger on at any time in a book he does not take the trouble to remember. The dead record does duty for the living function; and the power of mind is measured not by what it actually holds, but by what at any given moment it can command. MacCodrum's memory is still kindly cherished in his native country, where, on a slight elevation not far from the shore, and close to the village of Houghary, in an old churchyard overgrown with nettles, a rough piece of old gneiss is shown, with an uneven withered surface, spotted with nodules, but without any inscription, which the bard had himself picked out from the beach, and ordered to be laid over his grave.

Next upon the scene appears a poet who, like Cowper among ourselves, belongs as much—perhaps more—to the religious public, than to the Gaelic people at large; I mean Dugald Buchanan, born at Balquhidder, the country of the famous Rob Roy, in the south-west of Perthshire, in the year 1716. His father rented the farm of Ardoch, on the river Balvaig, a quiet inarticulate[1] streamlet, that, issuing from Loch Voil, bends its sluggish course down the valley of Strathyre towards Loch Lubnaig, a sheet of water well known to railway tourists, as they swing their way down by the north base of Ben Ledi from Killin to Callander. Our poet had the misfortune to lose his pious mother at an early age; and so his youth being deprived of that kindly care which a pious mother alone can give, he grew up early in an unshepherded sort of style, that led him out of the garden of good ways into broad black wastes of unsanctified sensualism. His early education he received from one of the schools established in his native parish by the Society for the Promotion of Christian Knowledge; and so rapid was his progress in what elementary knowledge could there be got, that when he was only twelve years of age, he proved himself in a condition to go forth into the world and make his bread in the capacity of a family tutor. But while drilling others in the elements of what is called useful knowledge, he was himself drifting away among loose and worthless companions into all sorts of excesses, and, as he himself says in his published diary, scarcely opening his mouth without uttering oaths and imprecations. In this respect he is a sort of Highland repetition of the famous Bedford tinker, John Bunyan; and like him also in the occasional fits of religious terrors and cold sweats of conscience that would seize him for a season, only to fling him back into the pool of swinish mire in which it had become his habit to wallow. One of these experiences may serve as a specimen of all the rest :—

---

[1] *Balbh* in Gaelic is inarticulate; Latin, *balbus*.

" On a Sabbath evening the mistress of the family read the Scriptures to the household, and spoke solemnly of eternity and judgment. She described the manner of the judgment, and the second coming of the Lord. She said it was the opinion of some that it would take place on a Sabbath, and in the winter season, and that His appearance would be heralded by thunder, lightning, and hail. That same night there was a violent storm, such as she described. Hail poured into the room in which he slept, and its walls were illuminated with vivid flashes of lightning. He trembled with apprehension, believing that at any moment Jesus might appear, and summon the dead to rise. ' O how happy should I be, if I could but be buried under the ruins of the house, and hide from the face of the Judge ! Horror seized me. Repentance, I thought, was too late.

" ' I remembered one of Mr. Gray's sermons, in which he describes the torments of the damned and their consternation at the coming of the Lord. I thought if my life were to begin again, how I should read, and pray, and keep the Sabbath. I heartily resolved against my sins ; but my resolutions were soon at an end. In less than eight days I was just what I was before.' "[1]

This state of helmless drifting of a reasonable soul could end only in two ways, either in the utter shattering and wreckage of the whole man, or in the restoration of the whole man to the legitimate rule of what the grand old Stoics called the *ἡγε μονικόν*, or sovereignty of practical reason. To Buchanan in the Highlands, and every Highlander, this restoration could of course come in no other shape than in conversion to the orthodox Christianity of his country, and a happy escape from the fearful terrors of the

[1] *Reminiscences of the Life and Labours of Dugald Buchanan,* by the Rev. A. Sinclair, Kenmore. 21st Edition. Edinburgh, 1875.

violated law, and the vain refuges of self-righteousness, to a full and unconditional reliance on the righteousness of Christ as the starting-point of an ethical regeneration, according to the lofty ideal of the Gospel. Dugald Buchanan, from a coarse sensualist and a reckless blasphemer, suddenly became a man of extraordinary godliness ; and not only a godly man, but a preacher of righteousness, and the happy rescuer of not a few souls from the mire of sensualism, in the swathes of which his own higher vitality had been so nearly smothered. He never indeed attained the position of an authorised preacher of the Gospel; he had to be content with the humbler status of a catechist and the minor dignity of a parochial schoolmaster ; but genius and inspiration can dispense with the trappings of office and the vantage-ground of conventional superiority. Buchanan was soon recognised as an effective popular preacher, of his powers in which capacity the following anecdote affords a striking illustration. He occasionally had meetings at the head of Loch Rannoch, where there was then a large but not a very harmonious population. Some local jealousies, the inheritance of old clan feuds, had so imbittered the social relationship of two adjacent districts that they could not rightly be brought together, even in the house of Christian worship, without the danger of the wrath of man breaking out in a most unrighteous fashion. Both parties, however, were anxious to hear the preaching schoolmaster; and the evangelist, with that wisdom of the serpent which should always accompany the harmlessness of the dove, wishing to impress both parties, and yet to prevent an outbreak of the old clannish enmity, posted himself for a pulpit on a great stone in the midst of the bed of a stream which divided the territories of the hostile hearers, and from this commanding position poured forth the pre-cepts of the gospel of peace upon the eager-listening clansmen.   The effect was notable.   Softened by the force of his appeals, and convinced of the antagonism between their bitter feelings to each other and the temper of regenerate men as pictured in the Gospel, they shed tears of shame, and clasped hands of reconciliation on the spot.[1]

In the year 1766, when the Reverend Mr. Stewart of Killin, one of the ablest Gaelic scholars of the last century, was in Edinburgh attending to the publication of his Gaelic translation of the New Testament, Buchanan, whose mastery of the rare old tongue was known, resided for a while in Edinburgh in order to assist in the revision of the press.   This led to an intimate connection with the Highlanders in Edinburgh, to whom he frequently preached, and became thus the nucleus of the Gaelic church in that city, now so favourably known to Celtic scholars by the incumbency of the learned editor of the Book of the Dean of Lismore.   He also, as a man of poetical talent, was introduced into the literary circle of the modern Athens, and, among others, had the honour to have an interview with the accomplished Scottish sceptic, David Hume.   In this interview the conversation naturally fell on the principles of taste and the beauties of poetical composition ; in the course of which the philosopher remarked, that he knew no lines which for combined sublimity and simplicity equalled the well-known verses of the great English dramatist :—

> " The cloud-capt towers, the gorgeous palaces,
> The solemn temples, the great globe itself,
> And all that it inherits, shall dissolve,
> And, like the baseless fabric of a vision,
> Leave not a wreck behind."

---

[1] Sinclair, p. 53.

Buchanan, of course, had nothing to say against the quiet weighty grandeur of these lines; but he thought he could make a quotation from an author, which even a great admirer of Shakespeare would confess to be superior. Hume smiled; and the Highlander forthwith, with great gravity and impressiveness, recited the words from the Book of Revelation :—

"I saw a great white throne, and him that sat on it, from whose face the earth and the heaven fled away, and there was found no place for them. And I saw the dead, small and great, stand before God : and the books were opened : and another book was opened, which is the book of life : and the dead were judged out of those things which were written in the books, according to their works. And the sea gave up the dead which were in it : and death and hell delivered up the dead which were in them : and they were judged every man according to their works."

The philosopher, it is said, acquiesced in the poet's judgment, and eagerly inquired who the author was of so sublime a passage; and was informed, to his surprise, that the passage was a well-known one from a book which he had been taught to look on, like many a modern witling, with feelings of morbid prejudice rather than of healthy admiration.[1]

This anecdote, of which there is no reason to doubt the truth, gives us a significant glimpse into the general character of the poet's mind, and the subjects most congenial to his Muse. "The Day of Judgment," "The Dream," "The Winter," "The Prayer," "The Skull," and "The Christian Hero," are the titles of his most notable pieces. If in these poems the terrors of the Law and the awfulness

---

[1] Sinclair, p. 56.

K

of eternity are predominant, we must bear in mind that there is a sort of poetical melancholy congenial to the Highlander, and that it was by the terrors of the Law and the awful visions raised by a violated conscience that Buchanan, like Bunyan, was plucked from the extreme edge of sensual corruption. It was the most natural thing in the world, therefore, that the poet should be anxious, by highly finished pictures of death, judgment, and eternity, to stir the seared sensibilities of the class of men who, as experience had taught himself, were not likely to be moved by any more gentle appeals. Above all things, the contemplation of a skull to an imaginative mind is most fitted to excite thoughts humiliating to the fleshly pride of man, and suggestive of higher destinies beyond the grave. The moralisings of Shakespeare and Byron on this theme are known to all. Let us hear the variations of the Rannoch catechist to the same tune :—

> " I sat all alone
>   By a cold grey stone,
> And behold a skull lay on the ground !
>   I took in my hand,
>   And pitiful scanned
> Its ruin, all round and round.
>
>   Without colour or ken,
>   Or notice of men,
> When a footstep may trample the ground ;
>   A jaw without tooth,
>   And no tongue in the mouth,
> And a throat with no function of sound.
>
>   In thy cheek is no red,
>   Smooth and cold is thy head,

Deaf thine ear when sweet music is nigh ;
   In thy nostril no breath,
   And the savour of death
In dark hollow where beamed the bright eye.

   No virtue now flashes
   'Neath eyelids and lashes,
No message of brightness is sped ;
   But worms to and fro
   Do busily go,
Where pictures of beauty were spread.

   And the brain that was there
   Into ashes or air
Is vanished, and now hath no mind
   To finish the plan
   It so boldly began,
And left—a proud folly—behind.

   From that blank look of thine
   I gather no sign
Of thy life-tale, its shame or its glory ;
   Proud Philip's great son
   And his slave are as one,
When a skull is the sum of their story.

   Thou who pliest the trade
   With shovel and spade,
To make beds for the dead in the land,
   Declare, if thou can,
   Be it maiden or man
Whose skull I now hold in my hand.

   A maiden wert thou,
   Of bright eye and fair brow,

And a witchcraft of smiles in thy face ?
   And was thine the fine art
   To enmesh the weak heart
Of each youth that might sigh for thy grace?

   And what art thou now,
   With no grace on thy brow,
And thy witchery turned to disgust ?
   Cry shame on black Death
   That stopped thy fair breath,
And trampled thy bloom in the dust !

   Or a lawyer wert thou,
   Wise and true to thy vow,
To hold all offenders in awe,
   Without favour or grudge
   To weigh and to judge,
And to keep the straight line of the law ?

   Or wert thou a knave,
   A tool and a slave
To the rich who could buy thee with gold,
   But no virtue couldst see
   In the poor man's plea,
And left him to starve in the cold ?

   If thou wert expert
   To refine and pervert,
Till right became wrong in thy hand,
   A court waits for thee
   Where no fictions can be,
And only the truth may stand.

   Or wert thou a leech,
   Keen to know and to teach

All the pharmacy tabled in science,
    With a balm in thy hand
    For each plague in the land,
Bidding death and disease defiance ?

    But alack for the man
    That so bravely could plan,
From disease and distemper to save ;
    In vain all his skill,
    With potion and pill,
To respite himself from the grave !

    Or a soldier wert thou,
    With storm on thy brow,
On the sword of thy vengeance relying,
    Careering with power,
    In victory's hour,
O'er heaps of the dead and the dying ?

    Was thy sword in thy sheath
    When confronted with death,
Or did thy heart faint in the day,
    When the stout heart must yield
    To light swarms in the field,
And vile armies that creep through the clay ?

    No whit care the worms
    For the strong man of arms,
On his brain they will banquet full well ;
    And the skull of the bold
    Is a garrison hold
For the black-mantled beetle to dwell.

    Some are digging beneath
    The fence of thy teeth,

Thine ears some are boring within,
　　And some creeping out,
　　In a revelling rout,
Are spoiling the bloom of thy skin.

　　Or wert thou a lord
　　Of strong drink, at the board
Where the cup was the deepest to drain,
　　With no heaven but this,
　　To wallow in bliss,
With the ferment of wine in thy brain?

　　And did oaths at thy board
　　Sweetest music accord
To thy filthy carousers and thee,
　　Till your senses were drowned,
　　And you reeled on the ground,
More swinish than swine may be?

　　Or wert thou a man
　　Of the temperate clan,
With the gentle control of the brain
　　To reason thy whim,
　　When passions o'erbrim,
And a king in thy kingdom to reign?

　　Or wert thou a glutton,
　　To gorge and to fatten
Thy carcass unseasoned by soul,
　　In thy belly to find
　　A god to thy mind,
And a worship in draining the bowl?

　　Now the belly, thy god,
　　Must rot in the sod,

With the cold ooze dripping round thee,
    Thy teeth may not bite,
    Nor thy tongue taste delight,
Where the fetters of death have bound thee.

    Or wert thou a man
    The chief of thy clan,
The broad-acred lord of the soil,
    A help still at hand
    To the good in the land,
But a rod and reproof to the vile?

    Or was it thy plan,
    A hard-faced man,
Thy people to grind and to flay,
    To exact to the letter
    Thy right from thy debtor,
While Mercy cried out for delay?

    And never from thee,
    In the pride of degree,
Could the old man's voice bring a tear,
    As he stood in the air
    With his bald head bare,
And the sharp east wind in his ear.

    But now the poor thrall
    Waits not in thy hall,
Forced honour and homage to pay;
    Death loved the poor man,
    When he bravely began
To level thy pride with the clay.

    Or wert thou a teacher
    Of truth, and a preacher,

With message of mercy to tell,
 With an arm swift and strong
 To pull back the throng,
That headlong were plunging to hell ?

 Or wert thou a man
 Of the moderate clan,
To shepherd the sheep at thy leisure ?
 If the fleece were but thine,
 Old Reynard might dine
On the lambs of the flock at his pleasure.

 But woe for thy doom
 When the judgment shall come,
And the eye of the Master shall find thee,
 To cast the amount
 Of thy hollow account,
When the fetters of death shall bind thee !

 Or wert thou a head,
 The hot-house and bed
Of evil devices, uncaring
 For statute or law
 To temper with awe
The restless career of thy daring ?

 A forger of lies,
 And the rumour that flies
On the pinions of calumny strong ;
 With lips of deceit
 And a smile bitter-sweet,
And the poison of asps on thy tongue ?

 But now still in death,
 With no voice to give breath,

That tongue shall no more be offender;
   While maggots shall go
   In thy mouth to and fro,
And gnaw at the root of thy slander.

   And if thou didst go
   All sin-laden so,
With a lie in thy throat to the tomb;
   The cold grave shall be
   The sole heaven for thee
Till the trumpet shall call thee to doom.

   Like an ugly old toad
   From thy miry abode,
Thou shalt crawl to reproof of the day;
   To encounter thy God
   When He comes with a rod
The reward of thy doings to pay.

   O then in thine ear,
   With voice sharp and clear,
The Judge shall thy doom deliver,
   With devils to dwell
   In the furnace of hell,
And His curse on thy head for ever.

   Nor deem that the fire
   Shall kindly conspire
To ashes unfeeling to turn thee,
   Thy flesh and thy bones
   Shall be hardened to stones,
And the flame that shall scorch may not burn thee!

   Or wert thou a wight,
   That strove for the right,

With God for thy guide in thy doing?
    Though now thou lie there,
    All bleached and bare,
In the blast a desolate ruin,

    From the tomb thou shalt rise
    And mount to the skies,
When the trump of the judgment shall bray;
    Thy body of sin
    Thou shalt slip like a skin,
And cast all corruption away.

    Thy form shall be bright,
    As the fair lady Light,
When in redness of morn she advances,
    Like stars when they shine,
    Thy far-seeing eyne
Shall pierce through the dim with their glances.

    Thy mouth shall o'erbrim
    From God with the hymn
Of His praise in the high habitations;
    He will open thine ear
    In rapture to hear
The pæan of deathless ovations!

    When in glory divine
    The Redeemer shall shine,
The hosts of His people to gather,
    When the trumpet hath blared,
    Like an eagle repaired
Thou shalt rise to the home of thy Father.

    He shall greet thee His own,
    From the light of the throne,

Whence joyfulness flows like a river;
Thou shalt bloom in His sight,
Without blast, without blight,
In an Eden of glory for ever.

O listen and learn,
And timefully turn,
From delusions that fondly deceive you!
While the Saviour stands
With welcoming hands
And a door open wide to receive you!"

It may seem hardly fair to the poor Highland school-master to have brought his work into comparison with two of the most striking passages in Shakespeare and Byron; it cannot be denied that the poet, in some of the above verses, loses himself in the preacher; and the poem would certainly have been improved by the curtailment of several stanzas, especially in the close. But his admirers are entitled to reply that the poet *was* a preacher; that his main object in this poem was to put a pictorial sermon into a graceful shape; and that he had as much right to mingle preaching with poetry as the prophet Isaiah had, or king Solomon. Certain it is that his countrymen have not been backward to assign to Buchanan one of the most notable niches in their poetical Pantheon; and if one were to judge by the number of editions which his poems have gone through, he was unquestionably, in their estimation, the greatest Celtic bard after Ossian. But everybody knows that religious works, whether in prose or verse, when they once get an acknowledgment, have a special circulation of their own, which cannot be accepted as a measure of literary merit. There are some well-known collections of spiritual songs in the Highlands, now going on to their twentieth edition, with nothing in them above commonplace as poetry, while Duncan Ban, one of the greatest masters of the Gaelic lyre, to whom we now make the transition, has waited a full century and more without coming to his tenth.[1]

This " Fair Duncan," or " Duncan of the Songs," as the Highlanders are fond of calling him, was born on the 20th of March 1724, at Drumliaghart near Inveroran, half-way between Tyndrum and Glencoe, where the Earl of Dudley has his shooting lodge to command the troops of antlered rangers that haunt the windings of the Black Forest. Of all the Highland poets this man is the one unquestionably who bears, even more distinctly than Ossian, the features of his Celtic origin on his face. He is in all respects as native to the land of Bens as the purple heather on the braes; he is a perfect uncorrupted, unqualified son of the mountains; with no Lowland manners or Lowland accomplishments to disturb the natural unity and completeness of his type. Like Homer, he could neither read nor write; and, unlike M‘Donald, he had neither school nor college to stimulate the natural vitality of his root or to trim the untutored expansion of his growth. In this respect he had even the advantage of Burns, whose ambition for English literary culture may seem sometimes to have led him into the use of a phraseology not quite in harmony with his rustic Muse. Nature is always right; culture not seldom wrong; dangerous always to a poet, if it either leads him away from the sympathies of general humanity, or, what is worse, teaches him to array his Muse in an incongruous tissue, composed partly of native rustic plaiding, partly of purple patches and curious network of out-

[1] Poems by Duncan M‘Intyre. First edition (Edinburgh, 1768). The last edition (Edinburgh, 1875), is the eighth. Sinclair's edition of Buchanan in 1875 is the twenty-first.

landish finery. In the life of Duncan Ban there was nothing to draw him away from feeding on anything but the native pabulum of a Highland bard. In his youth he had all the tastes and habits that belong to a budding sportsman; and when he grew up to manhood he attracted the attention of the then Earl of Breadalbane, who made him forester and gamekeeper in the districts of Coire Cheathaich and Ben Dorain, both which districts, now a large sheep-walk, were at that time in their original Highland condition as a deer forest. He served the Duke of Argyll also for a short while in the same capacity, as keeper of the Buachaill Etive, a wild mountain tract well known to tourists and deer-stalkers, at the south-east end of Glencoe. In the rebellion of '45, when Duncan was just emerging into manhood, he served on the Hanoverian side— somewhat jarring with his Celtic sympathies no doubt— under Colonel Campbell of Carwhin, and was present at the battle of Falkirk, or "the Spotted Kirk" as the Highlanders call it,[1] from which he returned without his sword. He had entered this service as substitute for a gentleman named Fletcher, a name still known in those parts, for the sum of 300 merks Scots, to be paid on his return. Along with the money-promise, Mr. Fletcher gave him his sword, and when M'Intyre came home without this weapon the owner of it shabbily refused to pay the poor poet the scanty wage of his substitution. It is dangerous to offend a rhymer; indignation makes verses; and the Fletcher was made to feel the lash of the M'Intyre as the Campbell in 1715 had winced under the castigation of Iain Lom. The poem of the "Battle of Falkirk," like Byron's "English Bards and Scotch Reviewers," made

---

[1] *Eaglais bhreac.* Mr. Skene pointed out to me the word *fal* in Schmidt's *Anglo-Saxon Dictionary*, meaning the same thing as *breac*, i.e. *spotted* or *brindled.*

M'Intyre famous and Fletcher contemptible; and not only was the imperious gentleman obliged to stand all the ridicule which in the Highlands a well-pointed stanza always carried with it, but the Earl of Breadalbane, taking counsel of men of law, forced the irate gentleman to pay the poor gamekeeper the sum of £16, 17s. 6d., which was his rightful wage.

Duncan Ban, like a genuine Highlander, who walked erect, brushing the heather and drinking the mountain breezes freely, lived to a good old age. In the year 1793 he joined the Earl of Breadalbane's regiment of Fencibles with the rank of serjeant, and served in it till the year 1799, when it was disbanded. For some time afterwards he belonged to the City Guard of Edinburgh, and, taking up his abode in this city, was moved to celebrate its more marked features in some characteristic verses—

> " Dunedin is a bonnie toun
>   In more fair ways than one;
>   A toun to it that must not bend
>   In all the realm is none;
>   So many gentlemen are there,
>   Whose purses swell with gold,
>   Right lusty lords who quaff stout wine
>   From Spain both rich and old."

The costume of the time he notes nicely, with the eye of a poetic observer; and finds as usual the fashion of the metropolitan dames not so much in harmony with graceful nature as the less pretentious array of the Highland milk-maids—

> " Here's many a gallant gentleman,
>   Full polished and well bred,
>   Wears powder plastered on his hair
>   To the high crown of his head;

With folds and plaits and many curls
Well woven overspread,
And on the top a knotted bunch
Like carded silken thread !

There's many a noble lady
A poor man here may meet,
In gown of silk and satin
That sweeps along the street ;
And every pretty thing wears stays
To keep her straight and spare,
And beauty-spots on her fair face
To make more beauty there.

Each one, as well beseems her,
Well-mannered with the best,
Stately and rich and ribbony,
And with gay roundness dressed.
The long robes on the maidens
Just showing to your eye
A strong and pointed well-made shoe,
—I thought the heel too high."[1]

The poet remained in the City Guard till the year 1806,
and died in Edinburgh in the year 1812, after seeing the
third edition of his poems. He lies buried in Greyfriars
Churchyard. A cenotaph has been erected to him in his
native county, on a rising ground above Dalmally, looking
down on the waters of the Orchy, as they pour their dark-

[1] Translated by Pattison, in *Selections from the Gaelic Bards* (Glasgow,
Sinclair, 1866). I have changed some lines and expressions. Some things
in Pattison are fine, but others show either a strange want of taste or an
ignorance of the English language. In not a few places the desire to be
literal has made him move in fetters, which utterly destroys all grace,
and makes lyric poetry worse than the worst prose.

brown floods here into the beautiful carse-ground at the north-east corner of Loch Awe.

The subjects of M'Intyre's poems, characteristically Highland as he is, are exactly such as might have been expected. The scenery of his native hills, the beauty of the mountain lasses and the bravery and manhood of the Highland "gaisgeach," all taken faithfully from the life, and touched with the fervour which it is the peculiar privilege of the poet's genius to impart, are his favourite themes. His tone of mind may most fitly be apprehended by shaping before the fancy something the very reverse of those qualities which gave such a brilliant and powerful but unkindly and uncomfortable character to the poetry of the Byronic school. If Byron represents the sublime of a tempestuous soul, interthreaded with exquisite gleams of beauty and glimpses of tenderness, Duncan Ban is pure beauty, pleasantness, and comfort : the fragrant bloom of May and the mellow fruitage of autumn hanging gracefully together on the same green branch. If not so bright as Burns, he is better rounded and more harmonious, and more sweetly at peace with himself, with Nature, and with God. One quaffs the rich bowl of his poetry, not like the sparkling stimulus of champagne, but as creamy milk warm from the motherly udder of the cow. His three most popular poems are the verses to his newly married wife, *Màiri bhàn òg*, or "Fair Young Mary," to *Coire Cheathaich*, or "The Misty Corrie," and perhaps the highest, certainly the longest effort of his Muse, *Ben Dòrain*. Both these two last poems are remarkable instances of the genius for descriptive poetry above noted, as so native in the Celtic bards ; and the great popularity of the former as a theme for recitation in the social meetings and other gatherings of the Highlanders, is ample proof that the taste for word-painting in landscape belongs as much to the genius of the mountain people as to the special talent of their bard. But in Ben Dorain we have the further element of mountain sports and deer-stalking, which should have rendered the bard of Glenorchy long ago the patron-saint of our sporting Nimrods in the north, had they not unfortunately been ignorant of the language and lyrical virtues of the noble people on whose soil they pursue their recreations. I shall be surprised to learn that there exists in any language, ancient or modern, a more original poem of the genus which we may call venatorial than the Ben Dorain of Duncan Ban. What Landseer, in a sister art, has done for animals in general, that M'Intyre, in this singular work, has done for the deer and the roe. Though not a deer-stalker myself, I had for many years been possessed by a strong admiration of this poem; and last summer, in intervals of leisure from various peregrinations, I summoned up courage not only to spell my way through it, but, with the assistance of some learned Galicians in the west country, to attempt a rhymed version of the whole. I am perfectly aware that a poem of this length, composed for pipe-music by a Highland piper, stands at a great disadvantage when placed before an English reader, as a thing to be read. Among other objections, he will naturally think there is too much of it, too little structure, and too much variation of one theme; but this objection could not occur to a lover of a Highland pibroch any more than the curious variations on a musical theme by a Beethoven or a Mendelssohn appear too much to an ear trained to appreciate the refined delicacies of rich musical harmonies; besides, the critic will kindly bear in mind that the same objection applies to Homer in many places; and there can be little doubt in my mind that, if one-third of the wrath of Achilles could be exsected from the poem as we now have it, without injuring the relative proportions of the whole, the *Iliad* as a readable book would be vastly improved. But as we know that the work of Homer was never written to be read as a whole, but composed without paper by a living man to be sung in living parts, and as Homeric criticism, since Wolf, takes equitable note of this peculiarity, so let the Highland Duncan be kindly condoned on a similar ground. And if there be a class of persons, accustomed to fare æsthetically on high-seasoned dishes, who deem no verses worthy of the name of poetry that do not bristle and twinkle all over with puzzling subtleties and brilliant surprises, let them consider that Duncan Ban in the Highlands, like Robert Burns and the authors of our best Scottish songs in the Lowlands, wrote in the language of the people, to be understood by the people, not in the language of a curiously cultivated art, to be praised by the fastidious Aristarchs of the hour and admired by a special circle of literary epicures. I have only to add that Ben Dorain is a beautiful conical mountain which rises sheer up from the glen, about four miles north of Tyndrum on the Glencoe road, looking down upon the stream of the Orchy, where it makes a sudden bend southward, and flings the mighty swirl of its mossy brown waters down to the green flats of Dalmally.

BEN DORAIN.

Honour be to Ben Dorain
  Above all Bens that be!
Beneath the sun mine eyes beheld
  No lovelier Ben than he;
With his long smooth stretch of moor,
And his nooks remote and sure
    For the deer,
When he smiles in face of day,

And the breeze sweeps o'er the brae
    Keen and clear ;
With his greenly-waving woods,
And his grassy solitudes,
And the stately herds that fare
    Feeding there ;
And the troop with white behind,
When they scent the common foe,
Then wheel to sudden flight
    In a row,
Proudly snuffing at the wind
    As they go.

Right mettlesome is he,
The stag with lightsome glee ;
    Who like him,
When he paces on the side
Of the Ben, with healthy pride,
So gallant and so gay,
In the fashion of the brae,
    Neat and trim ?
No cause hath he to fear
The wearing of his gear
    With the time,
When with mantle of the red,
Round his shoulders bravely spread,
    He doth climb.
And a youth doth walk behind,
With his face against the wind,
And with danger in his mind
    To the deer.
His hand is firm and steady,
And his eight-grooved gun is ready
    With its gear,

With its flint full sharp and keen,
And its trigger close and clean
        To the hand ;
When the hammer right and tight
On the pan's smooth lid shall smite
It will bring a deadly light
        At command ;
With a bore of honest fame,
And a stock that none may blame,
From a gun of goodly shape
No deer may find escape
        In the land.
For the hunter hath a skill
That will work his wary will
Though the quarry on the hill
        Flee like wind ;
And should Donald with his men,
Stoutly striding through the glen,
Mark his prey with cunning ken
        From behind,
O the bullets then will fly
Like lightning from the sky
        On thy head,
And the hind that walks the Ben
In her gory garment then
        Will lie dead !

II.

'Tis a nimble little hind,
Giddy-headed like her kind,
That goes sniffing up the wind
        In her scorning ;
With her nostrils sharp and keen,

Somewhat petulant I ween,
'Neath the crag's rim she is seen
    In the morning;
For she feareth to come down
From the broad and breezy crown
    Of Ben Dorain,
Lest the hunter's cruel shot
In the low encircled spot
    Should be pouring.
She hath breath in breast at will
As she scampers o'er the hill
    Without panting,—
Ruddy wealth of healthy blood
From the lusty fatherhood
Of Ben Dorain's antlered brood
    Finely vaunting;
And I stand with charmèd ear
    As I go,
If the echo I may hear
    Of her low.
And she seeketh round about
For the stag I little doubt,
When the season of the year
Brings hot passion to the deer;
The stag she seeks to please
In the flaunting of the breeze,
When he lifts his haughty head,
With his horns so grandly spread
    Loudly roaring;
And right well knoweth he
All the leafy nooks that be
    In Ben Dorain.
Though in sooth it passeth me
All the antlered troops to tell

That sweep through dale and dell
　　In Ben Dorain,
The hind I know full well,
With her slender shapely limb
So fashioned and so trim,
When she leads her dappled brood
Through the rough and tangled wood
　　Up the pass ;
You will never with your ken
Mark her flitting paces when
With lightsome tread she trips
O'er the light unbroken tips
　　Of the grass ;
Not in all the islands three,
Nor wide Europe, may it be
That a step so light and clean
　　Hath been seen,
When she sniffs the mountain breeze,
And goes wandering at her ease,
Or sports as she may please
　　On the green ;
Not she will ever feel
Fret or evil humour when
She makes a sudden wheel,
And flies with rapid heel
　　O'er the Ben ;
With her fine and frisking ways
She steals sorrow from her days,
Nor shall old age ever press
On her head with sore distress
　　In the glen.
And surely she doth wear
A dress both rich and rare
In firm flesh and healthy looks

Much excelling,
With the green and grassy nooks
Of the forest fresh and fair
For her dwelling.
And for choice food in sooth
She hath a dainty tooth
When she wanders at her will
Through the green depths of the hill,
Richly storing
For her fawns sweet milk that flows
From soft mountain grass that grows
On Ben Dorain;
Stout nurslings of the hill,
Whom the cold blasts may not chill
Of the mountain,
As they foot it to and fro,
Drinking vigour as they go,
From the pure untainted flow
Of the fountain;
With no sorrow in their heart,
As from glen to glen they dart
On the mountain.
Nor need they fear the snow,
Nor the swelling
Of the storm, nor winds that blow
Sharply yelling,
Though no shapely house their own
Of the well-compacted stone
They can show;
Yet with prudent haste they hurry
To their refuge in the corrie
Which they know,
'Neath the hollows of the rocks,
'Mid the rugged stumps and stocks

'Neath the boulders and the blocks
        Lying low.

III.

My delight it was to rise
With the early morning skies,
        All aglow,
And to brush the dewy height
Where the deer in airy state
        Wont to go ;
At least a hundred brace
Of the lofty-antlered race,
When they left their sleeping-place,
        Light and gay ;
When they stood in trim array,
And with low deep-breasted cry,
Flung their breath into the sky,
        From the brae :
When the hind, the pretty fool,
Would be rolling in the pool
        At her will ;
Or the stag in gallant pride,
Would be strutting at the side
Of his haughty-headed bride,
        On the hill.
And sweeter to my ear
Is the concert of the deer
        In their roaring,
Than when Erin from her lyre
Warmest strains of Celtic fire
   ·   May be pouring ;
And no organ sends a roll
So delightsome to my soul,
As the branchy-crested race,

When they quicken their proud pace
And bellow in the face
    Of Ben Dorain.
O what joy to view the stag
When he rises 'neath the crag,
And from depth of hollow chest
Sends his bell across the waste,
While he tosses high his crest,
    Proudly scorning.
And from milder throat the hind,
Lows an answer to his mind,
With the younglings of her kind
    In the morning;
With her vivid swelling eye,
While her antlered lord is nigh,
She sweeps both earth and sky,
    Far away;
And beneath her eyebrow grey
Lifts her lid to greet the day,
And to guide her turfy way
    O'er the brae.
O how lightsome is her tread,
When she gaily goes ahead
O'er the green and mossy bed
    Of the rills;
When she leaps with such a grace
You will own her pretty pace
Ne'er was hindmost in the race,
    When she wills;
Or when with sudden start
She defies the hunter's art,
And is vanished like a dart
    O'er the hills!
And her food full well she knows,

In the forest where she goes,
Where the rough old pasture grows
        To her mind.
Stiff grass of virtue rare,
Glossy fatness to prepare,
'Neath her coat of shining hair,
        To the hind ;
And for drink she hath the well,
Where the water-cresses dwell,
Far sweeter to her taste,
In the freshness of the waste,
        Than sweet wine ;
The blushing daisy-tips
Are a dainty to her lips,
As the nodding grass she clips,
        Very fine ;
St. John's wort too she knows,
And where the sweet primrose
And the spotted orchis grows,
        She will dine.
With such food and drink, I ween,
You will never find them lean,
But girt with pith and power,
To stand stoutly in the hour
        Of distress ;
And though laden on the back
With weighty fat no lack,
With well-compacted limb
They will wear it light and trim,
        Like a dress.
O how pleasant 'twas to see
How happy they would be,
When they gathered all together
To their home upon the heather,

In the gloaming !

At the bottom of the hill
They were safe from touch of ill,
In their nook of shelter tight,
When they rested for the night
From their roaming.

What though the nights were long,
And the winds were sharp and strong
In their roaring,

Wrapt in thick fur of the red,
Where the moor is widely spread,
Here they made their turfy bed,
And their sleep was sweet and sound,
With no wish beyond the bound
Of Ben Dorain.

IV.

For Ben Dorain lifts his head
In the air,

That no Ben was ever seen
With his grassy mantle spread,
And rich swell of leafy green,
May compare ;

And 'tis passing strange to me
When his sloping side I see,
That so grand

And beautiful a Ben
Should not flourish among men,
In the scutcheon and the ken
Of the land.

'Tis plenished o'er and o'er,
With rich gifts a fruitful store,
You will seek and far explore
Ere you find ;

Not a single spot is bare,
From the jewelled greenness there,
And blossoms waving fair
    In the wind;
Where the cock, the prideful-breasted,
    Swells his crow,
And the birds, the gentle-nested,
    Pour the flow
Of their voicing and rejoicing,
    As they go;
There the roebuck too is seen,
So nimble on the green
    Of the brae,
When he runs and never tumbles,
When he climbs and never stumbles,
    All the way;
With sharp horn upon his head,
And stout tramping hoof to tread,
With a soul of joyous brightness,
And long limbs of limber lightness,
And a tidy tripping tightness,
    He will climb,
Through the brushwood and the fern,
With brave dash of unconcern,
On the low and lushy meadow,
'Neath the mighty mountain shadow,
Or high upon the jag
Of the mist-engirdled crag,
    All sublime.
When the heat is in his blood,
He will dart from out the wood,
    Nothing slow;
He will gather up his might,
Like an arrow drawn for flight
    From the bow;

And then spring with lightsome skill
To the nook behind the hill,
Where he pleasures at his will
          With the doe.
And in sooth it suits her well
With her dappled brood to dwell
          In the glen,
This coquettish little doe,
That is waiting for her beau
          From the Ben.
With an eye so keen and clear,
With an ear so quick to hear,
And rapid hoofs that clear
The long bleak moor behind
          Like the wind.
If all the mighty race
Of the Fin should give her chase,
          Or the men
Who receive the golden pay
Of King George, in red array,
She would mock their lagging way
          On the Ben.
If only free from scot,
To their powder and their shot,
          She might go,
No man of mortal kin,
Would bring sorrow to the skin
          Of the doe ;
Such a web of shifting ways,
In the windings of the braes,
          She will try ;
And though she shy the race
Of the hounds in panting chase,
Up the steepest granite face
          She will fly,

Till she triumph o'er the foe,
This tricksy little doe,
As she tosses her light head
    In the air;
Then crouching she will lie,
With a wakeful watching eye,
And the dappled people nigh
    To her lair.

v.

This is my pretty doe,
With her fine fantastic ways,
As so lightly she will go,
With her slender shapely limb,
'Neath the green and shaggy rim
    Of the braes;
Sweet leafage of the wood
And crisp heather for her food,
    She will praise:
Very light of heart, I ween,
Right sprightly is her mien,
And her frown was never seen
    On the Ben,
Though a foolish thought will flit
Through her slight unsteady wit
In a gay and giddy fit,
    Now and then;
But right modest is my doe,
And in grace is nothing scant,
When she quietly will go
To her home and hidden haunt
    In the glen;
And my vagrant little doe,
When she wanders far and free

On the rough and mottled meadow,
Where the big rock flings a shadow,
On Monday and on Sunday
    You may see ;
And well she knows to find
The bushy coppice nigh,
Where in covert from the wind
    She may lie ;
The screened and shaded place
Which the tempest's rapid race
And the thunder's rolling pace
    Passes by.
And when she wills to drink,
Straight she stands upon the brink
    Of the fountain
That comes gushing from a chink
    In the mountain ;
And she taketh in a wealth
Of freshness and of health
    From the draught,
Such as mortal never knew
Strong ale of stiffest brew
    When he quaffed.
And when the mountain ranger
Brings glimpse of sudden danger
    To the doe,
She hath limbs of supple length
That will try the hunter's strength
    Round and round,
As he follows every fit
Of her rapid-shifting wit
    O'er the ground.
O ! how oft I felt the grace
Of her light-complexioned face,

And her warm coat's ruddy pride
On the heathy mountain side,
Not to mention winning ways,
And points of pretty praise
    Many mo ;
In Europe far and near
She hath fleetness without peer,
And the sharpest ear to hear.
    That I know.

VI.

Right pleasant was the view
Of that fleet red-mantled crew,
As with sounding hoof they trod
O'er the green and turfy sod
    Up the brae,
As they sped with lightsome hurry
Through the rock-engirded corrie,
With no lack of food, I ween,
When they cropped the banquet green
    All the way.
O grandly did they gather,
In a jocund troop together,
In the corrie of the Fern
With light-hearted unconcern ;
Or by the smooth green loan
Of Achalader were shown,
Or by the ruined station
Of the old heroic nation
    Of the Fin,
Or by the willow rock
Or the witch-tree on the knock,
The branchy crested flock
    Might be seen.

Nor will they stint the measure
Of their frolic and their pleasure
    And their play,
When with airy-footed amble
At their freakish will they ramble
    O'er the brae,
With their prancing and their dancing,
And their ramping and their stamping,
And their plashing and their washing
    In the pools,
Like lovers newly wedded,
Light-hearted, giddy-headed
    Little fools.
No thirst have they beside
The mill-brook's flowing tide
And the pure well's lucid pride
    Honey-sweet;
A spring of lively cheer,
Sparkling cool and clear,
And filtered through the sand
    At their feet;
'Tis a life-restoring flood
To repair the wasted blood
The cheapest and the best in all the land;
And vainly gold will try
For the Queen's own lips to buy
    Such a treat.
From the rim it trickles down
Of the mountain's granite crown
    Clear and cool;
Keen and eager though it go
Through your veins with lively flow,
Yet it knoweth not to reign
In the chambers of the brain
    With misrule;

M

Where dark water-cresses grow
You will trace its quiet flow,
With mossy border yellow,
So mild, and soft, and mellow,
          In its pouring.
With no slimy dregs to trouble
The brightness of its bubble
As it threads its silver way
From the granite shoulders grey
          Of Ben Dorain.
Then down the sloping side
It will slip with glassy slide
          Gently welling,
Till it gather strength to leap,
With a light and foamy sweep,
To the corrie broad and deep
          Proudly swelling;
Then bends amid the boulders,
'Neath the shadow of the shoulders
          Of the Ben,
Through a country rough and shaggy,
So jaggy and so knaggy,
Full of hummocks and of hunches,
Full of stumps and tufts and bunches,
Full of bushes and of rushes,
          In the glen,
Through rich green solitudes,
And wildly hanging woods
With blossom and with bell,
In rich redundant swell,
          And the pride
Of the mountain daisy there,
And the forest everywhere,
With the dress and with the air
          Of a bride.

VII.

On the moor both broad and bare
Swept by breezy mountain air,
Where the rifted hollow goes,
And the rocks with jutting nose
　　Sharply run,
There the bonnie heather corrie
Spreads forth its purple glory
　　To the sun,
Where the air is sweet and mild,
Where the fawn, the mountain child,
　　Comes to view,
And the dappled people wild
　　Not a few.
Right snug the shelter there
Boon Nature did prepare
　　For the hind
From the driving and the tearing,
And the cutting edge unsparing
　　Of the wind;
She, the sweetheart of the stag,
When he gazes down the crag,
With hoof untaught to lag
　　On the Ben;
No cassocked priest they need
To make their marriage speed
　　There and then.
A healthy bride is she,
Right fine and fair to see,
　　Nice and sweet;
If you kissed her you would know
That the breath from her doth go
　　Very sweet.

This corrie is the praise
        Of all men
Who trained in hunting ways
Ever came to feed their gaze
        On a Ben;
And 'tis here in autumn weather
That the hunters come together,
When the breeze is racing shrill
Through the big gaps of the hill
        Down the glen.
All fruitfulness is there
That springeth fresh and fair,
Where the rainy virtue rare
        Will be pouring;
All pleasantness it knows
Of the scent that largely flows
From the wild-rasp and the rose
        On Ben Dorain;
With stream and streamlet too
Where fishes not a few
        Suffer scath,
When the flashing light will bribe
The thoughtless finny tribe
        To the death;
Where a stalworth youth shall stand
With a strong spear in his hand
        Right and tight,
And will pierce them with the pine,
Where the gleaming torches shine,
        Through the night.
Right pleasant too to watch
        At the station
Of the eddy dark and deep
Where the salmon love to rise,

And the spotted trout will leap,
A dainty meal to catch
        With surprise
From the light and buzzing nation
        Of the flies.
Such is my corrie fine;
        In the bound
Of the broad earth and the brine
No virtue like to thine,
Thou heather corrie fine,
        May be found.

VIII.

The hind that dwelleth in this glen
        Is light of foot and airy;
Who tracks her way upon the Ben
        Must be full wise and wary.
Softly, softly on her traces
He must steal with noiseless paces,
        Nigh and still more nigh,
Lest she turn with sudden starting,
And, like feathered arrow darting,
        Cheat his eager eye.
He must know to dodge behind
Rock and block in face of wind,
In the ditch and in the pit
Dripping lie and soaking sit,
        Stoop, and creep, and crawl,
Ever with quick eye to note
Face of earth and clouds that float
        In the azure hall.
Wisely, wisely wending round
Where she surely will be found;
        And then planted surely

Where with fixed and steady aim
He may mark the dappled game
          For his own securely;
Then his gun he well must know
How to handle 'gainst the foe,
With his firm forefinger's end
He the trigger back must bend;
New and closely locked the flint,
Smart and sharp the hammer's dint,
Stroke whence flies a spark that never
Failed to kindle flame, however
          Small the smutty grain;
Powder dry—well-seasoned stuff—
Rammed with tow both rough and tough,
That without fail both loud and large
May speed the deadly dun discharge
          Of smoke and leaden rain;
'Tis a pleasant sight, I ween,
When the lusty youth are seen
          In their hunting gear
Brushing briskly through the heather,
Planted on the grass together
          Watching of the deer,
With a gun that none may blame,
And a flash of sudden flame,
          Winged with mortal fear;
And the hounds, a restless crew,
Keen for bloody work to do,
Sharply nosing all the path,
Full of rapine and of wrath,
Yelping, howling at the sight,
Leaping with a wild delight;
With their tails they lash their side
          Bristling with their hair,

Their huge jaws they open wide,
    With lowering brows they frown,
With forward tongue and panting breath,
Exulting in the scent of death,
They for the feast of blood prepare
    When the deer is down.
And now their time is come; they know
Full well the winding way to go,
With rapid feet and sure,
Up and down, and to and fro
    Across the breezy moor;
The mighty Ben, the rocks reply,
As with tempest speed they fly,
To the howling and the yelling,
And the deathful bustle swelling
    O'er the breezy moor.
And now behold, with cunning wending,
    They have chased her down,
To the narrow glen descending
    From the mountain's crown.
In the pool of treacherous water
She must float and she must flounder
With a ring of death around her;
Looking in the face of slaughter
    She must now abide,
With her dear life's purple tide
    Welling from her side;
For now they hold her in their grasp
    With a grip of death;
While the yelping hounds confound her
She must plash and she must flounder,
She must pant and she must gasp,
    Till she find no breath.
But I must cease to flood your ear
With all I know about the deer

> And the fine craft of stalking;
> 'Twould leave you deaf the half to hear,
> And me drive from my senses sheer,
>   With such unmeasured talking.

I subjoin to this long venatorial pibroch a short lament made by the old deer-stalker over the desolation of his beloved haunts by the introduction of large sheep-farms. It is called the " Song of the Foxes," and, as connected with the much-vexed question of the proper management of Highland properties, may have to be referred to specially again in the concluding chapter of these sketches.

A SONG OF FOXES.

> Ho! ho! ho! the foxes!
> Would there were more of them,
> I'd give heavy gold
> For a hundred score of them!

My blessing with the foxes dwell,
For that they hunt the sheep so well!

Ill fa' the sheep, a grey-faced nation,
That swept our hills with desolation!

Who made the bonnie green glens clear,
And acres scarce, and houses dear;

The grey-faced sheep, who worked our woe,
Where men no more may reap or sow,

And made us leave for their grey pens
Our bonnie braes and grassy glens,

Where we were reared, and gladly grew,
And lived to kin and country true;

Who bared the houses to the wind,
Where hearths were warm, and hearts were kind,

And spread the braes with wreck and ruin,
The grey-faced sheep for our undoing!

And where they came were seen no more
Harrow or hoe on slope or shore,

And on the old and friendly places
New people sit with loveless faces;

And the good grey mare no more is seen
With its frisking foal on the open green,

And I seek in vain for the cow that lay
Licking its calf on the bonnie green brae!

And the bonnie milk-maids, ohon! ohon!
Are seen no more when the kine are gone!

And there's now no work for the lads to do
But to herd the sheep—some one or two!

And the goats, whose milk was good and cheap,
They too must go, to make way for the sheep!

And the roe in the rocky glade that lies
Is waked no more by the fawn when it cries.

For stags will flee, and mothers will weep,
When gentlemen live to make money by sheep!

And foresters now can earn no penny
Where stags are few and sheep are many.

He earns from me no kindly will
Who harms the fox upon the hill;

May he die the death of a hog
Against a fox who drives a dog!

On the hill-side may he rot
Who fires on Reynard with cruel shot !

And may the young cubs prosper well
Where snug in rocky holes they dwell !

And if my prayer with Heaven prevail
No trap shall grip their bushy tail !

And may they live on tasteful food,
And die as wise old foxes should ! [1]

---

[1] An excellent commentary on the sheep-mania here denounced by the old forester is found in the dialogue between Finlay the piper and an old friend, from the graphic pencil of the late Dr. Norman Macleod's father, in the *Teachdaire*. The atrocities perpetrated by those whose natural heartlessness made them fit instruments for carrying out such desolating reforms with a high hand were of course glossed over by interested parties, with whom one-sided theories of political economy served as an apology for all sorts of selfishness ; but the single witness of a man like Dr. Macleod, who was a wise man and a gentleman, and possessed of local knowledge, is alone sufficient to outweigh whole cartloads of daily columns or quarterly articles that ever were written, or ever can be written in defence of a style of management of Highland property alike barbarous and unpatriotic, impolitic and unprofitable. I translate from Dr. Clerk's edition, p. 253 :—

"There indeed you are right ; he was the man that had a kind heart. But this new man who has come in his place has a heart of remarkable hardness, and cares not a straw for the pipe or anything that belongs to the Highlands. He is a perfect fanatic in his passion for big sheep. It brings more enjoyment to him to look at a wether parading on the green braes than to listen to all the pibrochs that were ever played. If I were to compose a pibroch for him, I would call it LAMENT FOR THE BIG WETHER —the wether that fell over the rock the other day, the loss of which almost drove him mad. It's not I that would be caring to say this to everybody ; but as you happen to be with me on the spot, there can be no harm in telling you how he treated the poor people here. There is not now smoke coming out of a single cottage or sheiling in the whole glen, where you used to see scores of decent people working at honest work. This man would as soon give lodgment to a fox as to a poor crofter or a widow woman. You never heard in your life what a mangling and maiming he has made of the population of this glen. Not even a shepherd would he have from the people of the country ; he brought them all in from the South. Even his shepherd's dog does not understand a word of

We shall conclude these hasty notices of the great Celtic poets of the last century with a short account of the famous ROB DONN. I call him famous, both because he was a notable man in his own time and place, and because, for a remote Celtic bard, he received the remarkable honour of having his merits proclaimed on the great stage of the *Quarterly Review*, by a scholar of such subtle perception and wide range as John Gibson Lockhart.[1] The proper name of this poet was Robert Mackay, and, as bearing that name,

Gaelic! Mactalla of the Crag has not sent back a single Gaelic echo since good Donald went away. Everything must make way for the sheep. There is not a single brake now in which a bramble could grow; no tuft of brushwood on the slope where one could gather a nut; he has shaved the country as smooth and bare as the gable-wall of a house; and as for sloes, where sloes used to be, you may as well go and seek for grapes. The birds, too, have left us; they have gone to the wood on the other side of the sound; even the grey cuckoo cannot find a single stunted bush where it might lie. He has burnt all the wild-wood that ran so prettily up the slope from end to end of this property. You won't gather as many sticks from the brushwood as would serve to boil a pot of potatoes, or as many twigs as would make a fishing-basket. But no more of this; it makes my heart sick to think of it. Better to be talking of something else."

[1] *Quarterly Review*, vol. xlv. p. 358, July 1831. In this article a noteworthy passage occurs, which may in some sense be regarded as prophetic of that noble scheme for the creation of a Celtic professorship which is now being successfully realised by the University of Edinburgh :—

" When we reflect what benefits have already been derived from the institution of an Anglo-Saxon professorship at Oxford, it is impossible not to regret that neither in that nor in the sister University has the foundation of a Welsh chair been thought of. The want of a professorship of the Irish language and antiquities in the only University of Ireland is, no doubt, a circumstance still more discreditable; but, considering the enthusiastic interest which the Scotch have ever taken in the old monuments of their national existence, and the abundance of their academical apparatus for almost all purposes, even that does not surprise us so much as the absence of any Gaelic endowment among their four Universities. Surely the uumberless Highland and Celtic clubs, of whose proceedings for the improvement of black cattle and the encouragement of the philabeg the newspapers are continually reminding us, might do well to set apart a tithe, at least, of their annual funds for an object of such unquestionable importance."

he naturally belonged to the country of the Mackays, commonly called Lord Reay's country, in the north-west corner of the great county of Sutherland, now governed in such a kingly fashion by his Grace the present Duke. Rob Donn's birthplace was called *Allt-na-Caillich*.   His mother, as in the case of so many notable men, was a woman of remarkable talent, distinguished for the effectiveness with which she recited the poetry of Ossian and other popular literature of her country.   Like M'Intyre, the young Mackay enjoyed none of the advantages of a bookish culture; like Homer, he could neither read nor write; but this accident of his early training only added another to the many proofs literary biography presents of the fallacy of the prevailing notion that the reading of books is the only high-road to intelligence, and the natural nursery of literary talent.   The friction of living mind with mind, and the moral electricity educed by healthy social influences, are the grand educators.   So far is printed paper from being the prime educative power, that a certain tameness and timidity, and want of lusty vigour and natural freshness, has been observed to be the result of an education mainly bookish, after the favourite type of our English Universities.   There was no reason, therefore, why Rob Donn, brought up without scholastic appliances, under the fine social stimulants of the old clan system, should not have grown up not only a great poet, but an intelligent and a sagacious man.   Those who are fond of attributing all the evils under which the Highlands have suffered to what they alike contemptuously and ignorantly call feudalism may receive instruction from the following passage written by the reverend biographer of Rob Donn:—" I have of late frequently heard strangers express their surprise at the marked intelligence evinced in the works of a man devoid of every degree of early cultivation.   To this it may be answered, that the state of society was very different then from what it is now, progressively retrograding, as it has been for the last thirty years at least, in this country. *In the bard's time the lords, lairds, and gentlemen of this country not only interested themselves in the welfare and happiness of their clan and dependants, but they were always solicitous that their manners and intelligence should keep pace with their personal appearance.* I perfectly remember that my grandfather would every post-day evening go into the kitchen, where his servants and small tenants were assembled, and read the newspapers aloud to them, and it seems incredible with what propriety and acuteness they made remarks, and drew conclusions from the politics of the day. In a certain degree this was practised all over the country; the superiors regularly condescending to explain to their dependants whatever was going forward. The fact was, the chief knew his affinity to the different branches of his clan ; and it was deemed no inconsiderable part of duty in the higher classes of the community to elevate the minds, as well as assist in increasing the means, of their humbler relatives and clansmen. I am aware that many unacquainted with the dear ties of such a system, argue largely that the distinctions of rank appointed by God could not be maintained amidst such indiscriminate intercourse. Still, the habits of that day never produced a contrary effect. The chiefs here for many generations had been 'men fearing God, and hating covetousness.' Iniquity was ashamed, and obliged to hide its face. A dishonourable action excluded the guilty person from the invaluable privilege enjoyed by his equals, in the kind notice and approbation of their superiors. Grievances of any kind were minutely inquired into and redressed ; and the humblest orders of the community had a degree of external polish, and a manly mildness of

deportment, in domestic life, which few of the present generation have attained to, much as has been said of modern
improvements."[1]

Like Ovid and Pope, Rob was a versifier from his earliest years. The first effusion of his Muse goes so far back
as his third year, and arose as follows. It was the custom
of proper mothers in those days, after their young darlings
had emerged from their infancy into the germ of boyhood,
to attire them in a sort of short frock made close to the
body, and buttoned at the back. Such a habiliment had
been provided for our embryo poet; and with the pride
which a new vesture inspires in young gentlemen sometimes
of much riper years, he was eagerly employing himself in
fitting it to his little body. But he found the job (as new
buttons are apt to be stiff) too much for him; and the
mother and all the family had gone out to the turnips or
the potatoes. What was to be done? Robert took the
direct course; he marched out with only a short shirt to
cover his nakedness, and went straight to his mother in the
field. She of course sharply reproved him for his violation
of all social decencies; to which the boy, nothing abashed,
replied with the happy *impromptu*—

> *S'math dhomsa bhi 'n diugh gun aodach*
> *Le slaoidaireach Mhurchaid 'Ic Neill*
> *Mo bhroilleach chur air mo chùltaobh*
> *S' gun a dhùnadh agam fhéin.*

> " Nay, blame not me ; the tailor blame ;
>   A blundering loon was he,
> Who placed my buttons behind my back,
>   Where I had no eyes to see !"

[1] *Quarterly Review* as above ; and *Rob Donn's Works* (Inverness, 1829),
Preface, p. 69.

A youth of such precocious poetical power amongst a people to whom verse was the great engine of popular influence could not be long unpatronised. Lord Reay made him the superintendent, overseer, or bishop of his establishment of cows,—a position of honour and dignity amongst a patriarchal people, as many a schoolboy who has shaken hands with the δίος ὑφορβός in the *Odyssey* may know. In the year 1759 he enlisted as a private soldier in the first regiment of Sutherland Highlanders, and continued in that service till the year 1763. In the regiment he held a position, willingly conceded to his talents, as a sort of bard of the banner; and on one occasion, having been asked somewhat sharply by a newly appointed officer why he had not attended drill and to what company he belonged, he returned the haughty answer, " To every company! " and the new major soon found out that he had to do with a privileged person, one who was there, like Iain Lom at Inverlochy, not so much to gain victories as to celebrate them when gained. After his tenure of playing at war was over, Rob Donn returned to his own country, and spent his life partly in the service of Lord Reay's family, with whom, however, like a genuine brother of the irritable race, he had occasional differences, partly in rural isolation. He died at—for a Highland bard— the early age of sixty-four, and was followed to the grave by more than the whole country-side, as we say in the Lowlands; for he had been to the men of the north-west region of the Highlands a man, like Napoleon to the French, a unique character, whom they admired for his virtues, and loved in spite of his vices. For Rob Donn, according to all accounts, though outwardly of such fair respectability that he attained an honour, unknown to Robert Burns, of acting as an elder of the kirk, was not always so chaste in his words as he might seem to be in his deeds; he took his plash as a poet, and not always in the clearest waters; besides, he had a terrible lash at command, which he could wield with an effect at times that paid little respect to the bounds set in such matters by Christian charity, or even by social politeness. The consequence has been that much of the wit and humour of his pieces, however telling for its immediate purpose, has lost half of its interest by the disappearance of the persons to whom it referred. These personal allusions also import an additional difficulty into the language which he uses, and cause his productions, however belauded, to be less known amongst Highlanders generally than those of Duncan Ban and Dugald Buchanan. Severe moralists also very properly object to the undue license and occasional coarseness of his verses. Nevertheless, these very peculiarities add a special value to his works in the eyes of those who read poetry more for an illustration of local manners and customs than for an æsthetical luxury; and no man certainly should attempt to write the popular history of the Highlands during the last century without courting familiarity with the satirical and humorous verses of Rob Donn.

In respect of monumental fame a singular good fortune has followed the poet. His friends have published his well-deservings to posterity in four different languages, English, Greek, Gaelic, and Latin. We conclude with the inscription as a singularity in epitaphs, the false quantities in the Latin being quite characteristic of Scotland, where, though good Latin scholars were trained—especially in Aberdeen—the nice dexterities of classical tight-rope dancing were never largely practised.

[*First Side.*]

IN MEMORY

OF

ROB DONN OTHERWISE ROBERT MACKAY

OF DURNESS,

THE REAY GAELIC BARD,

THIS TOMB WAS ERECTED AT THE EXPENSE OF A FEW OF HIS
COUNTRYMEN, ARDENT ADMIRERS OF NATIVE TALENT
AND EXTRAORDINARY GENIUS.

1829.

[*Second Side.*]

POETA NASCITUR NON FIT.

OBIIT 1778.

[*Third Side.*]

Bu shluagh borb sinn gun breitheanas
Nun a dh' fhalb thu mur sgathadh sud oirnn.

Λέγεις· ἐγὼ γὰρ εἰμ' ὁ πορσύνας τάδε
Γνοὺς τὴν παρούσαν τέρψιν ἢ σ' εἶχεν πάλαι.

[*Fourth Side.*]

SISTE VIATOR ITER : JACET HIC SUB CESPITE DONNUS
QUI CECINIT FORMA PRAESTANTES RURE PUELLAS,
QUIQUE NOVOS LAETO CELEBRAVIT CARMINE SPONSOS,
QUIQUE BENE MERITOS LUGUBRI VOCE DEFLEVIT
ET ACRITER VARIIS MOMORDIT VITIA MODIS.

AETATIS 64.

N

CHAPTER IV.

MACPHERSON AND THE OSSIANIC QUESTION.

" Diogenes Laertius attributes the merit of the collecting and arranging of the Homeric poems to Solon ; Cicero gives it to Pisistratus ; and Plato to Hipparchus ; and they may possibly have been all concerned in it. But there would have been no occasion for each of these persons to have sought so diligently for the parts of these poems, if there had been a complete copy. If therefore Solon or Lycurgus and the other personages committed to writing and introduced into Greece what had been before only sung by the rhapsodists of Ionia—just as some curious fragments of ancient poetry have been recently collected in the Northern parts of this island— their reduction to order in Greece was a work of taste and judgment ; and those great names that we have mentioned might claim the same merit in regard to Homer that the ingenious editor of *Fingal* is entitled to from Ossian."—ROBERT WOOD.

THE interest generally excited by a great criminal trial is of two very different kinds. Setting aside those to whom a shocking murder or a great swindle is merely a novelty to stare at and to talk about, like a man with six fingers or a pig with two heads, the persons interested in a prisoner at the bar on trial for an alleged felony belong to two classes : either they have a warm sympathy with the fate of the individual, eager for his acquittal if they have reason to think him unjustly accused, or zealous for his condemnation if they have grounds to believe him an arrant knave and a conspirator against the peace of society ; or they have no feeling whatever for or against the unhappy individual, but they watch with keenness, and follow with satisfaction, the links in a long series of circumstantial evidence as they gradually move into their proper places, and form themselves into a chain of close-compacted facts, which no most cunning machinery of lies can either break down or overleap. Such persons follow the stages of the trial from day to day, or it may be from week to week, with a purely scientific interest, such as mathematicians feel in working out the steps of equipollency that lead to their conclusions, or the accomplished chess-player in calculating the far-reaching consequences of each move. Quite similar to this is the interest which attaches to certain notable questions of literary criticism. To a Christian, for instance, the question as to the authenticity of the Gospel of St. John, or any other notable part of the canon, possesses an interest so vital and so absorbing as often to deprive him of that coolness which is absolutely necessary for the exercise of a critical judgment, while to a sceptic, or the adherent of another creed, it is simply a question of evidence with which he may amuse or exercise his intellect for an hour, as his inclination may lead and his leisure allow. Of questions of this kind there are few in modern times more notable than that about the authenticity of the poems of Ossian, published by James Macpherson in the second half of the last century. At the present moment a real vital interest in these poems is confined to persons of genuine Highland descent, and a few thinkers and scholars fond of treading in unbeaten ways; to the great mass of persons of education in Europe, Ossian is but the faint echo of a storm that has long ago blown itself asleep. Whether this indifference of the public mind to a literary production which, in the days of our fathers and grandfathers, thrilled Europe with admiration, and struck chords of sympathy in such dissimilar bosoms as Goethe and Buonaparte, has arisen from the reaction that always follows on excessive admiration, in combination with the absence of that spur of novelty, always powerful to draw the gaze of the majority ; or whether Macpherson has just shared the fate of Plutarch and Dr. Blair, and many familiar respectable occupants of our library shelves in the last century, I shall not inquire ; but the fact is certain.   As among a thousand Germans, being readers of poetry, you will not find one now who has read Klopstock's *Messiah*, so among a thousand Englishmen or Scotsmen of average literary culture, not being Highlanders, you shall not stumble on one who has read a page of Ossian.   Nay, even among genuine Highlanders, hot as their blood will boil on occasions when we, ignorant or insolent Saxons, may treat them to a dish of sceptical cabbage heated up from the stale dogmatisms of Dr. Johnson and Malcolm Laing, even with such men, I apprehend, it will not seldom be found that their connection with Ossian is very similar to that sort of relation which exists between a certain not inconsiderable class of professing Christians and their Bible,—the relation not of living knowledge, but of traditional reverence. But however this be, it is certain that to the general public the Ossianic question has lost all vital interest ; Macpherson's Ossian is not read ; admired only partially by the very few who do read it ; and pronounced " trash " by hundreds who never heard of Wordsworth's crushing verdict,[1] and by most persons, I imagine, who are accepted· as mouth-pieces of the cultivated judgment of the present hour.   This, of course, does not settle the real value of the poems ; the critical appreciation of every age is generally one-sided, and like other things, is, to a certain extent, always the product of reaction, and may even be sometimes

---

[1] " The spirit of Ossian is glorious, but Macpherson's Ossian is trash." —Wordsworth to Dr. Norman Macleod. See *Macleod's Life*, vol. i. p. 68.

the mere creature of fashion; but it determines me in the present section of this work to expatiate rather on the secondary interest of Macpherson's Fingalian poems, as opening up a rare question for the appreciation of literary evidence, than on the intrinsic value of the poetry by such evidence accredited. And I do this the more willingly that the question as to the authenticity of these poems is in its most striking features a Gaelic repetition, or was rather a Gaelic harbinger of the famous question as to the character and genuineness of the Homeric poems raised by the mighty German Aristarch, Frederick Augustus Wolf. James Macpherson is unquestionably either the Homer or the Pisistratus of the Caledonian Celts; if the former, he is the Celtic poet who fused into epic wholes the floating ballad literature of the Grampians, just as the genius of the great Smyrnean minstrel caused the heroic traditions of the Greeks of the Ægean to crystallise round the plain of Troy and the rock of Ithaca; if only the Pisistratus, then he must be content with the lesser praise of having collected the scattered limbs of a previous Celtic Homer, and put the pieces together of a great work, to the creation of which he had no more pretensions than Cuvier to the construction of the Megatherium.

As the present generation for whom I write have grown up, I fear, in a general ignorance of all that belongs to Ossian and the Ossianic question, I must set out here with a clear and succinct statement of the facts of the case.

On the 2d day of October 1759, Dr. Carlyle of Inveresk, a Presbyterian clergyman of mark in those days, came from the neighbourhood of Dumfries to Moffat, and found there John Home, the author of *Douglas*, with whom he took up his quarters for the day. In the course of conversation, Home mentioned to Carlyle that he had long been on the scent for some old Gaelic poems, which Professor

Ferguson, an Atholl man, informed him were current in the Highlands, and that he had at last stumbled upon a person who could give him some definite information on the subject.   This was a young man, by name James Macpherson, from the district of Badenoch, in the centre of the Highlands, of good family, and well educated, an excellent classical scholar, and no stranger to the Muses,[1] and who was at that time acting as tutor to young Graham of Balgowan, afterwards Lord Lynedoch.   From this young man Home had learned that he had in his own possession some of these old poems, which Home eagerly solicited him to translate.   To these solicitations at first, the lad, whether from native modesty or from Highland pride, or a combination of both, was unwilling to yield ; at last, however, he gave in, and produced an English version of one of the most famous of the Ossianic ballads, known familiarly as the " Death of Oscar."   The author of *Douglas* was delighted at the amount of poetical genius displayed in this ballad ; the Inveresk Doctor of Theology agreed with him that it was " a precious discovery ;" the matter was communicated to Dr. Blair, the great arbiter of taste among the modern Athenians of those days ; and the result was that Macpherson was induced, under Blair's patronage, in June 1760, to give to the world a small volume of ancient Gaelic poems, under the title *Fragments of Ancient Poetry collected in the Highlands of Scotland.*   So introduced, such a volume, published in the capital of Scotland, could · not fail to attract attention ; young Macpherson, like Burns, was immediately afterwards laid hold of by the leaders of the Edinburgh literary circle, who, with hopeful

---

[1] Macpherson's first literary publication, *The Highlander, a Poem in Six Cantos*, was published in the previous year (1758), and though not calculated to set either the Thames or the Water of Leith on fire, was sufficient, considering the youth of the author, to make him known to a few as a literary aspirant of some promise.

foresight, saw in his fragments only the germs of a luxuriant growth that might quickly appear; and under the inspiration of a dinner-party, so necessary to all great undertakings in these islands, a subscription was raised towards defraying the expenses of a tour through the Highlands, to be made by young Macpherson with the express object of collecting ancient Celtic poetry, and publishing it in the most perfect shape possible to the world. Launched under such auspices, the vessel could scarcely fail to make a prosperous voyage; but besides the letters of entry to the best Highland society, with which his Edinburgh patrons supplied him, the young literary explorer was happy in being able to provide himself companions of travel more skilled in Gaelic literature than himself, and better able to make a satisfactory use of the manuscripts and dictations which might come into his hands. Of these the most noted was Lachlan Macpherson of Strathmashie, a Gaelic song-writer of some repute, Ewan Macpherson, a schoolmaster in Knoydart, and Captain Alexander Morrison, a nautical gentleman and excellent Gaelic scholar. With such able assistance Macpherson was able in the course of the summer months to visit the most important districts of the Central and Western Highlands, and succeeded in taking down, partly from oral recitation, partly from manuscripts with which he had been furnished by Clan Ranald and others, a mass of old traditional lore in the form of verse, which seemed to require only the sharp vision of accomplished Gaelic scholars, and the skilful hand of a judicious editor to make its *début* in the great world of books under the imposing title of Epic poetry. On his way from the far west, Macpherson remained some time in the house of the Reverend Mr. Gallie, minister of Laggan, who has left interesting testimony with regard to the procedure of his guest in trimming his literary treasures into the shape in which they could be appreciated by Saxon readers. In January 1761 he arrived in Edinburgh; and there, under the eye of Dr. Blair and Dr. Adam Ferguson, occupied himself with the prosecution of the work which he had commenced in the manse of Laggan; and, as the materials which he possessed, though of interesting quality, were not weighty in quantity, he found no difficulty in putting forth the first fruits of his Galician researches in the year 1762, under the title "*Fingal, an Ancient Epic Poem in Six Books,* together with several other Poems composed by Ossian, the son of Fingal, translated from the Gaelic Language by James Macpherson." To this volume an advertisement is prefixed, explaining that the author, in compliance with the suggestion of friends, had put forth proposals for printing by subscription the whole originals, but, as no subscribers appeared, he had to be content with retaining the originals for the purpose of transcribing them for the press, as soon as a design then on foot for printing them should be realised. The reception which this volume met with was more than sufficient to spur the author to give the finishing touch without delay to his great work of making the echoes of the old Celtic harp sweetly audible to Teutonic ears. He worked on the maxim of striking the iron when it is hot, and next year produced *Temora,* an epic poem of larger range than *Fingal,* along with some minor poems. Thus his Celtic labours were completed, and his European reputation as the Pisistratus or the Aristarchus of a Celtic Homer established; and thus in a sudden and strange way, from a little flickering light, so to speak, flitting over a Highland bog, he had become metamorphosed into a jar strongly laden with electricity, and flashing forth light and animation through the body and to the uttermost limbs and flourishes of the intellectual world. Unquestionably he had good reason to be satisfied; he had good reason to be proud; grave reason also to be modest, and, as St. Paul expresses it, to rejoice with trembling.

The scene which shortly followed is of an altogether different description. An old Greek, of the school of Herodotus, would not have hesitated to prophesy that some bane must swiftly come on the back of so much bliss; for the Divine nature is always jealous, $\Phi\theta o\nu\epsilon\rho\grave{o}\nu\ \tau\grave{o}\ \theta\epsilon\hat{\iota}o\nu$, and never allows to mortals the continued enjoyment of pleasure without pain. No doubt the highest literary authority in Scotland, Dr. Blair, had deliberately set his stamp and seal on all that Macpherson had done from beginning to end of the matter; but there is a sceptical element in human nature at all times which looks with peculiar jealousy on a reputation built on a loyal and reverential acceptance of the past; and in Scotland, the native country of Hume and the Mills, it is not likely that this element would be at zero. In fact, Hume was at that moment in the zenith of his reputation, and looked up to by the sceptical and cool section of the Scottish people as the most trustworthy spokesman of all that a small heterodox minority might dare to mutter or to growl against the dominant orthodoxies and respectabilities of the day. Nor was it at all likely that a man who had carried his ingenious but unsubstantial subtilty so far as to doubt whether the world were the production of an intelligent cause, would be willing to receive with simple faith the disentombed personality of a blind old Highland bard, alleged to have composed sublime epic poems hundreds of years before any modern European nation had crept out of its cradle. Accordingly we find that, when in London in the autumn of the very year in which Macpherson's second volume came out, the sceptical solver of sceptical doubts, in a letter to the literary theologian, expressed his grave doubts with regard to the authenticity of the poems published by the young Badenoch Celt, and endeavoured to impress strongly on Blair the necessity of bringing forth some proofs that might satisfy the men of letters in this and all other countries that the poems were not "forged within these five years by James Macpherson."[1] The place from which this letter is dated—London—clearly reveals another cause of the rude blasts of sceptical reproach which the young Celtic explorer was destined to encounter. It was not only the scepticism natural to the human mind at certain periods, and at that time preached in fashionable circles, by one of the most ingenious men of the age, that was muttering peals of growing thunder against the author of Fingal ; it was the natural jealousy of the Teutonic towards the Celtic race that was working secretly, and likewise the traditional ignorance and insolence of Englishmen with regard to the extra-Anglican world generally, and especially to all that concerns Scotland. Popular majorities, indeed, we may say, whether in England, America, or Germany, are as a rule ignorant, and generally insolent in proportion to their ignorance ; and, especially in this "tight little island," there has always been a strong and influential party, not now happily so strong as it once was, whose motto has been, " *D—n all foreigners !* " and similarly a party within ourselves whose motto has been, and still is, " *D—n all Celts !* " Dr. Blair, whose general good sense and judgment will be denied by none, even of those who are least apt to accept his literary verdicts, was, of course, from the first, altogether incapable of entertaining any such illiberal notions ;[2] but he was

---

[1] Letter from Hume, 19th September 1793. *Highland Society's Report*, p. 5.

[2] I do not know whether the great Moderate divine was in the habit of looking on the blood in his body as Celtic or Teutonic. BLAIR certainly is a Celtic name, of which the English equivalent is *Field ;* and this is

wise enough to know that, in such matters, deference is due to doubts entertained honestly by persons who are far removed from those sources of evidence which are best calculated to overcome their natural scepticism. He, accordingly, before publishing the second edition of his *Dissertation in Defence of Ossian*, which appeared in 1765, set himself seriously to collect information from the most trustworthy quarters with regard to the existence of Ossianic ballads in the Highlands, and specially with regard to the character and circumstances of the collection made by Macpherson. The result of these inquiries was to confirm the reverend Doctor in his original faith in the authenticity of the poems, and to enable him to state that belief with more emphatic confidence before the world.[1] But all this cautious inquiry and moderation on the part of the sensible Scotch Professor proved in vain. English ignorance and insolence indignantly bottled up must find vent; and the little Teutonic snake tumid with spite and bigotry must have free scope and large range to hiss and bite and spit venom, before cool reason could have a chance of being listened to in the matter. The instrument put forth by the just Destinies to be the spokesman of John Bull's ignorance on this occasion was the redoubtable Dr. Johnson, a strong-minded vigorous thinker, but gnarled through and through with stiff English prejudice, and accustomed to deal about him with a club—like the κορυνήτης in Homer —in a fashion that set all the laws of civilised intellectual warfare at defiance. The chosen instrument for the expression of Teutonic bile was Malcolm Laing, a native of

---

only one among hundreds of instances in Scotland where the name plainly indicates an original Celtic quality in persons who may have lost all living sentiment of the fountain whence they sprung.

[1] The letters which the Doctor received in answer to his inquiries appear in the *H. S. R.*, Appendix No. I., and contain some important points of evidence.

Scandinavian Orkney, an advocate, and an interpreter of historical documents, but who brought into the controversy against Macpherson all the partiality of a special pleader, all the bumptious obstinacy of a Scot, and all the unsubstantial dexterity so often necessary for the successful practice of the profession to which he belonged. But while these combatants were only preparing in secret for their future iconoclastic raids against the Celt, the great offender himself had been witched for a season out of the fray, having, in the year 1764, accepted a post in the public service of his country under Governor Johnstone, which necessitated his removal to Florida. In this situation, however, he remained only a few years, and from that time forward lived in the great world of London, more occupied with historical works and political discourses than with Highland ballads. However, in 1773 he published a new edition of Ossian ; and shortly on the back of that came the notable onslaught of the sturdy English Aristarchus, which led Macpherson to a stroke of conduct of the most vital significance in reference both to the temper of the parties concerned in the attack and the attitude of the assailed. But first let us give the very words of the redoubtable Doctor himself, which are worthy of being preserved as a warning monument of the great danger which attends strong-minded men—such as Porson, and Bentley, and Johnson—of conceiting themselves to be Popes because God has made them giants :—

" I suppose my opinion of the poems of Ossian is already discovered. I believe they never existed in any other form than that which we have seen. The editor or author never could show the original, nor can it be shown by any other. To revenge reasonable incredulity by refusing evidence is a degree of insolence with which the world is not yet acquainted, and stubborn audacity is the last refuge of guilt. It would be easy to show it if he had it, but whence could it be had? It is too long to be remembered, and the language formerly had nothing written. He has doubtless inserted names that circulate in popular stories, and may have translated some wandering ballads, if any can be found; and the names of some of the images being recollected make an inaccurate auditor imagine, by the help of Caledonian bigotry, that he has formerly heard the whole.

"It is said that some men of integrity profess to have heard parts of it; but they all heard them when they were boys, and it was never said that any of them could recite six lines.

"The Scots have something to plead for their easy reception of an improbable fiction : they are seduced by their fondness for their supposed ancestors. A Scotchman must be a very sturdy moralist who does not love Scotland better than truth ; he will always love it better than in-quiry, and, if falsehood flatters his vanity, will not be very diligent to detect it." [1]

It is written that "the wrath of man worketh not the righteousness of God ;" and certainly this tone of assumed infallibility against the poor Caledonian was not the way best calculated to charm any confessions from the breast of a proud and irascible Highlander. From the beginning of the affair, as we have seen, the alleged impostor had been anxious to publish the originals of his Celtic poems, and had been hindered only by the indifference of the public, who found it easier to admire or to denounce upon trust than to take the trouble of looking, or incur the risk of being asked to subscribe for their publication. Had a man of Macpherson's temper—a temper composed of the irritability and vanity of the poet with the pride and iras-

<hr>

[1] *Tour in the Hebrides* (London, 1775), p. 273.

cibility of a Highland Celt,[1]—after being thus publicly pilloried as an impostor, wrapt himself closely up in his own dignity, and refused to expose himself to any public inquisition at the hands of persons who could use such language, it would have been extremely unwise indeed, but nevertheless quite human.   But he prudently allowed his blood to cool, and then took the double course which, according to the laws of gentlemanly conduct then acknowledged, he was imperatively called on to take.   He sent a challenge to the Doctor, to answer for his impertinence with his life; and he deposited the Gaelic MSS. of Ossian with his London publisher, Mr. Becket.   To this challenge the Doctor replied by reiterating his charge that Ossian was an imposture, and refusing to fight with "a ruffian;" to the deposition of the Gaelic originals he replied by meeting fact with assertion, and measuring forth again his autocratic decree that "a nation which cannot write, or a language which was never written, has no manuscripts." And so the manuscripts which had been so imperiously called for, when produced were allowed to lie unnoticed; and, after waiting months, were recalled to the repositories of the person who was alleged to have forged them.   So far the blame for the non-appearance of the MSS. seems to have lain altogether with the public and with his accusers, not with Macpherson;[2] and if afterwards he showed a culp-

---

[1] Hume, in a well-known letter to Blair (*H. S. R.*), calls him "one of the most *perverse and heteroclite* mortals he had ever seen." .

[2] "What does Becket mean by the originals of *Fingal* and other poems of Ossian which he advertises to have lain in his shop?" Boswell to Johnson, Edinburgh, 27th January 1775. Confirmed by Dr. Blair (*H. S. R.*, p. 60, Appendix) and Dr. Graham (*Essay*, p. 259), who says that he had himself seen the advertisement in the *Literary Journal* for 1774. The authorities for the correspondence about the challenge are in Sir J. Sinclair's *Dissertation*, p. 220, where a letter is printed from Mr. Duncan, who bore the challenge from Macpherson; and Boswell's *Johnson*, Correspondence, February 1775.

able reluctance—or laziness rather—and remissness in the matter, it was only natural, considering how he had been treated, and how he might expect again to be treated by such ungentlemanly, unmanly, and insolent accusers. He seemed willing to forget all this poetical brawl and babblement for a season, by flinging himself into the more honourable and fruitful struggles of political life. He wrote some successful political pamphlets, and had the good fortune to be made political agent to the Nabob of Arcot; an appointment which brought him at once wealth and notoriety in a region where he might achieve honour unassailed by that host of pismires and hornets which his poetical explorations had called forth against him. He was now one of the notabilities of public life in London, and as such was considered of sufficient importance to be made M.P. for Camelford. This happened in 1780; and his re-election for the same place twice—in 1784 and 1790—showed that he had proved himself worthy of the confidence placed in him by the Tory powers of the day.[1] But, while the pride of political position might be an ample consolation to the haughty Celt for the persistent questioning of his honour by a sceptical section of the public, and while his self-esteem was strong enough no doubt to enable him to sit quiet under imputations which would have stung other men into some decided course of public justification, the blood of the great body of his countrymen was too fervid to assume this attitude of stoical indifference. It was not enough that all true Highlanders at home and abroad believed in Ossian as they believed in their Bible; they could not brook the idea that any Saxon, especially a Saxon of such weight and authority as Dr. Johnson, should be allowed without the most distinct contradiction to dis-

[1] Chambers's *Biographical Dictionary of Eminent Scotsmen*, Art. MACPHERSON.

pute either the genuineness of their national traditions or the honesty of their literary spokesman. Cæsar's wife must not only be chaste; she must be above the suspicion of unchastity. So in the year 1783, while Macpherson was in the zenith of his political celebrity, and little minded to recur to forgotten squabbles, the secretary of the Highland Society of London received a communication from certain influential Highland gentlemen in Calcutta, enclosing a bank-cheque for £1000, to be given to Macpherson in order to defray the expense of publishing the original Gaelic of the Ossianic poems. To this appeal from a body of the most fervid admirers of the great national poet whose remains he had rescued from oblivion, Macpherson of course could not remain deaf; and the following reply, of which the original lies in the Advocates' Library, Edinburgh, though not so cordial as one might have expected, indicates with sufficient clearness his position in reference to the matter :—

" NORFOLK STREET, 4th July 1784.

"I received the favour of your letter dated yesterday, and I am sorry the gentlemen should think of giving themselves the trouble of waiting on me, as a ceremony of that kind is altogether superfluous and unnecessary. I shall adhere to the promise I made several years ago to a deputation of the same kind, that is, to employ my first leisure time—and a considerable portion of time it must be to do it accurately—in arranging and printing the originals of the poems of Ossian as they have come into my hands. Funds having been provided for the expense, there can be no excuse but want of leisure for not commencing the work in a very few months.—I am, etc.,

" JAMES MACPHERSON."[1]

---

[1] Sir John Sinclair's *Dissertation*, p. 82.

This letter is in perfect consistency with all that he had previously said and written on the subject; the only apparently unaccountable thing being how it should have required so much *leisure* to arrange Gaelic MSS. of which a complete translation had been made and published more than twenty years before. The explanation of this seems to be partly that the translation was made hastily from scraps of original MSS. from various sources, mixed up with the MS. notes of himself and others taken down from the dictation of the popular reciters; and that to present a confused mass of this kind in a printable shape, to write it out, as the gentlemen of the quill say, in full clean copy, might be no easy affair, and an affair that would always become the more difficult the longer it was delayed. We must bear in mind also that whether from accidents in the course of his travels, of which there is distinct evidence,[1] or from the carelessness not uncommon among literary men, some of his original documents may have been misplaced, and, as MSS. have frequently a tendency to do, have crept into some corner of dust and decay, from which they were doomed never to be redeemed. Be this as it may, the unfortunate fact is, that though Macpherson lived twelve years after writing the above letter, that most reasonable request of his Celtic admirers in the far East never was complied with during the lifetime of the author. In 1796 his health began to decline, and he retired to his estate in the country of the Macphersons, near Kingussie, on the Spey, and there paid the debt of nature at the age of fifty-eight. As if willing to atone in some degree for his great remissness during his life, he left the MSS. of Ossian clearly written out for publication, with a sum of £1000 to defray expenses; and with a full consciousness that he had been a notable literary name in

---

[1] See Sir John Sinclair's *Dissertation.*

his day, he ordered in his will that his remains should be interred in Westminster Abbey; which request was complied with.[1]

The person to whose care the deceased left his MSS. for publication was John Mackenzie, Esq., of the Temple; and, as this gentleman was a faithful friend of the deceased, and an excellent scholar, it seemed now that the way was clear for the final publication. But the destiny of delay still followed the business. Mr. Mackenzie's scrupulous anxiety to execute his friend's dying commission served more to raise difficulties than to expedite work; and so, while still engaged in all sorts of protracted discussions with regard to the proper spelling of Gaelic words, the proper type, and the proper letters (Macpherson had had a whim of using Greek letters!), the proper quality of paper, and a proper Latin translation, the Celtic executor died with no execution done. The publication of the MSS. then devolved on the Highland Society of London, who appointed a committee of their number to superintend the business, of which committee the celebrated Sir John Sinclair was the most active member. This was in the month of May 1804; and indeed it was high time to go seriously to work, for in the meanwhile—1800—Mr. Malcolm Laing had come forward with his hard-headed History of Scotland, and appended to it a critical dissertation on the authenticity of Ossian's poems, which, from the point of view of a Lowlander and an unpoetical barrister, seemed to deal much more effective blows against the arch-

---

[1] That any one should have had the power of bequeathing his body to the great national Valhalla in Westminster does seem very strange; all that Dean Stanley and Dr. Carruthers, Inverness, to whom I wrote on the subject, have to say is, that such things were done easily in those days, and that Macpherson had good friends in high quarters, who, provided only the fees were paid, might be quite willing to do this homage to his memory.

impostor Macpherson than could have come from the stout dogmatism and the wrathful bluster of a declared enemy of everything Scotch, like Dr. Johnson. Nevertheless the great Celtic book could not be spurred; and three years more were required till, in 1807, the *Poems of Ossian* were at length put forth, in three volumes royal octavo, with a Latin translation for the benefit of the learned in all parts of the world. This final act took place eleven years after Macpherson's death, and, whatever else it proves, may serve in no small degree to justify, or at least to palliate, the author's own delay, when in the year 1784, as we have seen, he had been earnestly requested to give publicity to the originals. To put his manuscripts into shape, and send the book forth in all that amplitude of form and with all that fulness of illustration which the author desired, was evidently no easy job, and implied a considerable encroachment on what men of business call leisure.

Thus ends the personal history of the Celtic Homer or Pisistratus, and the final revelation of his manuscript treasures. But before the notables of the Highland Society in London had completed their work, the Highland Society of Scotland had come forward to play their part in so patriotic a business, and in doing so, had made inquiries, and examined witnesses, and printed a report on the subject of the authenticity of the Ossianic poems, which for clearness, completeness, judiciousness, and impartiality, presents a most gratifying contrast to the character and general tone of the documents put forth in this literary warfare. This report was published in 1805,[1] and ought to be carefully studied by all those who wish to form a just judgment, not only on this special question, but on all

---

[1] Report of the Committee of the Highland Society of Scotland appointed to inquire into the Nature and Authenticity of the Poems of Ossian, Edinburgh, 1805 ; referred to in my notes as *H. S. R.*

questions of which the genesis and growth of popular poetical tradition forms an important element. Immediately on the back of this, and before the publication of the great edition of the Gaelic, there was put forth an essay on the authenticity of *Ossian*, by Dr. Patrick Graham of Aberfoyle, which will still reward perusal, specially with reference to the objections from internal evidence advanced by Mr. Laing.

There is no necessity, for the purposes of the present sketch, that I should make an enumeration of the complete literary fates of Macpherson's *Ossian*, from the year 1807 up to the present hour. I am afraid the truth is, it was slowly and surely sinking into oblivion, and with many into contempt. Since Macpherson wrote a great change had come over the English taste in reference to poetry; nobody, since the commencement of the present century, has been moved either to tears or suicide by the *Sorrows of Werther;* and of the old Celtic epics that shot an electric thrill of admiration through the whole of Europe, Wordsworth, as we have seen, could say in the face of Norman Macleod, that "they were trash," and move no man's bile. But the time was coming when, if not Macpherson's *Ossian*, certainly Ossianic ballads, would come in for a fair share of revived public interest. As the chief spokesman of this new epoch, we greet with no common pleasure J. F. Campbell, Esquire, of an ancient and illustrious Highland family, who has gone about the business of collecting and tabulating the traditional literature of his country, both prose and verse, with a thoroughness and completeness which, with all genuine admirers of popular lore, throws the labours of Macpherson and his fellow-interpreters into the shade. Mr. Campbell, inspired by a quick sympathy with the people, and using their language with the graceful facility of a native (an example, alas! which only a few of the Highland proprietors have had the wisdom to follow), has, year after year, by sea and land, in Scotland and in Ireland, measured with unwearied foot the length and breadth of the countries inhabited by the Celts, and collected from the living recital of the people whatever of ancient song or story he could lay hands on. His first publication in this interesting vein of discovery was entitled *Popular Tales of the West Highlands*, orally collected (Edinburgh, 1862); and, though the contents of the four volumes of this work are not heroic poetry, like Macpherson's materials, but *Sgeulachdan*, or prose stories, with the narrative of which the healthy-minded Highlanders used to amuse their firesides in the long winter evenings, they do nevertheless contain, as indeed they could not but contain, not a little Ossianic matter, which gives occasion to the learned author in the fourth volume to present a most valuable and comprehensive survey of Ossianic literature, and of recent Gaelic poetry generally— a survey full of the good sense, sagacity, and manly distinctness which distinguish all the writings of the author. But the great work of Mr. Campbell—a work which gives him in the literary history of the Celt the same proud position that the strong genius of Wolf achieved in the domain of the Greek epos—is the *Leabhar na Feinne*, being the Gaelic texts of heroic ballads collected in Scotland at different times, from 1512 to 1571.[1] In this great work —only vol. i. yet published—Mr. Campbell has set forth a systematic collection of all the old popular verse narratives current in Scotland, most of which are more or less connected with the materials used by Macpherson; while he has at the same time arranged his materials and discussed his authorities in a fashion every way satisfactory to whosoever can appreciate hard work, and will be content with nothing less than a thorough excavation, and a

---

[1] Printed for the author by Spottiswoode and Co., London, 1872.

sifting examination in matters of this kind. Whatever judgment people may come to with regard to the character and composition of the work of Macpherson, they must take with them as an indispensable element of judgment this admirable collection of Mr. Campbell.

The appearance of this great work had been preceded in 1870 by a noticeable new translation of Macpherson's *Ossian*, under the patronage of the Marquis of Bute, and executed by the Rev. Dr. Archibald Clerk of Kilmallie, brother-in-law of the distinguished Dr. Norman Macleod. This edition contains, besides a new translation, the Gaelic text with Macpherson's translation in the margin, along with a valuable introduction and notes, in which the author vindicates the authenticity of his text against the objections of Laing and other sceptical writers of the extreme left. The translation itself performs admirable service in liberating the English reader at once as well from the stilted solemnity of Macpherson's English as from the stiff and ungrateful literalness of Macfarlane's Latin. A similar service to the English reader had been previously performed in the translation of *The Genuine Remains of Ossian*, by Patrick Macgregor, M.A., London, 1841, and by the author of the verse translation, published by Black, Edinburgh, 1858.

Thus much for the historical succession of the facts and the character and condition of the witnesses from which we are to form a judgment on this remarkable literary controversy. It remains now that we state in articulate propositions the clear results at which the evidence, contained in the various works we have enumerated, when carefully weighed enables us to arrive :—

PROPOSITION I.—The Highlanders of Scotland, like the pre-Homeric Greeks, and all other intelligent peoples before the currency of a written or printed literature, were possessed of a great mass of floating lyrical and narrative tradition, which was transmitted from father to son, through many generations, and formed the staple of a native, natural, healthy-minded, and invigorating popular education. Of this rich oral literature the traditions about Ossian and the Feinn, and the warlike struggles between Scandinavians and Celts in the early history of Scotland and Ireland—which in those early days were one Celtic country[1]—formed a prominent part.

Of this proposition it is unnecessary to bring forward any detailed proof. Even Dr. Johnson, with all his sturdy English prejudice and his scholastic notions about the indispensability of books and bookish machinery to a healthy popular culture, did not deny the fundamental fact stated in the proposition. What he denied, and living as he did before the great German Homerist, Frederick August Wolf, had cleared the ideas of the literary world on the genesis and growth of popular poetry, might well be pardoned for denying, was the immense mass of narrative matter that was faithfully retained in the popular memory, and capable at any time of being fixed down in the shape of manuscript record for preservation.

PROPOSITION II.—It is established by an accumulation of evidence from various quarters, such as would satisfy the most scrupulous jury, that there existed in the Highlands, before the time of Macpherson, considerable collections of Gaelic songs and ballads and other traditional records in the form of manuscript; that Macpherson in his literary explorations through the islands got possession of some of the most important of these; that others of them were seen by various persons in the possession of

---

[1] This now well-known historical fact puts an end to the famous dispute whether Ossian was an Irishman or a Scotchman; he was both, just as Homer was as a worker at once an Asiatic and an European Greek.

individuals who had no connection with Macpherson, and before he appeared on the scene ; further, that Macpherson before publishing his *Ossian* spent many months, in the presence of various parties, employed in the decipherment and translation of these manuscripts; and finally, that by carelessness and such accidents as constantly happen to old papers, especially when their possessor flits frequently from place to place, the most important of these manuscripts, those at least which would now be most serviceable for the settling of the Ossianic controversy, have been lost.

This proposition it was which Dr. Johnson denied. It is however hardly necessary to prove it now in the face of the Gaelic manuscripts which the scholarly zeal of Mr. Skene has deposited in the Advocates' Library, Edinburgh, not to .mention the evidence now patent to the world by the publication of the Book of the Dean of Lismore. From the special evidence with regard to Macpherson's use of the documents collected by him the following extracts are the most instructive :—

(A.) From the evidence of the Rev. Andrew Gallie, minister of Kincardine in Ross-shire, 12th March 1799 :—

" When he [Macpherson] returned from his tour through the Western Highlands and Islands, he came to my house in Brae-Badenoch : I inquired the success of his journey, and he produced several volumes, small octavo, or rather large duodecimo, in the Gaelic language and characters, being the poems of Ossian and other ancient bards.

"I remember perfectly, that many of those volumes were, at the close, said to have been collected by Paul Macmhuirich Bard Clanraonuil, and about the beginning of the fourteenth century. Mr. Macpherson and I were of opinion, that though the bard collected them, yet that they must have been writ by an ecclesiastic, for the characters and spelling were most beautiful and correct.

Every poem had its first letter of its first word most elegantly flourished and gilded; some red, some yellow, some blue, and some green : the material writ on seemed to be a limber, yet coarse and dark vellum : the volumes were bound in strong parchment : Mr. Macpherson had them from Clanranald.

"At that time I could read the Gaelic characters, though with difficulty, and did often amuse myself with reading here and there in those poems, while Mr. Macpherson was employed on his translation. At times we differed as to the meaning of certain words in the original."

And in another letter, dated 4th March 1801, he added the following characteristic anecdote along with his own notions about the propriety of Macpherson's procedure in the handling of the translation :—

"I remember Mr. Macpherson when reading the MSS. found in Clanranald's, execrating the bard who dictated to the amanuensis, saying, 'D—n the scoundrel; it is he himself that now speaks, and not Ossian.' This took place in my house, in two or three instances : I thence conjecture that the MSS. were kept up, lest they should fall under the view of such as would be more ready to publish their deformities than to point out their beauties.

"It was, and I believe still is, well known, that the ancient poems of Ossian, handed down from one generation to another, got corrupted. In the state of the Highlands and its language, this evil, I apprehend, could not be avoided; and I think great credit is due, in such a case, to him who restores a work of merit to its original purity."

(B.) Evidence of Dr. Hugh Blair, 20th December 1797:—

" When he returned to Edinburgh in winter, laden with his poetical treasures, he took lodgings in a house immediately below where I then lived, at the head of Blackfriar's Wynd, and busied himself in translating from the Gaelic into English. I saw him very frequently : he gave me accounts from time to time how he proceeded, and used frequently at dinner to read or repeat to me parts of what he had that day translated. Being myself entirely ignorant of the Gaelic language, I never examined or looked into his papers; but some gentlemen who knew that language, particularly Professor Adam Fergusson, told me that they did look into his papers, and saw some which appeared to them to be old manuscripts; and that, in comparing his version with the original, they found it exact and faithful, in any parts which they read."

(C.) Evidence of Dr. Adam Fergusson, Professor of Moral Philosophy in the University of Edinburgh :—

" The fragments I afterwards saw in Mr. Macpherson's hands by no means appeared of recent writing : the paper was much stained with smoke, and daubed with Scots snuff."

(D.) Evidence of Lachlan Macpherson of Strathmashie, 12th October 1763 :—

" In the year 1760, I had the pleasure of accompanying my friend Mr. Macpherson during some part of his journey in search of the poems of Ossian, through the Highlands. I assisted him in collecting them; and took down from oral tradition, and transcribed from old manuscripts, by far the greatest part of those pieces he has published. Since the publication, I have carefully compared the translation with the copies of the originals in my hands, and find it amazingly literal, even in such a degree as to preserve, in some measure, the cadence of the Gaelic versification. I need not aver, sir, that these poems are taken in this country to be of the utmost antiquity. This is notorious to almost all those who speak the Gaelic language in Scotland. In the Highlands, the scene of every action is pointed out to this day; and the Historical Poems of Ossian have been, for ages, the winter evening amusement of the clans. Some of the hereditary bards retained by the chiefs committed very early to writing some of the works of Ossian. One manuscript in particular was written as far back as the year 1410, which I saw in Mr. Macpherson's possession."

(E.) Evidence of Captain A. Morrison, Greenock, 7th January 1801 :—

"That Mr. James Macpherson, on his tour through the Highlands and Isles, was a night in his house in Skinnader, Skye; was then collecting the ancient poems, but when in his house had only a few of them : that he gave him (Captain Morrison) some, which he afterwards translated and published; together with Fingalian or old heroic poems, not published in his translations, one of them Dargo. That afterwards in London, he had access to Mr. Macpherson's papers; saw the several manuscripts which he translated, in different handwritings, some of them in his own hand, some not, as they were either gathered by himself, or sent him from his friends in the Highlands, some of them taken from oral recitation, some from MSS."

As a supplement to this must be added the interesting account of the procedure of the translators in making their version, given by Mr. Graham at p. 283 of his dissertation :—

"I have further to state that the Rev. Mr. Irvine, of Little Dunkeld in Perthshire, permits me to say that Captain Morrison was his intimate friend; that he now possesses in the original MS. much of the correspondence which passed between Macpherson and Morrison during the progress of the collection and translation of Ossian's poems; that Mr. Morrison assured him that Macpherson understood the Gaelic language very imperfectly; that he,

Mr. Morrison, wrote out the Gaelic for him for the most part on account of Macpherson's inability to write or spell the Gaelic properly; that Captain Morrison assisted him much in translating; and that it was their general practice, when any passage occurred which they did not well understand, either to pass it over entirely, or to gloss it over with any expressions that might appear to coalesce easily with the context."

Besides this general evidence, there is special proof with reference to a large folio volume of old historical notes and ballads, given to Macpherson by the Clan Ranald of that day, and known among the bards of that district under the name of the LEABHAR DEARG, or RED BOOK. The testimony with regard to this given by the old bard of the Clan Ranald family is so full of interesting matter with regard to the quality and character of that manuscript literature of the Highlander, whose existence Dr. Johnson refused to believe, that I shall give it here in full.

(F.) Declaration of Lachlan Mac Vuirich, made at Torlum in Barra, 9th August 1800 :—

"In the house of Patrick Nicolson, at Torlum, near Castle-Burgh, in the shire of Inverness, on the 9th day of August, compeared in the fifty-ninth year of his age, Lachlan, son of Niel, son of Lachlan, son of Niel, son of Donald, son of Lachlan, son of Niel *Mòr*, son of Lachlan, son of Donald, of the surname of Mac Vuirich, before Roderick M'Neil, Esq. of Barra, and declared, That, according to the best of his knowledge, he is the eighteenth in descent from Muireach, whose posterity had officiated as bards to the family of Clanranald; and that they had from that time, as the salary of their office, the farm of Staoiligary and four pennies of Drimisdale during fifteen generations; that the sixteenth descendant lost the four pennies of Drimisdale, but that the seventeenth descendant retained the farm of Staoiligary for nineteen years of his life. That there was right given them over these lands as long as there should be any of the posterity of Muireach to preserve and continue the genealogy and history of the Macdonalds, on condition that the bard, failing of male issue, was to educate his brother's son, or representative, in order to preserve their title to the lands; and that it was in pursuance of this custom that his own father, Niel, had been taught to read and write history and poetry by Donald son of Niel, son of Donald, his father's brother.

"He remembers well that works of Ossian written on parchment were in the custody of his father, as received from his predecessors; that some of the parchments were made up in the form of books, and that others were loose and separate, which contained the works of other bards besides those of Ossian.

"He remembers that his father had a book which was called the *Red Book*, made of paper, which he had from his predecessors, and which, as his father informed him, contained a good deal of the history of the Highland Clans, together with part of the works of Ossian. That none of those books are to be found at this day, because when they [his family] were deprived of their lands, they lost their alacrity and zeal. That he is not certain what became of the parchments, but thinks that some of them were carried away by Alexander, son of the Rev. Alexander Macdonald, and others by Ronald his son; and he saw two or three of them cut down by tailors for measures. That he remembers well that Clanranald made his father give up the red book to James Macpherson from Badenoch; that it was near as thick as a Bible, but that it was longer and broader, though not so thick in the cover. That the parchments and the red book were written in the hand in which the Gaelic used to be written of old both in Scotland and Ireland before people began to use the English hand in writing Gaelic; and that his father knew well how to read the old hand. That he himself had some of the parchments after his father's death, but that because he had not been taught to read them, and had no reason to set any value upon them, they were lost. He says that none of his forefathers had the name of Paul, but that there were two of them who were called Cathal.

"He says that the red book was not written by one man, but that it was written from age to age by the family of Clan Mhuirich, who were preserving and continuing the history of the Macdonalds, and of other heads of Highland Clans.

"After the above declaration was taken down it was read to him, and he acknowledged it was right, in presence of Donald M'Donald of Balronald, James M'Donald of Garyhelich, Ewan Mac Donald of Griminish, Alexander Mac Lean of Hoster, Mr. Alexander Nicolson minister of Benbecula, and Mr. Allan Mac Queen minister of North-Uist, who wrote this declaration.

his
LACHLAN × MAC VUIRICH.
mark.

RODERICK MAC NIEL, J.P."

In addition to all this there is in the dissertation of Sir John Sinclair, prefixed to the great edition of 1807, a most minute and circumstantial account, confirmed by the confronting of various witnesses, of a manuscript of Ossianic poems in Gaelic, originally collected by Mr. John Farquharson, a Roman Catholic missionary in Strathglass, before the rising of 1745. These poems were carried by Mr. Farquharson to Douay in France, where he acted as prefect of studies in the theological college; and when the British atmosphere began to buzz with Macpherson's Ossianic publications, Farquharson took to his old book, and employed his idle hours in carefully comparing Macpherson's performance in *Fingal* and *Temora* with the originals in his collection, and recognised throughout their fundamental identity. Mr. Farquharson left France to return to his native country, and deposited his Celtic MS. in the college of Douay, imagining that it might be in safest keeping there; but in this he was mistaken: a generation of students came into the collegiate quarters who knew no Gaelic; they put their fingers upon it, as one would do on an old newspaper, and tore it up for any base occasion, till at last, reduced to a fragment of its original self, it was swept away by the harpies of the French Revolution, and was recoverable from space no longer.[1]   I have been at some pains to state all this evidence in detail, because persons of a sceptical and suspicious temperament are apt to conclude that because no MSS. were forthcoming when they called for them, therefore no MSS. ever existed.   But, if this sort of logic is to pass current, we shall have to make a clean sweep not only of Macpherson's *Ossian*, but of much that is now reputed most genuine and most valuable among the literary treasures of the world.   Books disappear every day, even from the hands of private persons who keep their libraries with care; and that old yellowed MS. papers should vanish from beneath the fingers of persons to whom they are as precious as Linnæus' dried plants were to the besom of his housemaid, is just as natural an occurrence as that a golden guinea should fall into the mire through a hole in the pocket of an ill-stitched pair of breeches. And as to literary men like Macpherson, I have known

[1] See Edition of 1807, vol. i. pp. 40-58.   Of the whole evidence there is an excellent digest in an admirable little work in *Notes on the Authenticity of Ossian*, by the late Archibald M'Neil, brother of the late Lord Colonsay. Printed for the author.   Edinburgh, 1868.

not a few of them who were no more careful of their old papers than a schoolboy is of his Latin books.

PROPOSITION III.—From the fact that the most important of the original MSS., from which Macpherson made his translations, have disappeared, so that the originals published by Sir John Sinclair were only the clean copy prepared for the press by the author's own hands or those of his amanuensis, it is impossible to say exactly how closely the translator adhered to the original MSS., or how freely he allowed himself to handle them. But there is every probability, arising both from the general fragmentary and scrappy condition of his materials, and from the notions of literary men in those days with regard to the function and duties of a translator, that the author took much larger liberties with his authorities than would now be thought justifiable. Perhaps we may best conceive of his procedure by comparing it with that of a modern sculptor, finding himself suddenly in the midst of an excavated ruin of old Greek masterpieces : instantly he sets to work, piecing here and patching there, till he builds up a whole, with head, arms, and legs, all compact, that takes its stand with admiration among the most venerated relics of the chisel of Phidias.

Of this proposition it is altogether unnecessary to produce any proof. Those who doubt it may find the evidence cropping out here and there in various parts of the Report. For myself, I have not the shadow of a doubt that Macpherson acted with the most perfect good faith in the matter according to his lights. He found the long-neglected Celtic Muse of the Highlands in a very forlorn, defaced, ragged, and unsavoury condition ; and he thought it only his duty, before presenting her to a critical modern public, to wash her well, and scrub her stoutly, and dress her trimly in fresh habiliments, of which himself was proud to be the milliner. No man can blame him for this; but what he is to be blamed for, and what no doubt, through the length of literary time, he will have to pay for severely, is simply this, that when he was accused of downright imposture and forgery, he certainly did not show the proper forwardness in adopting that course of conduct which alone could have cleared him completely in the eyes of a strongly prejudiced company of accusers. Instead of the frank and manly procedure which he might have adopted with perfect leisure after his return from Florida, he allowed the matter to lie over, wrapping himself up belike in the notion that he would not be concussed into showing anything that he might choose to withhold, forgetful that, while fencing himself behind this bulwark of false dignity, he was exposing himself for ever to the imputation of dishonesty from a large class of persons not much accustomed to season their judgments with charity. So true is it always that in letters, as in trade, and even in politics, honesty and openness, in the long run, are the best policy.

PROPOSITION IV.—The evidence taken by the Highland Society of Scotland, or from other sources, does not tend in the slightest degree to settle the question as to the antiquity of the poems of Ossian, at least in the shape published by Macpherson. If the charge of wholesale imposture and forgery, as brought forward by Johnson and Laing, may be considered as triumphantly refuted; and if it may with all willingness be conceded that the original materials of the Ossianic ballads, whether as published by Macpherson, or in other collections from Dean Macgregor's book downwards, contain not a little both in matter and in tone that may justly be considered as older than the establishment of Christianity in those north-western regions; there is not a scrap of evidence to prove that the poems, in their present form, may not have been composed by some Celtic gentleman, of literary culture, living any time between the Reformation and the 1745, who might have performed the same kindly office to the minstrelsy of the Bens and glens that Walter Scott did to the minstrelsy of the Border, when he composed the *Lay of the Last Minstrel.*

This proposition aims principally at a theory with regard to the construction of such large poems—minor epics, we may call them—as *Fingal* and *Temora*. None of the Ossianic poems collected by Mr. Campbell, nor of those specially Ossianic in the Dean of Lismore's collection, are of this magnitude and pretension; and it appears pretty plain, from the nature of the case, and from the habits of the Highlanders, who were not a reading people, that such large poems as *Fingal* and *Temora*, whoever composed them, never could get into general circulation. And in perfect harmony with this, Mr. Campbell distinctly asserts that, amid all his perambulations among the Highland peasantry, continued for twelve years, he never could find that the people had any living familiarity with Macpherson's particular form of the Ossianic ballads. It appears indeed plainly from his testimony, which must for the present be accepted as final in the matter, that in respect not only of extent and pretension, but not less of tone, style, and sentiment, the Ossianic poems of Macpherson must be considered as occupying a perfectly distinct platform from the great mass of Ossianic poetry that has for ages entertained and elevated the Gaelic-speaking population of the Highlands. If so, who wrote it? and how did it come into shape? One thing seems certain, that the Gaelic was not composed by Macpherson, who never professed to be more than a translator, and who, according no less to the express testimony of competent persons than to the *ex facie* probabilities of the case, could no more "have written a poem, like one of Ossian's, than he could have composed the Prophecies of Isaiah, or created the isle of Skye."[1]   Either, therefore, Macpherson, aided by Strathmashie, Captain Morrison, and other good Celtic scholars, pieced these larger poems together from smaller ones, having a common theme (like the ballads of Robin Hood, for instance), and this, from the remarkable prevalence of episodes in those pieces, always appeared to me the most probable supposition ; or, if Macpherson, as he seems to say, really "was *lucky enough to lay his hands on a pretty complete poem, and truly epic, concerning Fingal,*"[2] then we are bound to believe—unless we persist in saying that he was a systematic liar, of which, from beginning to end of the matter, I do not see a shadow of proof—that certainly the greater part of *Fingal* was composed by some cultivated Highland gentleman at such seasons of intellectual recreation as gave birth, in those districts, to the elegant poem of the *Old Man's Wish*, to *Mordubh*, whose authorship is unknown, and to *Collath*, composed in recent times by a well-known Inverness-shire clergyman, named Macallum.[3] For though the Gaels generally were neither a writing nor a reading people, there can be no doubt, as the works of M‘Donald and M‘Intyre show, that for poetry, which they had practised from the earliest times, they had a highly cultivated taste ; and there is no such transcendental merit in *Fingal* or *Temora* as to bar the supposition that they were composed out of old bardic materials by

[1] Captain Morrison's Evidence, Report, p. 177. But I am not equally sure that he could not have composed the English, had it been his ambition, after the failure of "the Highlander," to put together an original poem in that language.

[2] Letter to the Rev. Mr. M‘Lagan, Edinburgh, 16th January 1761. Report, App. p. 155.

[3] On *Mordubh* and *Collath*, see before, p. 99.

some kilted gentleman of poetic susceptibilities, whose
ears habitually drank in the music of the moaning seas,
as his eyes were fed with the drifting clouds and floating
mists of the sublime west coast of the Highlands some-
where betwixt Loch Maree and the Crinan Canal.[1]

It remains that we complete this summation of the
results of the external evidence in this curious case with
some notice of what light may be thrown on the origin of
the poems, whether from a philological test in the character
of the language, or from a critical estimate of its style and
contents.   So far as philology is able to contribute to the
illustration of the question two things seem certain : first,
that Macpherson's English bears all the marks of a translation from a Gaelic original, such as occasional Celticisms,
mistranslations, skipping of difficult phrases, lowering poetry
into prose, departure from the simplicity of the original,
an affectation of improvement, and other signs of translated
work familiar to scholars ;[2] second, that there is no such
difference between the Gaelic now spoken in the Highlands and the Gaelic of Macpherson's book as exists
between the English of Macaulay and the English of
Chaucer, or betwixt the Greek of Plato and the Greek of
Homer, and, therefore, that, if any argument is to be drawn
from the Gaelic idiom of the book, it is rather against
than in favour of any great antiquity that may be claimed
for it ; at the same time it must be borne in mind that
whoever put *Fingal* into its present shape would naturally
so modify the language of the old materials which he used

---

[1] It has been remarked by several persons that the frequent allusions to
the sea, and the perfect mastery of sea imagery and phraseology in the
poems, certainly do not indicate the author to be a young man of Badenoch,
which is the very centre of the Highlands.

[2] On this subject I read a paper before the Royal Society of Edinburgh,
1st May 1876, which was printed at full length in the *Celtic Magazine* for
July and August 1876.

as to make them enjoyable by his contemporaries. How far the Celtic dialect spoken in the Highlands may, from exceptional causes, have preserved its form with comparatively little change through long centuries, is a question of historical philology which I leave to profound Galicians. My own knowledge of the language, though quite sufficient to enable me to judge of the character of a translation, does not qualify me to form a critical estimate of the epoch of a style.

As for the contents of Macpherson's epics, and the pictures which they exhibit of ancient Celtic manners and sentiments, these form the principal subject of the severe onslaught made by Laing in his dissertation on "the greatest literary impostor of modern times." But after what has been said of the general character of Macpherson's materials and the method of his procedure, a very few words will now suffice to blow aside all this apparently formidable artillery. The hard-faced barrister, in the first place, enters into a serious exposure of the historical mistakes or incongruities, as he imagines, woven into the tissue of Macpherson's poems. Let it be so. No person expects exact history in a collection of popular ballads, whether presented separately or worked up into the form of an epic organism. Macpherson's individual notions about the exact epoch of some of the poems published, and his identification of certain proper names with old Roman Emperors, are mere notions, which, if true, prove only the antiquity of a certain small residue of very ancient matter discernible in the mass of what is in all likelihood a later conglomerate; if false, are mere wind and waste paper, which history will not be sorry to lose, and which poetry should never have cherished the ambition to claim. As to the manners of the heroes and heroines of the Ossianic ballads, which Laing represents as bearing the same relation to the true persons that walked and talked in those pre-Christian and mediæval times that Tennyson's dainty-footed knights and dames do to the lusty life that held its revels in the atmosphere of Charlemagne's Round Table, we must bear in mind, on the one hand, that we know not in the least either what age the poet meant to depict, nor at what particular date he wrote; also that the scenery of the poems is both Irish and Scotch, and no objections taken only from the topographical character of the Scottish glens can have any value; and again, that the notions vulgarly entertained by the people of the South with regard to the barbarism and savagery of the race of men whose bare legs startled the shopkeepers of Manchester and Derby in 1745, are altogether unfounded; that there is no necessary connection between chivalrous sentiment towards women or heroic self-devotion in men, and that machinery of smooth and comfortable externalities which we call civilisation; that the clan system which prevailed in the Highlands, whatever might be its faults, was certainly characterised by bonds of mutual esteem and respect between the different classes of society not surpassed in the social relations of any time; that even now the Highland crofter, who has often been treated so scurvily by ungracious lairds and unkindly factors, is a gentleman in his manners compared either with the Yorkshire boor or the Scottish Lowland labourer; and generally that the morals, character, and manners of our Highlanders, of which Great Britain has every reason to be proud, are the natural legacy of those chivalrous sentiments which the clan system fostered, and which the poetry of Ossian has eternised,—a legacy which those who preach political economy and cash payment as the only bond betwixt man and man, only show their own poverty of spirit when they despise.

There is one point falling under the rubric of the internal evidence which deserves a special word. In Homer and the old epic nothing is more prominent than religion; in the language of a certain school of critics the gods formed a sort of necessary machinery without which an epic poem could no more exist than the earth without the sky. In Ossian, as everybody knows, religion performs au extremely subordinate and altogether unsubstantial part: consisting principally in the occasional apparition of the dim forms of floating ghosts mantled in mist, peering out from behind some grey lichen-crested granite block on the brown slope of the Ben, and holding dim communications with human flesh and blood at some momentous crisis of their fate. This absence of religion in the poetry of a people now remarkable for their nice religious sensibilities may be accounted for in many ways, some of which may be used as a convenient weapon against "the great impostor," and others made to tell as powerfully in his favour. For my own part, endeavouring to cast an impartial glance on this matter, the most natural explanation seems the following :—Either the most ancient pre-Christian Celts, of whom we know little or nothing, had no religion beyond the worship of ancestral shades,—and in this case the poetry represents the real state of the most ancient fact; or, what I think by far the preferable supposition, when the introduction of Christianity by St. Columba, and the dominance of the sacerdotal order in the middle ages, threw everything connected with the old heathen religion into discredit, the family bards, to avoid giving offence to the Church, while retaining in form, outline, and in full breadth all the warlike exploits and the general secular doughtiness of the oldest Fenian ballads, reduced religion in them to the minimum of hero-worship, which in an age largely practising saint-worship was not likely to strike the ear as a very gross form of heresy.   That the Highland bards were an essentially secular body, and habitually abstained from all handling of religious topics, is the thesis maintained by Mr. Mackinnon in an able paper quoted below,[1] and which I have every reason to believe is consistent with the fact.

There remains one notable argument in favour of the authenticity and antiquity of Macpherson's *Ossian*, recently advanced by a gentleman of great eloquence and decided original genius, which it would be unpardonable to omit here.   I allude to the learned and ingenious work entitled *Ossian and the Clyde*, put forth in 1875, by the enterprising Glasgow publisher, Mr. Maclehose.   The substance of this book is an attempt to identify certain districts in the island of Arran and the north-east of Ireland with famous sites in *Fingal* and *Temora*, and some of the minor poems published by Macpherson.   The identification is carried through partly by minute topographical examination illustrating the text, partly by the aid of popular traditions collected round particular monumental spots.   Now, supposing this recovery, so to speak, of the exact scenery of the Ossianic epics to be geographically reliable,—though for myself I must confess, considering both the general vagueness of local reference in Ossian as compared with Homer, and the necessity that Dr. Waddell has felt of bringing notable changes of the geological relations of land and water to his aid, the foundation feels to me somewhat uncertain; but accepting his topography as a fact, the argument raised upon it is that as Macpherson was evidently ignorant of the topographical consistency of his framework, he cannot be charged with having invented what he did not understand.   This argument seems perfectly fair; but it affects only the sources from which the author drew, and does not at all exclude the possi-

[1] *The Gaidheal*, vol. v. No. 49.

bility of his having dealt in a grand style of freedom with
materials which he only half understood.   So that Dr.
Waddell's argument, so far as the question of authenticity
is concerned, merely amounts to a demonstration of the
general truthfulness of local tradition forming the basis of
Macpherson's poems, as against the charges of wholesale
forgery brought by Johnson, Laing, Pinkerton, and other
men of the extreme left.   But as these extreme views
brought to light in the imbittered element of national
jealousy and personal animosity have long ago ceased to
give a red hue to the sceptical side of this question, Dr.
Waddell's book, if more sober inquiry should bear out its
results, will assert an archæological rather than a literary
interest, and leaves the question as to Macpherson's share
in the present form of the poems pretty much as he found
it—in the mist.   No one can now withdraw the veil
behind which a dead man of letters chose to hide the
secrets of his workshop.

It may naturally be expected, in concluding this chapter,
that I should give some critical estimate of the value of
Macpherson's *Ossian* as poetry, altogether independent of
its real or supposed authorship.   Anyhow, it is a genuine
Celtic production; if by Macpherson, then the natural
outcome of a youth spent in Badenoch, behind the mist-
covered caps of the Grampians, and beside the swift-
rushing waters of the Spey; if in the main, both in tone
and materials, much more ancient (as I believe), and
standing on the broad basis of popular tradition, then it
possesses all the interest that belongs to every form of
popular poetry as an exponent of a certain type of popular
life.   As mere creations of fancy, however, I cannot say
that I have any particular admiration either for *Fingal* or
Temora; and, just because I do not particularly admire
them, it is better, perhaps, that I should not attempt to

give a formal verdict on their merits. What a man does
not admire, he will be wiser, in the general case, quietly
to drop rather than hastily to condemn ; for the absence of
admiration may arise as naturally from deficiency in the
spectator as from a fault in the spectacle. Something I
do admire in *Ossian*, viz., its sustained tone of sombre
sympathy with some of the most sublime aspects of nature
in the Highlands, and not less the combination of heroic
manliness and delicate sensibility in the poetical personages. I will say, also, that to my ear there is a rich melodious flow of descriptive verse in many parts of the original,
very far removed from the pseudo-sublime staccato-stride
of the English prose. On the other hand, there is a prolonged monotone about these epics which is really oppres-
sive : there is extremely little variety either of character
or incident : there appears in *Fingal*, as already remarked,
an artificial stuffing up and padding out of a very meagre
plot, with a disproportionate array of episodes ; and,
worse than all, there is to my feeling, in some places, a certain melodramatic air about the poems, and a vein of over-
refined, almost sickly, sentiment, here and there, which I
cannot away with. At the same time, I am very far from
setting up my own taste as a norm for other people. I
know not a few gentlemen, of high original genius, who
derive intellectual nourishment from Ossian and other
types of poetry against which my stomach rebels. Some
men cannot read Tennyson ; most men find it difficult to
digest Browning ; and other men say that Walter Scott
was no poet. Diversities in such matters need not be
contradictions ; and I hope the enthusiastic admirers of
Ossian may willingly condone the fault of my temperament when I say that I, in every view, prefer the simple
natural grace of Duncan Ban M'Intyre's cheerful Muse to
the sombre and somewhat stilted sublimity of the author
of *Fingal*, whoever he may be.

CHAPTER V.

GAELIC LITERATURE IN ITS MOST RECENT PHASES; POETRY AND PROSE.

Thìr steallaireach, alltach, ard-choillteach thiugh sprèidheach
Thìr àiridheach, fraoch-shliosach, ghorm lochach àrd ;
Thìr, bhreacanach, cheolraidheach, oranach, aoidheach
Bu tu tìr nan sgéul dachaidh ghreadnach nam Bàrd !
Ach cò an tir chéin a ni 'n sgeulachd a dhusgadh ?
Co thogas an t'òran bheodh sòlasach tùirseach ?
Co 'bhcanas do'n chlàrsaich 's na h'òighean air ùrlar ?
No ghleusas a'phìob 'thogail inntinn nan sàr ?

EWAN M'COLL.

I PITY the man who can ramble among the waving woods fresh-tipt with green, in the month of May, and resonant with vocal life, and not wish to be a bird ; and him I pity more who, at no moment of his life—not even once in the exuberant fulness of opening youth—has felt those bird-like motions in his soul which naturally issue in song. Song, in fact, is the very triumph of life with itself, the harmonised issue of a happy vitality thrilling in all its strings ; it is the unfolding of the cased wings of the creature that on common occasions can only walk or creep ; for which reason, no doubt, Plato calls the poet a winged animal ;[1] and every man is a poet when he sings. What the single song poured out of a full heart, and curiously vibrated through the cunning apparatus of the throat, is to each individual who sings, that the popular

[1] Ζῷον πτερωτὸν ὁ ποιητής.—ION.

song and the national air is to the people. It is the stirring of the great national life in its deepest fountains ; it
is the upbillowing of the grand river of popular energy
with fertility in its flood ; it is the feeder of the inspiration of the mighty phalanx of an organised humanity, as
it marches on its way through the phases of heroic struggle
and manly conflict to the goal of national independence
from without, and reasonable liberty from within. What
the nation wishes and wills, what it desires and what it
achieves, what it triumphs in and what it weeps over, fitly
expresses itself in song. Music in fact is the only art that
can make even sorrow enjoyable; there is a miraculous
power in it which changes all water into wine, and a
touch that clothes even the basest object with a coating of
living gold.

Every one has heard the definition of the old French
constitution, struck out in the usual happy way by some
wit of the saloons—*monarchy limited by a chanson.* If
song was mighty in modern France, as in ancient Greece,
it was not less potent among the Highlanders of the middle
ages, the progenitors of those best of national soldiers who
made the British name immortal, in the great European
war against Napoleonic despotism, on the memorable fields
of Spain and Belgium. If sermons did much to form the
character of Scotsmen and Highlanders, songs I imagine
did no less. I do not scruple in all soberness to agree
with the stout remark of a manly Highlander, that " the
old Gaelic system of cultivating the hearts of the people
by means of poetry and music was, so far as the masses
are concerned, infinitely superior to a lettered education."[1]
Nothing is more natural than that people who have unfortunately in this hard country been strangers to the

---

[1] *Language, Poetry, and Music of the Highland Clans,* by Donald
Campbell. Edinburgh : 1862.

educating power of music in their own homes, should be unable to estimate its action in forming the noble and chivalrous character of the genuine old Highlander. But modern opinions and dry scholastic notions are no test of truth. It was a musical education that made Achilles and Agamemnon, Homer and Pythagoras, Heraclitus and Plato. The Greeks no doubt invented logic also; but they used that only as a tool for intellectual fence; their instrument for popular education was music—μουσική—that is, a poetry essentially popular, and a music wedded to words of a predominantly national significance. Herein lay the secret of their greatness; and our own Highlanders, though performing a less prominent part on the great stage of human life, used the same method, and achieved to a great extent the same result. It always must be so. Nature, however ignored by fashion, over-ridden by red-tape, and tortured by schoolmasters, will always assert her supremacy. She alone can make men; school boards easily, if they fail to follow her indications, may invent a patent machinery to unmake them.

The Celt is essentially a lyrical animal; and, had the Government of this country, or the lords of the soil, who were the natural overseers (or bishops) of the people in civil matters, been anxious to do common educational justice to the sons of the brave fellows who so freely shed their blood in our defence, the last thing they would have suffered to be neglected in Highland schools (where there were any) was the national music. For national purposes the "March of the Cameron Men," and scores of such heroic lays, in the true old Greek style of *ἐν μύρτου κλαδὶ τὸ ξίφος φορήσω*, were worth all the Latin grammars that ever were printed. But an evil destiny hung over this noble fountain of national inspiration, a blight fell with deadening swoop over the brightness and the joy and the luxuriance of Highland life; and not only on the brave land beyond " the rough boundaries," but in Scotland also, the land of Burns, and in once merry England, from a combination of causes that we shall now endeavour to enumerate. That song—genuine national song rousing enthusiasm and forming character, does not reign among us now with that sway which it once possessed, and with that divine right which belongs to it, is but too evident. To what causes is this to be traced? First, I think there is the democratico-political spirit which arose in Europe with the French Revolution, and is still working with a fretful fermentation amongst us. No doubt the Revolution had its songs, and some of the best; but the continuous struggle for power which democracy begets, the bitterness of party strife on which it feeds, and the habit of fault-finding which it cherishes, are not favourable to that sweet and sympathetic temper which delights in a song. There is a hardness, a sharpness, and sometimes a sourness about politics with which music can have no fellowship; and democracy, which makes every man a politician, will have a tendency to substitute party recriminations for social entertainment, and Parliamentary debates for songs. Then again with the French Revolution there came upon our poets a strange rage of tugging at the roots of things, laying all sorts of new imaginary foundations for Church and State, now soaring up to heaven and now diving down to hell with all sorts of perturbed questionings; in short, they became metaphysicians and theologians; and, though this could not annihilate poetry, but rather created a new species of it, attempting in a more brilliant style the cosmic problems which in the earliest times had stirred the soul of an Empedocles and a Heraclitus, it certainly was not favourable to song. It had rather a decided tendency to ignore singing generally, and to substitute in its place a sort of half-dreaming half-preaching speculation; only of course within a special circle; for a nation is never metaphysical. Hence it has come about, amongst a large section of our literary men and persons of culture, that the sense for the genuine old song has died out: to men who are familiarly fed with the ingenious subtleties, Titanic wrestlings, and ambitious exaggerations of a metaphysico-political poetry, a simple song is apt to appear insipid; even as a man whose appetite has been spiced for years with the artificial preparations of French cookery will not relish the most excellent pudding made by the best of wives with fresh-laid eggs and the richest cream to float it down. So much for politics and metaphysics; but on the back of these two mighty disintegrating forces came a wave of much wider swell, and, so far as song is concerned, for the time of baneful influence. Suddenly, with the help of Lord Brougham and Messrs. Chambers, Cassells, and Nelson, we found ourselves in an age of cheap books, with a general craving after all sorts of knowledge, specially of physical science and things tangible. It is needless to point out formally that there is a certain antagonism between the knowing man and the singing man. We all know who it was that the philosophic bard of the Lakes described most characteristically as

> " Contented to enjoy
> What others understand."

The age of Aristotle was not the age of Homer or of Pindar; and the age of universal reading, peripatetic lectures, and physical science, with or without God, is not the age of popular song. I knew a very clever fellow who could talk and write books on every possible subject; he was in fact a sort of walking encyclopædia, who had tabulated and framed into a logically disposed inventory all things knowable. He was dining with me one day, and after he had bid adieu to dinner and to us, I asked a lady of fine culture and nice discrimination who happened to be staying with us how she liked him. "Not at all," was the reply; "he is like a circular case of lancets; he cuts all round." Here was a man who knew everything, but whose intellect was aptly compared to a cutting instrument, not to a singing bird. Of course there is no need of supposing any natural necessity for a choice between universal knowledge and sweet sounds. Solomon in ancient times and Goethe in these latter days grandly prove the contrary; but such minds are rare. The great majority of men at any given moment in the history of society will be found to live under the influence of some one dominant tendency, which, so long as it lasts, stints and starves, and even annihilates every other, especially that which is none of its natural allies. The union of contraries, no doubt, is perfection; but the division of contraries is the natural law of the process of individualising by limits which makes a rich and various manifestation of the divine Logos possible. So we must content ourselves with the recognition of the great fact, that where a general rage for exercising the cognitive faculty prevails the capacity for lyrical enjoyment will be subordinated in the masses. Individuals, of course, whether from a more broad natural endowment or from favourable circumstances, will escape the contagion; and in such case it is their duty and their privilege stoutly to protest against the tyrannous monotony of the prevalent fashion; but the current will carry the multitude inevitably along, and the man who will sing and enjoy while the whole world is eager to inquire and to know and to discuss, must retire into some leafy corner and croon out his delight to the birds. The next anti-lyrical force that we have to notice is the schoolmaster—not the schoolmaster generally indeed, but the British schoolmaster, whether English or Scotch, the Scotch more particularly. In England, from the milder form which the Reformation assumed in that country, the unnatural divorce between Religion and the Fine Arts, the most repulsive feature of extreme Protestantism, did not take place. Organs and cathedral chants maintained their ground, and in the great public schools there might often be regular training in choral song. Still there was a prevailing tendency in the great classical masters to teach from dead Greek and Latin books without the living power of English song; and we need not therefore wonder if in that country also, notwithstanding the more rich and genial flavour of their culture, music, in the shape of popular songs and national airs, met with very shabby treatment. In fact, not only were the great national songs not sung in the schools, but the noble art of public speaking, so dear to the Greeks, was neglected, and men got themselves crammed with Aristotle's Rhetoric and passed severe examinations to end in becoming dumb. All this was merely the manifestation on a large scale of the besetting sin of all modern teachers, since the discovery of printing,—the inclination to substitute dead books for living functions; and to this, in the case of the great English schools, there was added the special idolatry of the classical scholars to give to the study of the great Greek and Roman masters a practical monopoly of the teaching hours, so that there was no time for anything else; and thus it was no wonder that after being artificially tortured with the minutiæ of Greek rhythm which was driven into him in most cases through the understanding, not by the ear, your accomplished classical scholar came out into the English world utterly incapable of a single stave of the "Battle of the Baltic," or the "Battle of the Nile," or the "Arethusa," or any patriotic melody that should naturally have expanded the lungs of a well-conditioned young Englishman in this nineteenth century; and thus a scholarship grew up systematically trained to disown the best elements of our nationality, and a student life was developed making itself known stoutly (for which we are thankful so far) by click of cricket-bats and flash of oars, but sadly devoid of the charm of popular air or the inspiration of national song. In Scotland matters were worse. The Scot, with more of the fine Celtic fire in his blood, and less of the stiff Teutonic clay in his muscle, roused into indignation by the brutal murder of his great moral heroes under Episcopalian no less than under Romanist rule, flung himself with an emphatic rebound into the opposite position; threw the organ out of the cathedrals and the choral chant along with it; and what had been thus in the name of God done for the church could not fail to be carried out with faithful imitation in the school. Gradually the singing-schools which existed some time after the Reformation in connection with the old cathedral churches came to be disused; in the churches no trained choruses appeared; in the schools singing was never heard; and the more learned the school, and the more ambitious of classical reputation, the less chance was there of either a sacred chant or a " guid auld Scotch sang " being heard there. The classical teachers in Scotland, indeed, principally, and the schoolmasters have chiefly to bear the blame of the lamentable fact that a generation of disnatured fledglings is growing up benorth the Tweed who know not Burns, and in whose breasts the name of Bruce lights no flame and that of Knox stirs no reverence; artificial creatures who can spell their way daintily through the pretty Arcadianism of an old Doric Theocritus, but who know nothing of " The Twa Dogs " and " Tam o' Shanter " (idylls as superior to anything in Theocritus as Hercules is to a pigmy), and who, though curiously trained to the strange trick of compaginating Latin hexameters or Greek iambics, could not, though it were to save their lives, voice forth a single stanza of a native melody, whether melting the heart with the tenderest Scottish pathos, tickling the nerves with the rich redundance of Scottish humour, or bracing the breast with the stoutest resolves of Scottish manhood. To such soulless trickery must men come when they put grey paper in the place of green life, and fill the empty benches of their souls with foreign compositions where a vigorous native growth should be. But there remains yet another vial of woe poured plentifully out upon our national song in these latter days. Music, which was once only the servant of poetry, has become her mistress; nay, assumes the right to walk alone, disdaining the companionship of an art which cannot so easily separate itself from the severe mastership of reason, and revel in those honeyed exercitations of measured sound, which with all their curious excellence are the furthest removed from any definite thinking. This is one of the evils which accompany the unwise application of the great principle of the division of labour, a principle which has got a great deal more praise than it deserves; for it requires no sharp eyes to see that in the great majority of cases, as we see it developed in this country, while it multiplies the product immensely, it degrades and debases the producer. The Celtic girl who stands by a spinning-machine in some Titanic Glasgow manufactory, merely to correct its occasional false strokes, is a much less healthy, a much less noble, and a much less interesting creature in every respect than the Highland nighean of a hundred years ago in a breezy hill cottage, who could spin and weave with her own hands, and milk the cow and attend the dairy, and do half-a-dozen other things besides. And where the dexterities of the individual, who has gone through certain courses of intellectual drill, are not, as in the case supposed, altogether annihilated, in no case does the extreme division of labour and the exclusive cultivation of specialities leave the human being undamaged. With all our researches and all our discoveries, it is only too plain that if we have many more accomplished men in this nineteenth century we have few complete men. Among other things, music without words, even when practised by a Beethoven, is an incomplete, and, unless in the case of the great artist himself, an unnatural art. It is plain also that the habit of cultivating music apart from words must have two bad effects. It must confine the enjoyment of music more and more to a trained few, and by separating the art from the musical habits of the masses it must force on a divorce betwixt music and the popular song. No doubt men of the most original musical genius, artists of the calibre of Mozart, Rossini, and Beethoven, will be the first to recognise the peculiar and inimitable charm of the simple popular air; but the common musical artist will be apt to look with contempt on those wildings which wear their stamp direct from God without any aid from the professional training-master. It is with music as with all other dexterities,—the artist possessed with a vain desire to exhibit his acquired skill departs from Nature and glories in himself. A common example of this we see in the professional ballet-dancer, who stretches and strains herself by a long process of training, not that she may learn to dance gracefully or teach others to do so, but that she may make display of the elastic springiness of her soles and the deft versatility of her hip-joints. And verily she has her reward. She makes the multitude stare and applaud, which they would not do at mere graceful dancing. But that staring and applauding multitude, if it is to learn, I shall not say to dance, but to walk or to march gracefully, must go to quite other masters. And so the great mass of the people, if music is to be an educative power amongst them, must be taught not from the intricate and delicate movements of the professional musician, but from the scientific use of the popular song. For the popular song is not only music already existing in the popular ear, and thrilling the fibres of the popular heart, but it is a great deal more : it is history and heroism; it is wit and wisdom; it is humour and character; it is chastening sorrow and noble aspiration; everything that a human being requires, to be what he ought to be, where God has placed him in the world. For no man, not even an encyclopædic genius, can in the world of action put himself forward as a cosmopolite. A man acts, where he acts, not as a man, but as an English man, French man, German man, or Scottish man, according to the congruities, the fitnesses, and the opportunities of his position. But it is not only by the cultivation of mere dexterities of the throat or fingers that the popular song suffers in this country. It is by the irruption of foreign teachers, and the servile adoption of foreign melodies and foreign words thence resulting. No doubt the cause of this is sufficiently obvious : a mercantile nation will always know how to adopt largely what it produces only scantily at home; no man blames the foreign musician for training the ears of Scottish young ladies to delight in foreign rather than in native melodies. It is the fact only that we wish to state here. If fair young creatures, whose education consists mainly in prinking themselves with showy accomplishments in order that they may attract admiration from hopeful expectants of the other sex, submit themselves with the most amiable servility to the indoctrination of their foreign music-masters ; and, after they have entirely lost all sense of their beautiful native Scotch by intoning *amore* and *dolore*, *donzella* and *ritornella, lontano* and *invano*, according to the strictest science of the scales for the appointed number of months and years, are elevated to the regular attendance on the Italian Opera in Drury Lane or the Haymarket as the initiation into the sublimest mysteries of the musical art of which the fashionable world is capable,—who can wonder if creatures so educated, feeding for years on foreign sentiment, and never accustomed to connect the idea of music with anything beyond the luxury of the ear and the entertainment of the hour, should end in being utterly incapable of enjoying those native melodies which, however simple, require at least character and soul to sing them, and mean not merely to tickle the sense, but to purify the emotions, to brace the nerves, and to harmonise the life of the persons who sing them?   Add to all this artificiality of a forced education, the notion, only too apt to grow up in the minds of the middle and higher classes of society, that the popular songs and the language in which they are composed are something vulgar, which ought not to overleap the fence of the teeth of ladies and gentlemen. Of all snobberies that I know in our modern society this is one of the most contemptible; difficult however to eradicate, because it hides a sentiment essentially vulgar under a vesture of aristocratic gentility. The Greek sophists, the rhetorical snobs of ancient Athens in the fifth century before Christ, used to laugh at Socrates, the wisest man of the wisest people the world ever saw, because he used familiar illustrations and what they called vulgar similes; those who think the songs of Robert Burns, Tannahill, Ballantine, and a legion of others vulgar, stand on the same stage of superficial feeling and false culture. Whatever bears the type and stamp of catholic nature can never be vulgar; but the highest accomplishment of fashionable education may readily be unnatural. The brightest gem in the crown of Robert Burns is that he redeemed the popular Scottish song from whatever coarseness cleaved to it from times of greater robustness and less refinement than those in which we live; no vulgarity attaches to it; but vulgarity of mind and hollowness of character certainly does attach to those Scottish ladies who can prefer scraps of Italian operas, however well sung with the throat, to strains of genuine Scottish music thrilled forth from the heart; as she unquestionably is a poor creature who, because she feeds her eye on the vegetable luxury of Kew Gardens, has no admiration to spare for a green bank spotted with primroses, or the hollows of a hundred lochlets blooming with white water-lilies on a brown Ross-shire moor.

I have been led into this train of remark by observing how unfaithful the Scottish people in this generation, and especially the would-be genteel in the middle and upper classes, have been to the rich inheritance of popular song which they have received from their fathers. But the Highlanders, with whom I have specially to do in these pages, have suffered not merely from the same contagious influences which are denationalising the Lowlander; they have had all this potentiated by sorrows peculiar to themselves, by causes whose slow insidious working has gradually brought matters to such a pass that, with the finest original melodies in the world, and the richest collection of national songs, continually streaming out like spring-water from the brae, it is not seldom a difficult thing, even within the walls of a Highland manse, to find a cultivated young lady who will sing a good Highland song! This arises from obvious causes; in the first place, because the Highland proprietors in the majority of cases receive no proper Celtic education, and grow up utterly estranged from the best life of the people from whom they draw both their

blood and their rents; their example, by the usual charm of
aristocracy, infects the ministers' wives and their daughters,
who all wish to be fine English ladies, forsooth! rather
than natural and noble Highland women. Again, in many
parts of the Highlands, from the large size of the properties, non-residence, false notions of political economy, and
other causes, there is actually no middle class; and with the
disappearance of this class, the best soil was swept away
from which the bloom of popular culture proceeds; for the
upper classes are too estranged by English habits, and the
lower classes are too depressed by poverty, and disheartened
by neglect, to be fit organs for showing any luxuriant outcome of joyous popular life. The soul has been literally
sucked out of them; and like the Israelites by Babel's
streams, they know not what singing means. Then in the
schools, the same anti-popular practices are observed as in
the Lowlands, only in a much worse form; for in the
Highlands many a schoolmaster is set over Gaelic-speaking
children, who either does not know a word of the mother
tongue of the children, or has been taught to despise it.
Latin may be taught, perhaps, and even Greek sometimes,
as I have seen it; but a Highland *oran* or *luinneag*, or a
good tramping chorus of a *caismeachd*, is the very last thing
you may expect to hear in a Highland school. Not to
draw out the true nature, but to force in a false nature, is
the educational principle of many teachers in those parts;
and of course, as men do not gather grapes of thorns, so
neither do we look for or find fine Celtic culture from crude
Saxon pedagogues. Lastly, to bring down the rich lyrical
poetry of the Highlander even to a lower than this lowest
depth, there come certain ecclesiastical and clerical persons
in some places, believing in nothing but sermons, and
looking with a narrow-minded ungenial jealousy on all
popular poetry as more or less profane. Thus the poor

Highlander, in addition to a grey climate and a deserted country, has not seldom a God preached up to him whose heaven is a dome of lead, whose rule is a rod of iron, and whose Gospel is not a message of glad tidings, but a system of unnatural repression, an abnegation of all healthy instinct, and a clipping of the wings of every natural joy.

As it is not my purpose in this work to exhaust a subject, but only to excite an interest and to open a vista, I will arrange what seems proper to be said in this concluding chapter in three parts. *First*, I will give a few biographical notices, principally from Mackenzie,[1] of the most notable names in the lyric poetry of the Gaels from Macpherson's time to the present hour. After that I will print a few specimens of translations which I have made from such of the works of any of these minstrels, or others

[1] Of Mackenzie I find the following notices in the *Highlander* newspaper, published at Inverness, a publication to which all who take any interest in the Highlands and in Celtic literature owe a deep debt of gratitude, not only for the effect which it has had in strengthening the self-esteem of the poor neglected Celts, but for the great amount of valuable pieces of Celtic literature which it has preserved, and is continually preserving in its columns :—

"JOHN MACKENZIE, of *The Gaelic Beauties*, was born at Melon, in the parish of Gairloch, or now in the *quoad sacra* parish of Poolewe, Ross-shire. He is buried in the churchyard of Gairloch, where a monumental stone is erected to his memory. A brother and sister are living at Poolewe. I have no doubt they possess some of his MSS. As affording some insight into his mind, besides what his published works give, I may mention it was at a sacramental gathering that I first met John Mackenzie. I remember he was perfectly horrified at the outpourings of damnation, as he called them, which he heard then proceeding from reverend lips. Such fiery utterances met with no response in his young and gentle bosom. He looked, he said, upon their declamation as nothing short of blasphemy against his Heavenly Father. 'What a tyrant,' he said, 'they make their God! My God is a God of love and summer; such a God as they paint would be my devil.' W. C."

"JOHN MACKENZIE, Editor of *The Beauties of Gaelic Poetry*, was a native of Gairloch, Ross-shire, and died at Poolewe, on the 19th of August 1848. He mentions several MSS. in his *Aosdana*. They are to be found in the Advocates' Library, Edinburgh. N. C."

of less celebrity, as seemed remarkable for popularity, or happened to strike my fancy. To a critical appreciation of each of these writers I do not feel myself equal at present; and besides, abstract estimates of lyrical writers, without effective specimens of truly lyrical translation, are a mere grey skeleton of notions that could do the reader little good. I will then give some hint of the character of Gaelic prose, so far as its scanty development may require, and conclude by giving a translation from one of the most classical of their prose writers.

First on the roll stands LAUCHLAN MACPHERSON of Strathmashie, in the parish of Laggan, Inverness-shire, a district well worthy of its designation (*maiseach*, beautiful), as indeed the whole drive from Fort-William up the Spean, and by Loch Laggan to Kingussie, is one of the finest in the central Highlands. This gentleman, whom we already know (above, p. 199) in connection with the Ossianic question, was born in the year 1723, and therefore considerably older than the more famous James of his clan, and died at the latter end of the last century. He was not by profession a poet; but the lyrical form being the native and traditional organ of literary expression in the Highlands, his compositions took that shape, and arose out of those occasions of real life which are the best security for natural incident and healthy sentiment. In fact the best poems of the Highlands are what the wise Goethe predicated of his own works; they are *Gelegenheits-Gedichte*. Lauchlan Macpherson's genius was nothing like that of the Ossianic poets whom he assisted James Macpherson to translate, his poems being almost all in the humorous vein. Like most Highlanders he had the accomplishment of being bilingual; and I have myself read an old yellowed paper, bearing date 1763, containing in very fair Popian verses a humorous account of a flood which came sweeping down the Spey, carrying hay and corn along with it. At a certain part of its course, where the current of the river was impeded, the farmers and crofters, the fruits of whose labours had been ruthlessly carried away, congregated by scores, and began to fish out the drenched corn-sheaves with scythes and shepherds' crooks, and every sort of rural implement. The angling was successful; but, as in the case of Achilles and Agamemnon, there arose an angry fray about the division of the spoil, and with the desperate battle of the claimants for property that could not possibly be identified, the poem ends. The subject is unquestionably a good one, and worthy of the most delicate handling from the author of the *Rape of the Lock*, a delicacy, however, which no native Highland singer, using the foreign weapon of the *Beurla*, could hope to reach.[1]

JOHN ROY STUART, like James Macpherson a Badenoch man, and like many other Highlanders both soldier and poet, is well known to history by the active part which he took in the brilliant blunder of 1745. Stuart of course was a Jacobite, and a red-hot one. He had been fighting in Flanders, and when on the field of Culloden he signalised himself, hewing down the red-coats by tens, as only a Highlander can do. The Duke of Cumberland, his eye wandering over the field, and having had his glance fixed on the bloody execution doing in a hotly-exercised quarter, cried out to his aide-de-camp, "*Good God ! look yonder ; who the devil is that ?*" "That is John Roy Stuart, your Grace,"

---

[1] The MS. of this poem was shown to me by Mr. James Macpherson of the Union Bank, Edinburgh, a relation of the celebrated James, and a gentleman who boasts the possession of some of the rarest and most valuable books in the Gaelic language.

was the reply. "*Stuart! the devil! the man whom I left in Flanders doing the butcheries of ten heroes! Can he possibly have dogged me here?*" We may imagine such a man, when he wrote poetry, would not write it weakly, but something in the vein of the grand old soldier-dramatist who fought at Salamis, and afterwards wrote a drama "full of war" in every line. "His martial strains," says Mackenzie, "thunder along with the impetuosity of the mountain-torrent—racy, sinewy, and full of nerve." After the battle of Culloden, like the unfortunate Prince whom he followed, he made escape after escape, often by a mere hairbreadth, that would make the fortune of any novelist to rehearse; and on one occasion he hid himself behind the waters of a cascade while his pursuers were looking at the face of it! On this occasion he composed the verses of gratitude for his providential deliverance, commonly called *John Roy's Psalm*, commencing with the lines,

> "The Lord's my targe, I will be stout
>   With dirk and trusty blade;
> Though Campbells swarm in flocks about,
>   I will not be afraid."

After slipping successfully through all the traps laid by the hunters who pursued him, he found his way to France, and died, like his master, with that consecration of pity which human sympathy seldom withholds from the disasters of those who have suffered nobly, though in a foolish cause.

KENNETH MACKENZIE, born at *Caistel Leauir*, near Inverness, in the year 1758, was, unlike most Highlanders, a sailor, not a soldier. When he went to sea he had a library consisting of three volumes,—the Bible, the poems of Alexander M'Donald, and those of Duncan M'Intyre.

This circumstance is well worthy of notice. A better
library for a young Highlander, whether by land or sea,
I could not conceive; but it is such a library as the young
Celt of the next generation is not likely to possess, that is,
if our school-boards go on disowning everything that is
native and characteristic, and extinguishing by the imposi-
tion of a common external mould all the vigour and variety
of British local life; under such a monotonous drill, without inspiration and without character, the Highlander of
the coming century will grow up an emasculated and a
dispirited creature, whom no man will be able to distinguish from the lowest type of an English boor. Mackenzie
composed his songs to the cradling music of the waves of
the mighty ocean; and when he returned home in the
year 1789, not being able to find a publisher, he had to
go about soliciting subscriptions. Beggars are never agreeable callers; and beggars, in the shape of poor poets, have
not always more respect paid to them than is accorded to
other less reputable members of the fraternity. On one
occasion our poet called on a certain individual of the
name of M'Intosh, whom he believed to be a gentleman,
and presented his petition. "D—n poetry!" said the
M'Intosh. "There, do you see the door? Don't bother
me any more!" and with that he showed him out. The
consequence was what might have been expected. Mac-
kenzie·felt as Byron did when the clever Editor of the
Edinburgh tried to snuff him out with an article : he would
not be snuffed out, but only blazed more fiercely. A
terrible satire, in the style of which the Highlanders have
always been masters, came forth against the ungracious
M'Intosh; he was worse than hewed to pieces; and in
three days after the appearance of the satire died of a
broken heart. It is a pleasant thing to think that on this
model critics may sometimes die of remorse for their harsh

sayings, and not always poets of chagrin for being harshly criticised. Mackenzie was now, however, in a position not much less comfortable than his victim. The cry of the country he knew would be too strong for him ; so he made the round of his subscribers, and bought up all the copies he could lay his hands on, as the only possible reparation for the involuntary murder of which his verses had been the occasion. Did Lord Byron ever do anything equally noble ?

Shortly after this unfortunate event, which happened in 1792, Mackenzie, by his talents and good character, attracted the notice of Lord Seaforth and the Earl of Buchan, by whose influence he was appointed an officer in the 78th Highlanders. Afterwards, leaving the army, he accepted the situation of postmaster in an Irish provincial town, and lived there considerably beyond the usual term of human life, in the lusty exercise of those virtues of hospitality, fraternity, and good-fellowship, for which the genuine uncorrupted Highlander has ever been remarkable.

WILLIAM ROSS is one of those overfinely strung natures who died young, and has furnished a text, along with not a few others in recent times, for some hasty generalisers to lay down the proposition that poets die young. This is not true : Ross died young, like Keats, from a frail organisation and native delicacy of fibre, though no doubt in such cases poetry and love may assist. He was born at Broadford in Skye, a place well known to tourists, in the year 1762. His father, like the hero of Wordsworth's *Excursion*, was a travelling pedlar ; his mother, a native of Gairloch in Ross-shire, a daughter of the famous blind Allan the piper, whom we shall have to notice immediately. Young Ross, though of this humble parentage, managed to get an excellent education in the Grammar

School of Forres, where he picked up much more Greek and Latin in a few months than the sons of most rich and mighty men did about the same period at Eton and Oxford in as many years. Polished with school drill, he returned home, and made the tour of the Hebrides, specially Skye and Lewis, along with his merchant-father. This mode of life was of great advantage to him as a poet, keeping him in fresh communion with men and nature after the healthy old fashion of Homer and the Cyclic poets, in an age when books were little known and less used, and all influences came fresh on the mind, eye, and impressible fancy of the poet. After finishing his wanderings Ross settled as a schoolmaster in Gairloch, where, by his poetical and musical accomplishments, general intelligence, pleasant humour, and admirable good-fellowship, he attracted the love and esteem of a large circle of friends and admirers. But his career was destined to be short. Asthma and consumption preyed on the delicate substructure of his frame, and he died at the early age of twenty-eight. A simple upright stone in the churchyard of Gairloch stands over his remains.

The quality of his poetry in the region to which it belongs is praised highly by Gaelic scholars. " In purity of diction, felicity of conception, and mellowness of expres sion," says Mackenzie, "he stands unrivalled." What he wanted no doubt was robustness; but it is difficult in one soul to combine the grace of a weeping willow with the strength of a gnarled oak. Like Tasso, he had the misfortune to perch his love on one who was too high, or at least thought herself too high, to wed the son of a pedlar; and copious streams of finely modulated sorrow from the poet's lips were the result. As in the amorous, so in the convivial strain he vied with Burns; and MAC-NA-BRACHA (son of malt) received the praises of the

Celtic bard in a similar vein as John Barleycorn from the Lowlander.

> *Mac-na-brach an gille gasda*
> *Cha bu rapairean a chlunn !*

ALLAN MACDOUGALL, commonly called *Ailean dall*, or Blind Allan, Ross's father-in-law, was made of different stuff. He was a native of Glencoe, born about the year 1750, and departed this life in the year 1829. He was a tailor by profession (St. Paul was a tentmaker); but he escaped the general curse of tailoring, arising from sedentary habits; like his son-in-law he perambulated the country, and kept his limbs and external machinery in good trim, and saw the world to boot, as a poet knows how to see it. He was a fellow of most lively wit, sharp in his sallies, and, though a tailor, not to be trifled with. On one occasion a fellow-craftsman of the thread and needle, happening to throw a little bit of impertinence in his face, young Macdougall, with the double irritability of a poet and a Celt, flung back a scourge for his whip in such a style that the original offender in retaliation thrust his needle into the poet's right eye ; the consequence of which was that the injured organ completely lost its function, and the left eye from a strong fellow-feeling sorrowed itself away into a similar blankness. But a true poet, a *puer animosus*, as Horace has it, is not easily daunted. Blind Allan soon knew to turn his bane into a blessing. To his natural genius for poetry he added the accomplishment of instrumental music ; from tailoring he turned to fiddling, and earned his livelihood, as Bentley says Homer did, by playing at country weddings and raffles for a small fee. But poetical merit, accompanied by endurance and true manhood, has a wonderful faculty of rising. Colonel Ronaldson Macdonell of Glengarry, a notable man in his day, laid hold of Allan, and made him his family piper. The tailor was now as great a man as the poet-laureate ; he was in fact both poet and piper laureate to the most famous *Ceann-tighe* in the Highlands; and as such on terms of greater intimacy and more jovial communion with his chief than any English laureate can hope to be with the Majesty that sits on the British throne. He was also—a happy circumstance in his position—never tired of singing the praises of his patron. Like Horace with Mecænas, or Goethe with the Great Duke of Weimar, he could fairly indulge his humour for praise without being accused of flattery. Sometimes, naturally enough, the chief thought that praise less frequently and more delicately bestowed might be of more value. On one occasion, after the games were ended, and the bard had to finish the proceedings with the customary Pindaric ode (for Pindar really composed under similar influences), Glengarry came forward and said publicly, "Now, Allan, I will give you the best cow on my estate if you sing the doings of this day without once mentioning my name." To which the poet with ready adroitness replied—

> *Dheanainn latha gun ghrian*
> *A's muir bhi an gun 'bhi sailt*
> *Mu'n gabhainn do na Gàidheil dàn*
> *Gun fhear mo gràidh 'n aird mo rainn !*

> " Sooner the day without the sun,
>   Or without salt the sea,
> Than a song from me, most honoured Chief,
>   Without the praise of thee !"

JAMES SHAW, commonly called the bard of Loch Nell,— for the Celts are fond of substituting a topographical for the personal designation,—born at Mull in the year 1758, seems to have been a worthless fellow, as indeed it happens with rhymers not seldom; so far at least as my observation goes, when they are not better they are apt to be worse than their less gifted brethren. Shaw lived at Ardchattan, partly supported by the kindness of General Campbell of Loch Nell, whose family still dominates in that part; but, as he disgraced the pious fraternity of bards, by having no regular occupation unless perhaps drinking and abusing persons who would not give him money, we shall let him pass. Many a good song has been written by a great fool, and Shaw has written a few.

JAMES MACGREGOR, according to the account given by Mackenzie, seems to have been a most noble character, and worthy of being placed in the same niche of fame with the most heroic of Christian missionaries. Born in Perthshire in the year 1762, at a small farm-house near Comrie, and being of a thoughtful and serious turn of mind, he early devoted himself to theological studies, and was licensed to preach by the ecclesiastical authorities of the Anabaptist church to which he belonged. Soon after his license, he was sent to Nova Scotia, to superintend the ethical life of the Scotsmen who abound in that quarter. The diocese of this Anabaptist bishop was large enough for the ambition of any servant of the Roman Pope; not only Nova Scotia but Prince Edward's Island and the isle of Cape Breton being included in his jurisdiction. And how different from the soft walks through smooth lawns of fat parishes, which a modern English Bishop has to perambulate at his ease, was the evangelical wayfaring of the devout Macgregor! Through a country with a population more scanty and far apart than now in the most desolate part of the Highlands, without roads, without bridges, without inns, with only a notched tree for a milestone, a pocket-compass for a guide, a hard plank for a bed, and a potato for a dinner, yet he did it—honour be to his name! —and amused the road by weaving songs of gracious evangelic fragrance as he plodded along. This particular form of the redundant lyrical genius of the Celt we have already noted in Buchanan; my friend the Rev. Arch. Farquharson of Tiree entertains his thoughtful walks on the remote strand of Tiree by crooning Gospel chants in the same way; and I remember well on one occasion, when at Tobermory, in Mull, that most beautiful of all tiny harbours, I strayed into a bookseller's shop, or more properly the shop of a general merchant, where some books were to be had, and there picked up a little volume called *Dàin Spioradail*, Spiritual Songs, by the Rev. Patrick Grant, Strathspey. Now, no doubt, these spiritual songs are sometimes merely Scripture history put into verse, and scarce worthy of the name of poetry; but on other occasions they rise into a true lyric elevation, sustained in a lofty region of peace and purity, and are pervaded by a genuine spirit of piety such as that of Cimabue and the pre-Raphaelite painters of the Roman Church. Anyhow they stand a notable witness to the wide range of lyrical expression in the Gaelic language, and to the marked Celtic partiality for verse.[1] Next to Dugald Buchanan, Macgregor seems to hold the highest place among the sacred bards of his country; the fifth edition of his poems lies now on my table.[2] There is one anecdote connected with this excellent evangelist which I would rather not mention, because it brings to view a dark side of Celtic piety in

[1] On *the Laoidhean*, or hymnology of the Gaels, see the excellent articles of Mr. Mackinnon in the *Gaidheal*, vol. iv.

[2] *Dana a Chomhnadh Crabhaidh nan Gaël.* Edinburgh : 1870.

Scotland, which superficial scoffers are only too ready to fasten upon as a type of the whole. In order to improve his style in the writing of Gaelic verse, the reverend hymn-writer, in the most natural and innocent way possible, had ordered from the mother country some books of Gaelic poetry and music, and among others the works of Duncan Ban M'Intyre and Donald M'Donald, the Strathconan bard. These were lying open one day shortly after their arrival on the table of the minister's study, and happening to catch the eye of the servant-girl who ministered to the cleanliness of the habitation, she forthwith, in the gossiping way so dear to servants, spread abroad the news through the whole district that their pastor, a man publicly so high in repute for piety, did actually entertain his private hours, not with the Psalms of David, but with profane songs of secular poets! And this affair actually caused a schism in the Baptist Church of Nova Scotia! This is the same kind of superstition which prevents many a sensible clergyman, even in the Lowlands, from taking a quiet stroll on a fine Sunday evening, or playing the piano on the Lord's Day : the godly people of his congregation would be offended at such profane liberties! Nothing does religion more harm than when it is seen in fellowship with such grim imaginations. Godliness and gaiety should always walk together ; as indeed the good Macgregor himself says in the verses on the titlepage of his book—

Fhir a tha suigeartach ceòlar
Ceannaich-sa mo leabhar òran
Theag' gu'n dean e feum ri'd' bheò dhut
Ged nach mòr a phrìs.

" Who can sing and would be merry,
Buy my book, the price is small ;

> When your foot is worn and weary
> It will keep your fancy cheery,
> And lift you when you fall!"

Macgregor died at Pictou, March 3, 1828, in the sixty-eighth year of his age. The University of Glasgow had previously done itself honour by conferring on him the degree of D.D.

EWAN MACLACHLAN, who stands next on our roll, was a native of the Lochiel country, commonly called Lochaber. He was born in 1775, and picked up the rudiments of a learned education in the parish school of Kilmallie, near Fort-William. The zeal and success with which he followed out classical studies in private, not to mention his poetical and musical accomplishments, attracted the attention of Macdonell of Glengarry, who, with that generosity for which the old Highland chiefs were notable, furnished the scholar with what little pecuniary aid he required in order to pursue his studies at the University. In the year 1796 he proceeded to King's College, Old Aberdeen, where young Celts ambitious of intellectual distinction still delight to congregate. Here he forthwith announced himself as a candidate for one of those *bursaries* or scholarships which abound in those parts; and, after the usual trial in Latin composition, for which the Granite City of the North was always famous, to the great surprise and mortification of the shrewd young Lowlanders, who had enjoyed far better opportunities of juvenile indoctrination, the raw Highlander came out first on the roll of merit. From that moment he was a marked man. After going through the regular classes, and taking the degree of A.M., he entered the Divinity Hall. In the year 1800 he received a royal bursary in the gift of the Barons of Exchequer, and was shortly afterwards appointed to the office of teacher in the Grammar School of Old Aberdeen, and assistant-librarian to King's College. In England these would have been offices as lucrative as they were honourable ; but it has long been an ugly characteristic of social morality in Scotland, while putting the highest value on education, to overwork and underpay the educator. MacLachlan, like every genuine Scot, was a hard worker. After going through the tear and wear of his daily routine, he found leisure to carry on his classical studies to a height not commonly attained in Scotland. But, though devoted to Greek, as in his view the most valuable of intellectual acquisitions, he never forgot, as some people foolishly do, the learning he had brought with him from the Bens and the glens of his early boyhood. He wedded the study of Gaelic to that of Greek, by employing himself—like the present Arch-bishop of Tuam—in making a poetical Celtic version of the *Iliad ;* a work held in high estimation by his countrymen, though only a few selections from it have been published.[1]

MacLachlan was not only a scholar but a poet, and, like all true poets, felt the might of the mother tongue. His proficiency as a Celtic scholar was so great that he was selected by the Highland Society of Scotland to superintend the Gaelic-English part of their Scoto-Celtic Dictionary, published in the year 1828, a circumstance which one can hardly mention without expressing a very natural wonder that the Society which exerted itself so meritoriously in the registration of the words of the Gaelic language did not follow their noble inspiration further by the erection of a Celtic chair in one of the Scottish Uni-versities. MacLachlan was the very man for such a post ; and there can be no doubt that, had the British Govern-

---

[1] In the *Gaidheal,* vol. ii. No. 113, and subsequent numbers. The whole amount translated, only seven books, is in the possession of a clergyman in Falkland, with whom I had some correspondence on the subject.

ment of that day been as quick-sighted in searching out intellectual excellence as the Prussian is now, this distinguished poet-scholar would have been transplanted to the metropolitan seat of learning, there to found a national school of Celtic philology, which is only now being dreamt of. As it was, MacLachlan died of overwork, on the 29th day of March 1822, in the forty-ninth year of his age. His remains were carried to his own Highland home, and interred in their native soil with all the honours which affection and respect could gather round a departed magnate. A monument was raised to him near Fort-William, before which every educated man who makes the ascent of the chief of Scottish Bens will reverently take off his hat.

ALEXANDER MACKINNON, born at Morar, in the district of Arisaig, in the year 1770, brings us back to the military profession, in which the Caledonian Celt always appears more typically himself than among books. Mackinnon fought stoutly on the famous battle-fields of Egypt in the beginning of the present century, being a corporal in the gallant 92d. He afterwards took service in the 6th Royal Veteran Battalion, but died at the early age of forty-four. He was buried at Fort-William with military honours. His poems belong to the history of Great Britain, being the lusty growth of the stout soldier-life which he led, and are, according to Mackenzie's report, full of that fire and pith which only the experience of actual warfare can inspire.

DONALD MACDONALD, or the Strathconan bard, was born at Strathconan in the south-east of Ross-shire, in the year 1780. He was a sawyer by profession, and lived in those happy days, and in those fortunate places, where a man could cherish his native genius in a natural way without having English thrust down his throat, whether he required it or not. In the year 1832, happening to be in Edinburgh at the time when the cholera was raging, he was seized by that black pestilence and prematurely carried away. Like Mackinnon, the battle of Alexandria inspired his early Muse, and his best known lyric, the *Oran do Bhonipart* owes its existence to the splendour of British achievement in those parts.

The parish of Durness in Skye, like that of the same name in the Mackay country, boasts of a bard bearing the characteristic name of the district—Macleod. DONALD MACLEOD, called the Skye bard, was born in 1785, and after emigrating to America returned to his native county, where he settled as a merchant at Glendale near Dunvegan. He died three years ago, at the advanced age of ninety, retaining all his faculties to the last, and ever ready to give a poetic expression to any incident in his circle that presented materials capable of being poetically handled.

We come now to the men who kept alive, and are still keeping alive, the fervour of the Celtic lyre in these latest days, when red-tape and centralisation and Examination Boards seem conspiring to chase all nationality, all freshness of original colour, and all interesting variety of type out of the country. The first on this most recent roll is LIVINGSTONE, or, as he insisted on writing his name in Gaelic, Mac-Dhunleibhe, not Mac-an-Leighe.

In this man we have another example of that wonderful power of fiery persistency,—the *perfervidum ingenium,* —which, so often quoted as applicable to Scotsmen generally, has always appeared to me to be specially descriptive of the Celtic element in our mixed blood. Livingstone, like Blind Allan, was by profession a tailor, and, like the same bard in his youth, practised his craft in the salubrious way of travelling, as Homer did, from house to house, and from land to land, and gathering knowledge of men and of the world, while he carried, so to speak, his shop in his pocket. Livingstone was a native of Islay, born in 1808, and saw with his own eyes the sorrow of the passage of the land from its hereditary lords into the hands of new men, with the consequences, always disagreeable to the old inhabitants, which accompany a new dynasty. Whether anything was done in the way of clearance at that time harsh or impolitic, I do not know; but Livingstone, as a poet and a patriot, naturally thought so, and he poured forth his wail for the country of his love in verses that will long echo in the ears of the islanders :—

> " Though the sun is shining brightly,
>   And bright flow'rets gem the lea,
> And a thousand sheep are feeding
>   On the land, so dear to me;
> Though the shag-haired nolt are browsing
>   On the brae and in the glen,
> I have seen, and I will sing it,
>   Islay, thou hast lost thy MEN ! "

Home history and local tradition are the natural food of the poetic mind. So Livingstone devoted himself with all the ardour of the poetic temperament to the study of Scottish history, as it is recorded in Fordun and other ancient annalists. With his own feet also he walked over most of the battle-fields of his country's glory in Scotland and the north of England. To master this subject properly, he applied himself in his leisure hours to Latin; and not only so, but he took a taste of Greek and Hebrew, that he might stand on as sure a footing as the parish minister in the interpretation of the Scriptures, and " take him over the fundamentals," if necessary. This shows what Presbyterianism, with its stout individual energy,

and its stiff ransacking of the Great Book, does for the
people. French also he knew, and Welsh. In his authorship, besides poetry, he put forth *A Plea for the Gael*,
and some numbers of a *Scottish History*, which was never
finished. In those works he showed himself a most fervid
Celt and a good hater, ready to eat the Saxon up, as
Marshal Blücher was the French in that bloody affair at
Katzbach, in the Great Liberation War. Nobody expects
an Aristotelian temper in a poet ; and a Highlander may
well be pardoned for an occasional cordial curse cast at
a people who have dispossessed him of his inheritance,
appropriated his titles, gained their most glorious victories
by spilling Celtic blood, and then rewarded him by ignor-
ing his language, scoffing at his genius, and maligning his
character. When a true Highlander looks round about
him, and sees, as he imagines, what may be also not
seldom literally true, the interests of deer and sheep, and
black cattle and salmon in his country systematically
attended to, and protected by a law which he regards as
an invasion of the historical rights and privileges of each
member of the clan, while a deaf ear is turned to the
natural claims and the strong cries of a human population,
it is more than human to expect that he should love the
men whom he regards as the authors of such wrong.

As a poet, Livingstone is placed by his countrymen on
the same pedestal with Alastair M'Donald and Duncan Ban,
and even Ossian. He is equally powerful, says my authority,[1]
in the expression of ruthless fierceness and tearful sorrow.
He died in the year 1870, in the month of July ; and his
countrymen showed their respect for his memory by pur-
chasing for his remains a burial-place in the Janefield Ceme-
tery, at the north-east end of the great semi-Celtic city of
Glasgow. A memorial stone, with a short inscription in

---

[1] Three articles in the *Gaidheal* for 1873, signed R. I.

Gaelic and English, marks the resting-place of this sturdy protester against the inevitable dominance of the Teut.

Not inferior in reputation to Livingstone, and four years younger in point of time, is EWAN MACCOLL, commonly called Bard of Loch Fyne, from his birth at Kenmore, on that lovely arm of the sea, in a country rich with every most picturesque variety of Highland scenery. His father, a trifle more comfortable than most Highland peasants, not being satisfied with the modicum of learning that was doled out at the village school, hired a private tutor at a small fee, from whom the young poet learned English, and had the good fortune, at the same time, to meet in with an itinerant Paisley weaver, from whom he bought the *British Essayists* and the works of Burns. By this plentiful fuel the literary ambition, so common in the souls of young Highlanders, was fanned into a flame ; and in 1837, when he was twenty-five years of age, he commenced contributing to the *Gaelic Magazine*, then appearing in Glasgow, and in 1839 he came before the Celtic public in the well-known volume *Clarsach nan Beann*. His poems, both in Gaelic and English, showed such decided genius that gentlemen of the district, quick to spy rising merit, particularly the late Angus Fletcher of Dunans and Mr. Campbell of Islay, procured him a situation in the Custom-House, Liverpool. In 1850 he paid a visit to Canada ; and finding there not only more of the Caledonian spirit than in the commercial atmosphere of Liverpool, but the language of the Gaels in greater vigour than in some parts of his native Highlands, he managed to get himself transported across the Atlantic, where he remains to the present hour, holding a situation in the Customs at Kingston similar to what he held at Liverpool, and from time to time stirring the hearts of the loyal Scots in that quarter with strains full of patriotic fervour, and rich with such imagery as only a poet born and bred in the Highlands knows how to employ.[1]

So much for the singers. Now for the songs. And I may commence with one or two love-songs, which I have often heard sung in those delightful Highland gatherings in the busy metropolis of the West, where the soul of the genial old Highland life still delights to disport itself amidst the whirr of multitudinous spinning-jennies, and beneath the pitchy mouths of a thousand smoking vents. But in doing so in this artificial age, when all soul rushes into grey paper, and the laziness of dumb reading has numbed the unused wing of quickening song, I must premise that songs are meant to be sung, and that any person who merely reads them, and applies to them the principles of criticism which he may be accustomed to apply to modern poetry, mostly written to be read, is doing them and their authors great injustice; is in fact comporting himself only a little more reasonably than the mathematician who asked what Milton's great epic demonstrated. In modern poetry written to be read, we are accustomed to look more to the originality of the conception, the brilliancy of luxuriant imagery, and the striking appositeness of significant metaphors, than to the nature, truthfulness, healthy light and warmth, or, in one word, genuine fervid humanity, of the composition. In popular songs it is all the reverse. No doubt, in virtue of these qualities, modern written poems have their advantages; they may be compared to a grand exhibition of fireworks played off with all the effect which belongs to a scientific

---

[1] Besides Mackenzie's authority here, I have a short and meagre notice of MacColl in the *Gaidheal* for June 1873, and some notices in the *Scottish American Journal*, New York, which have been kindly sent me by Celtic friends across the water.

pyrotechny, while your popular song is only a very bright and cheery fire on a homely hearth; but the popular poetry of the Highlanders, and I may add of Burns and our other song-writers, has the compensating element of sweet music, without which it is the colourless photograph of a bright-hued original. I therefore set down in a note some of those collections of Highland airs which I happen to have seen, with the expression of my fervent wish that we may soon see in some popular shape, adapted for general circulation, some such cheap editions of the songs of the Gael as we have of Scotch and Irish melodies.[1]

The song of *Mairi laghach*, Bonnie Mary, in its oldest form, was composed by one MURDOCH MACKENZIE, a Loch Broom drover, not to his sweetheart, but to his own daughter, who in addition to her personal charms, in the labours of the shieling and the dairy displayed an expertness from which a Gaelic Homer would have constructed a whole book of a Gaelic Odyssey; but the version which I translate, and which has with general consent taken the

[1] (1.) Collection of Highland Vocal Airs, by Patrick Macdonald, minister of Kilmore in Argyllshire. Edinburgh, 1781. Very rare.

(2.) A Collection of Ancient Martial Music of Caledonia, by Donald Macdonald. Edinburgh, 1806.

(3.) Albyn's Anthology: a Select Collection of Melodies and Vocal Poetry peculiar to Scotland and the Isles, by Alexander Campbell. Edinburgh, Oliver and Boyd, 1816. This collection contains several pieces by Walter, not then Sir Walter, Scott.

(4.) Orain nan l'Albainn: Gaelic Songs, English and Gaelic, by Finlay Dun. The words to some of the airs in this collection are by Dr. Moir, Musselburgh, the well-known Delta of *Blackwood*.

(5.) A Treatise on the Language, Poetry, and Music of the Highland Clans, by Donald Campbell, Lieutenant 57th Regiment. Edinburgh, 1862.

(6.) Melodies of the Highlands and Islands of Scotland, by Captain Fraser of Knocking. New Edition, Inverness, 1874.

(7.) In the *Gaidheal*, a Gaelic monthly periodical, published in Edinburgh (Maclachlan and Stewart) and in the *Highlander* newspaper, Inverness, there are several Gaelic airs, with music and words, scattered here and there.

place of the original set, was written by John Macdonald, tacksman of Scoraig, in the same beautiful district of north-western Ross.   The air is simple, but to my ear uncommonly beautiful.

MARY LAGHACH.

CHORUS.

Ho ! my bonnie Mary,
My dainty love, my queen,
The fairest, rarest Mary
On earth was ever seen.
Ho ! my queenly Mary
That made me king of men,
To call thee mine own Mary
Born in the bonnie glen !

I.

Young was I and Mary,
    In the windings of Glensmeoil,
When came that imp of Venus,
    And caught us with his wile,
And pierced us with his arrows
    That we thrilled in every pore,
And loved as mortals never loved
    On this green earth before.

II.

Ofttimes myself and Mary
    Strayed up the bonnie glen,
Our hearts as pure and innocent
    As little children then ;
Boy Cupid finely taught us
    To dally and to toy,
When the shade fell from the green tree,
    And the sun was in the sky.

III.

If all the wealth of Albyn
　Were mine, and treasures rare,
What boots all gold and silver,
　If sweet love be not there?
More dear to me than rubies
　In deepest veins that shine
Is one kiss from the lovely lips
　That rightly I call mine.

IV.

Thy bosom's heaving whiteness
　With beauty overbrims,
Like swan upon the waters
　When gentliest it swims;
Like cotton on the moorland,
　Thy skin is soft and fine,
Thy neck is like the sea-gull
　When dipping in the brine.

V.

The locks about thy dainty ears
　Do richly curl and twine;
Dame Nature rarely grew a wealth
　Of ringlets like to thine.
There needs no haud of hireling
　To twist and plait thy hair,
But where it grew it winds and falls
　In wavy beauty there!

VI.

Like snow upon the mountains,
　Thy teeth are pure and white;

Thy breath is like the cinnamon,
   Thy mouth buds with delight.
Thy cheeks are like the cherries,
   Thine eyelids soft and fair,
And smooth thy brow, untaught to frown,
   Beneath thy golden hair.

VII.

The pomp of mighty kaisers
   Our state doth far surpass,
When beneath the leafy coppice
   We lie upon the grass;
The purple flowers around us
   Outspread their rich array,
Where the lusty mountain streamlet
   Is leaping from the brae.

VIII.

Nor harp, nor pipe, nor organ
   From touch of cunning men,
Made music half so eloquent
   As our hearts thrilled with then;
When the blithe lark lightly soaring,
   And the mavis on the spray,
And the cuckoo in the greenwood,
   Sang hymns to greet the May.

The next song was composed by Ewan MacLachlan, and is perhaps oftener sung at social gatherings in the West than any other. The air has a touch of the Scottish tune to which the humorous song "The Laird of Cockpen" is sung, but is in every respect superior :—

I.

My love she is fairer
Than swan when it swims,

Or the foam of the sea
When on pebbles it brims;
Like milk in the milk-pail
When purest its flow,
Or tips of the pine-tree
New sprinkled with snow.

II.

Her ringlets are floating
In golden display,
Like cloudlets that sail
O'er the blossomy brae!
Her cheeks like the roses
When freshest their hue,
And the sun on May morning
Is kissing the dew.

III.

Like Venus when brightest
She looks from the sky,
Is the charm of her look
And the trick of her eye.
Her neck it is jewelled
With beauty and grace,
Like the bright silver moon
When the stars hide their face.

IV.

The lark and the mavis,
In field and on spray,
Pour greeting full-throated
In praise of the May;
But the lark has no skill,
And the mavis no glee,

When my lass thrills the air
With sweet soul-melodie !

V.

When summer with daisies
Has spotted the lea,
And the home of the warbler
Is flooded with glee,
I wander alone
'Neath the green-waving tree,
And I sing of the maid
That brings summer to me !

The next amorous ditty is from the other side of the house : the Highland lassie sings her sailor lover. It is a song very generally known, and appears in all the cheap song-books that have a considerable sale among that most lyrical people. It is called *Fear-a-bhata*. I am afraid my version is at fault in one respect; each verse should have a trochaic ending exactly to suit the music; but the singer will find another translation in Finlay Dun's Collection of Gaelic Airs, of which the title is given in the note to p. 269.

FEAR-A-BHATA.—THE BOATMAN.

I.

Ofttimes I look down from the hill to see
When my boatman brave may come back to me ;
He may come to-day, he may come to-morrow,
But if he comes not, 'tis my heart's own sorrow.

II.

Full sharp is the sorrow my heart is knowing,
And the tear from my eye comes bitterly flowing ;

Wilt thou come to-night? or again must I,
Shut the door upon hope with a sob and a sigh?

III.

Ofttimes I ask the sailors to tell
If they have seen thee, and if thou art well,
But with cruel gibe and jeer they reprove me,
And call me a witless wench that I love thee.

IV.

My boatman vowed when he left the town,
To bring me a shawl and a new silk gown,
And his own fair face in a gold ring set ;
But I fear sometimes he may forget.

V.

There is no town in creek or kyle
Where thou wilt not rest with thy boat awhile ;
And thou wilt be humming a sweet song there,
That may win the heart of some maiden fair.

VI.

They say thou art light, and a light thing will move
    thee,
But say what they will, I will say that I love thee ;
Thee in my midnight dreams I see,
And I wake with the dawn to look for thee !

VII.

I loved my boatman, I held him dear,
Not since a day, or a month, or a year ;
But I loved him young, and I'll love him when old,
Till love with me shall lie down in the mould.

VIII.

My friends are saying, and ceasing never,
I must cast thee off from my thoughts for ever;
 But this word to me is even as idle
As to stem the flow of the tide with a bridle.

IX.

In sadness and sorrow my days are spent,
Like a swan on the loch, when its plumes are rent,
When it sighs its death-song to the wind,
And leaves its love in the reeds behind.

Mo chailinn dilis donn is another great favourite, and
may be looked on as a sort of nautical response to the
previous one on the part of the roving young sailor, who
quite justifies the faith of the bonnie lassie when from the
hill-top she is looking out eagerly for his return.

MO CHAILINN DILIS DONN.

I.

May health and joy be with you,
My bonnie nut-brown maid,
With your dress so trim and tidy,
And your hair of bonnie braid.
Thy voice to me is music
When heavy I may be,
And it heals my heart's deep sorrow
To speak a word with thee.

II.

'Tis in sadness that I'm rocking
This night upon the sea,

Right scanty is my slumber
When thy smile is far from me ;
'Tis on thee that I am thinking,
'Tis thy face that I behold,
And if I may not find thee
May I lie beneath the mould.

III.

Thine eyes are like the blaeberry
Full and fresh upon the brae ;
Thy cheeks blush like the rowans
On a mellow autumn day.
If the gossips say I hate thee,
'Tis an ugly lie they tell,
Each day's a year to me since
I left my lovely Nell.

IV.

They said that I did leave thee
To feed on lovelier cheer,
That I turned my back upon thee
For thy kiss was no more dear ;
O never heed their tattle,
My bonnie, bonnie lass,
Thy breath to me is sweeter
Than the dew upon the grass.

V.

Before we heaved our anchor
Their evil speech began,
That you no more should see me,
The false and faithless man ;
Droop not thy head, my darling,
My heart is all thine own,

No power from thee can part me
But cruel death alone.

VI.

There are story-telling people
In the world, great and small,
Their heart it swells with poison,
And their mouth it droppeth gall ;
Ev'n let them spin their lies now,
They'll see the thing that's true,
When the minister shall speak the word
That maketh one of two.

VII.

The knot of love that binds us
Is tied full sure and tight ;
What matters if they wrong me,
When I know that I am right ?
There's many a rich curmudgeon
Frets his heart with bitter spleen ;
But I can live, and love, and laugh,
Although my purse be lean.

Not few are the stormy nights on the grim grey sea
which this ditty has enabled the young Celtic sailor to
pass with his fancy pleasantly cradled in kindest memories.
It is, however, essentially a love-song, not a boat-song ;
and as your genuine West-country Celt is a sort of amphi-
bious creature, living as much on the water—at least where
locomotion is necessary—as on the land, it may be as well
here to complete the picture of sea-life in those parts by
giving a specimen of a genuine boat-song. The author of
the following piece is the Rev. JOHN MACLEOD of Morvern,
on the Sound of Mull, and uncle to Norman, the late
lamented minister of the Barony Parish, Glasgow. Through

all that clerical family, indeed, a rich vein of robust vital poetry can be traced,—a vein of more value, sometimes, than a hundred sermons. The air of the song is that of *Mary Laghach :—*

CHORUS.

Ho, my bonnie boatie,
Thou bonnie boatie mine !
So trim and tight a boatie
Was never launched on brine.
Ho, my bonnie boatie,
My praise is justly thine
Above all bonnie boaties
Were builded on Loch Fyne !

To build thee up so firmly,
I knew the stuff was good ;
Thy keel of stoutest elm-tree,
Well fixed in oaken wood ;
And timbers ripely seasoned
Of cleanest Norway pine,
Well cased in ruddy copper,
To plough the deep were thine !

How lovely was my boatie
At rest upon the shore,
Before my bonnie boatie
Had known wild ocean's roar.
And deck so smooth and stainless,
With such fine bend thy rim,
Thy seams that know no gaping,
Thy masts so tall and trim !

And bonnie was my boatie,
Afloat upon the bay,

When smooth as mirror round her
The heaving ocean lay ;
While round the cradled boatie
Light troops of plumy things,
To praise the bonnie boatie
Made music with their wings.

How eager was my boatie
To plough the swelling seas,
When o'er the curling waters
Full sharply blew the breeze !
O, 'twas she that stood to windward,
The first among her peers,
When shrill the blasty music
Came piping round her ears !

And when the sea came surging
In mountains from the west,
And reared the racing billow
Its high and hissing crest ;
She turned her head so deftly,
With skill so firmly shown,
The billows they went their way,
The boatie went her own.

And when the sudden squall came
Black swooping from the Ben,
And white the foam was spinning
Around thy top-mast then,
O never knew my boatie
A thought of ugly dread,
But dashed right through the billow,
With the hot spray round her head !

Yet wert thou never headstrong
To stand with forward will,

When yielding was thy wisdom
And caution was my skill.
How neatly and how nimbly
Thou turned thee to the wind,
With thy leeside in the water,
And a swirling trail behind !

What though a lowly dwelling
On barren shore I own,
My kingdom is the blue wave,
My boatie is my throne !
I'll never want a dainty dish
To breakfast or to dine,
While men may man my boatie
And fish swim in Loch Fyne ! "

Drinking-songs come next; but they are out of fashion now-a-days, and perhaps with no great loss. It is difficult, however, to conceive the typical Highlander without whisky. Like a German who does not drink beer, a Scotsman who takes no part in ecclesiastical politics, or an Englishman who does not read the *Times*, he may be a very excellent person, but cannot be accepted as a normal specimen of the type to which he belongs. CALUM O GHLINNE, or Malcolm Maclean, of Kinloch Ewe, in Rossshire, the author of the following extremely popular song, was no doubt a very undutiful parent to his toasted daughter, the beauty of Loch Maree; and it might have been much better for him, had his wife possessed a little less of that saintly forbearance for which she was celebrated; but there was a fulness of grand vital enjoyment about this magnificent toper, with which, in its lyrical Avatar at least, and at a distance from the occasional consequential sorrows of Bacchanalian delights, we cannot help sympathising. One feels at least more comfortable in

such company for the moment, than when in the presence
of a certain type of gospellers not unfrequent in some parts
of the Highlands, who declaim against all forms of popular
amusement (dancing and singing as well as drinking),
and tolerate no utterance of thoughtful breath from a
man's breast, except in the shape of grim sermons and
lugubrious psalms.

CALLUM O' THE GLEN.

CHORUS.

My bonnie dark maid,
   My precious, my pretty,
I'll sing in your praise
   A light-hearted ditty ;
Fair daughter whom none
   Had the sense yet to marry ;
And I'll tell you the cause
   Why their love did miscarry,
      My bonnie dark maid !

I.

For sure thou art beautiful,
   Faultless to see ;
No malice can fasten
   A blot upon thee.
Thy bosom's soft whiteness
   The sea-gull may shame,
And for thou art lordless
   'Tis I am to blame.

II.

And indeed I am sorry,
   My fault I deplore,
Who won thee no tocher
   By swelling my store ;

With drinking and drinking
 My tin slipped away,
And so there's small boast
 Of my sporan to-day.

III.

While I sit at the board,
 Well seasoned with drinking,
And wish for the thing
 That lies nearest my thinking,
'Tis the little brown jug
 That my eye will detain,
And when once I have seen it,
 I'd see it again !

IV.

The men of the country
 May jeer and may gibe,
That I rank with the penniless,
 Beggarly tribe ;
But though few are my cattle,
 I'll still find a way
For a drop in my bottle,
 Till I'm under the clay.

V.

There's a grumpy old fellow,
 As proud as a king,
Whose lambs will be dying
 By scores in the spring,
Drinks three bottles a year,
 Most sober of men,
But dies a poor sinner
 Like Callum o' Glen.

VI.

When I'm at the market,
  With a dozen like me,
Of proper good fellows
  That love barley-bree,
I sit round the table,
  And drink without fear,
For my good-wife says only
  " God bless you, my dear ! "

VII.

Though I'm poor, what of that?
  I can live and not steal,
Though pinched at a time
  By the high price of meal.
There's good luck with God,
  And He gives without measure;
And while He gives health,
  I can pay for my pleasure.

VIII.

Very true that my drink
  Makes my money go quicker;
Yet I'll not take a vow
  To dispense with good liquor;
In my own liquid way
  I'd be great amongst men.
—Now you know what to think
  Of good Callum o' Glen.

The following song is not indicative of the general tone
or style of Ross's poetry; but as a specimen of the hearty
drinking-song of the last century—and some of Burns's are
nothing better—it may have a place here.

MAC-AN-TOSAICH.

CHORUS.

Seize the bottle and brim the bumper !
Hence, each churlish loon and sour !
Son of Malt, right noble fellow,
Mighty warriors own thy power !

Who would compare a man of thy mettle
To the French wines, so thin and weak ?
Who would sneer at Mac-an-Tosaich,
But a whey-faced loon and a heartless sneak ?

Prigs and pedants may condemn thee,
Smooth and false, a hateful clan ;
But although they slander loudly,
They'll sip thee gently when they can.
Seize, etc.

Even the clergy, the black-coated,
Now and then beneath the moon,
I have known them in thy service
Stout as any bold dragoon.
Seize, etc.

How could mortals make a wedding,
How could bonds be binding, when
The writer lad who scrawled the parchment
Had no smeddum in his pen ?
Seize, etc.

Son of my heart, may I be ever
Of thy jolly company !
Oft have I danced sans fife or fiddle
With my legs made light by thee.

The intense love of country, which is one of the deeply-rooted passions in a Highland breast, and which makes it so cruel to eject them out of their old haunts without urgent cause, has produced many beautiful pieces, growing out of local reminiscence, which, even when destitute of any very striking poetical merit, have a fervour of feeling about them, and a truthfulness of description imparting to them a value far above the commonplaces of sentimental feebleness, which too often usurp the place of healthy national music in the dainty atmosphere of West End saloons. I give three pieces of this kind, the first by DUGALD MACPHAIL, the other by a native of beautiful Ballachulish, bearing, as one naturally does in that country, the noble name of CAMERON, a name now no less famous in the records of geographical exploration than it has long been in the annals of chivalrous adventure and military achievement, and the third by JOHN CAMPBELL of Ledaig, a picturesque spot betwixt Connel Ferry and Loch Creran, close to the old vitrified fort which the guide-books have christened Berigonium.

THE ISLAND OF MULL.

BY DUGALD MACPHAIL.[1]

O the Island of Mull is an isle of delight,
With the wave on the shore, and the sun on the height,
With the breeze on the hills, and the blast on the Bens,
And the old green woods, and the old grassy glens.

---

[1] DUGALD MACPHAIL, from whom I have a letter containing some notes of his life, was born in the year 1818 at Torosay in Mull. He was bred to the joiner trade ; but by that noble instinct of intellectual ambition so characteristic of the Highlanders, he raised himself to a superior position, lived twelve months in England as clerk of works and surveyor, and now practises in the same line in Glasgow. In 1859 he gained a prize, given by the Celtic Society, Edinburgh, for an original essay on the HIGHLAND CLEARANCES, and has been a considerable contributor to the well-known Celtic periodical entitled the *Gael*, under the signature of Muileach.

Though exiled I live from the land of my race,
In Newcastle, a grey and a grimy old place,
My heart, thou fair island, is ever with thee,
And thy beautiful Bens with their roots in the sea !
O the Island, etc.

There was health in thy breeze, and the breath of thy
  bowers
Was fragrant and fresh 'neath the light summer showers,
When I wandered a boy, unencumbered and free
At the base of the Ben 'neath the old holly-tree !
O the Island, etc.

Where the Lussa was swirling in deep rocky bed,
There the white-bellied salmon, with spots of the red
And veins of dark blue, in young lustihood strong
Was darting and leaping and frisking along !
O the Island, etc.

And a deft-handed youth there would gallantly stand
With a triple-pronged spear, smooth and sharp in his hand,
And swiftly he pounced, like a hawk, on his prey—
And glancing and big on the bank there it lay !
O the Island, etc.

And the red hen was there 'neath the wood's leafy pride,
And the cock he was crooning and cooing beside ;
And though forest or fence there was none on the Ben,
The red deer were trooping far up in the glen !
O the Island, etc.

O then 'twas my joy in the prime of the May
To list to the sweet-throated birds on the spray,
And to brush the cool dew from the low-winding glen,
When the first ray of morning streamed down from the Ben !
O the Island, etc.

Bright joys of my youth, ye are gone like a dream,
Like a bubble that burst on the breast of the stream ;
But my blessing, fair Mull, shall be constant with thee,
And thy green-mantled Bens with their roots in the sea !

O the Island, etc.

SONG IN EXPECTATION OF SEEING BALLACHULISH.

BY JOHN CAMERON.

CHORUS.

O I shall see, shall see the mountains,
The great sky-cleaving grey-coned mountains,
The corries and the foaming fountains,
And the white mists floating by !

Dear land of my birth, how soon shall I greet thee,
In a tongue that I know where kind welcome shall meet me,
And a thrill of delight at the vision shall stir me,
That mountains of gold could not buy !

I shall see the sun rise on the granite peaks hoary,
And set in the wave all ablaze with his glory,
Not veiled in the smoke of this huge-heaving city,
That blots all the breadth of the sky.

Though the cuckoo is gone that of spring would be telling,
The groves of the Duthag with music are swelling,
The mavis is pouring his lay more delightsome
Than harper or piper to me !

My nets I will spread where the herrings are plenty,
My line I will cast where the trouts are not scanty,
And here I would live to the reach of my fancy,
While breath in my body shall be.

I shall see the green glades that the bright waves are laving,
The far-stretching roods with the yellow corn waving,
The stag, the grand-antlered, the king of the corrie,
    Through the mantle of mist I shall see!

The green sloping braes I shall see in their beauty,
The men never false to their love and their duty,
With light-bounding step I shall hasten to greet them
    Whose eyes have been watching for me!

I shall leave the big town with its wheeling and whirring,
For solitudes where scarce a whisper is stirring,
The dark of the lane, and the din of the causeway,
    For the peace of the green-winding glens!

Hail to the blue-capped grey-coned mountains,
The dark-nodding woods, and the clear-gushing fountains.
Hail to the shieling securely reposing
    In the mighty embrace of the Bens!

THE GAEL TO HIS COUNTRY AND HIS COUNTRYMEN.

My heart's in the Highlands, I love every glen,
Every corrie and crag in the land of the Ben,
Each brave kilted laddie, stout-hearted and true,
With rich curly locks 'neath his bonnet of blue.

A brave Highland boy, when light-footed he goes,
With plaid, and with kilt, dirk, sporan, and hose;
O who will compare with my Highlander then,
When he comes fresh and fair like a breeze from the Ben?

When foemen were banded to spoil and annoy,
Who then fronted death like my brave Highland boy?
For his cause and his country, in battle's rude shock,
When kingdoms were reeling, he stood like a rock.

T

And the dear Highland lasses, bad luck to the day,
When I look in their faces and wish them away;
I'll cross the wide seas to the far coral isles,
With Mary to lighten the road with her smiles.

And the songs of the Gael on their pinions of fire,
How oft have they lifted my heart from the mire;
On the lap of my mother I lisped them to God;
Let them float round my grave, when I sleep 'neath the sod.

And dear to my heart are the chivalrous ways,
And the kindly regards of the old Highland days,
When the worth of the chief and the strength of the clan,
Brought glory and gain to the brave Highlandman.

But now with mere sheep they have peopled the brae,
And flung the brave clansmen like rubbish away;
But should foes we have vanquished the struggle renew,
They'll sigh for the boys with the bonnets of blue!

At Alma's red steep, and at red Waterloo,
The Gael still was first where hot work was to do!
And when Ganga and Jumna revolted, who then
Were more loyal and true than the sons of the Ben?

Where the East and the West by broad billows are bounded,
The Gael shall be known and his fame shall be sounded;
While thrones shall have honour, and right shall prevail,
Long ages shall echo the praise of the Gael.

And when need comes again for the law of the sword,
Though few now the clansmen that follow their lord,
The brave kilted boys for defence will be nigh,
And shoulder to shoulder will conquer or die!

In the next poem the same author, himself a Campbell, celebrates the return of one of that prosperous race from the sickly steam of London dinner-parties to the bright breezy freshness of the pebbly beach of Loch Nell :—

My love is a lady, my love is a Campbell,
    And she has come back to the Highlands again;
For the blood will run thin in the veins of a Campbell
    When away from the heather that purples the Ben.

Mid the pomp of huge London her heart still was yearning
    For her home in the corrie, the crag, and the glen;
Though fair be the daughters of England, the fairest
    And stateliest walks in the land of the Ben.

What poet may praise her? her virtues to number
    Would baffle the cunning of pencil or pen;
Though fair be the casket, the jewel is fairer—
    The best of true hearts for the best of good men.

She is comely and kind, and of gracefulest greeting,
    Erect and well-girt as a Campbell should show,
And a heart with warm blood, and a pulse ever beating
    With loving reply to the high and the low.

Long ages have gone since the sires of thy people
    First pitched at Ardmucnas their tents on the shore,
When Diarmad himself, with his spear and his harness,
    O'er the heights of the Garvaird gave chase to the boar.

The swan on the loch that belongs to thy people
    Made vocal the billow to welcome thee home,
And Mucairn and Benderloch shouted together,
    'The Campbells are coming! the Campbell is come!'

Thanks to the man who had sense for to find thee,
  And steal back from England so dainty a flower,
To live where the ties of thy kindred shall bind thee,
  And the love of thy people shall gird thee with power.

And we pray to the God who gives blessing and bounty
  That the seed nobly planted may gallantly grow,
And that never a Campbell may fail on Loch Creran
  While breezes shall wander and waters shall flow.

The elevating feeling of attachment to a noble race of local aristocracy (which, alas! the lords of the soil in Celtic districts have not always been wise to cultivate) that peeps out in this little poem spreads its wings out more grandly in the following epithalamic ode, composed by MRS. MARY MAKELLAR in honour of the marriage of the Marquis of Lorne to Her Royal Highness the Princess Louisa, on the 21st March of the year 1871. Mary Makellar, no unworthy inheritor of the genius of the celebrated Mary Macleod of Skye, is a native of Fort-William. Her father and mother and grandfather, who lived at Corrybeg on Loch Eil side, belonged to the grand old school of true Highlanders, who, by their familiarity with the fine lyrical poetry of their country, and the chivalrous traditions of their native glens, along with sound scriptural training in Gaelic, did more to educate a noble race of mountain peasantry than can ever be hoped for from any formal bookish nurture prescribed by gentle-men in London and Edinburgh, altogether ignorant and sys-tematically regardless of the living fountains from which all that is best in the Highland character flows. Mary, who was a Cameron by birth—the name native to that quarter—had early experience of the rough ways of life, from the death of her father at the age of forty-one. The shop which he kept at Ballachulish was thus left mainly in young Mary's charge, where she had to learn the wisdom most useful for a poet, of practical life, and where she had ample opportunity of studying human nature as it displays itself with undisguised simplicity in the various incidents of a populous village life. At an early age Mary was married to a sea-captain named Makellar, in whose companionship she has visited many distant parts of the world, living more on the water than on the land. In the year 1868 their ship was wrecked in the river Weser in Germany, and after hanging ten hours on the rigging they were rescued with much loss. She has recently remitted her sea wanderings, and lives at present in Edinburgh.

As a Highland poetess Mary had to encounter the strange, grim superstition, more than once alluded to in these pages, that secular song is a thing essentially ungodly, and that nothing ought to be sung but psalms. This nightmare oppressed her in such a fashion that though, to use her own words,[1] "the desire to write songs was strong upon her, she crushed it down in deference to the opinions of the pious Highlanders, who declared a song to be a sin." However, Nature is strong, and He who is the author of Nature, and from whom cometh down every good and perfect gift, enabled Mary to feel and to show to the sour-faced Pharisees of the hills, that there is no inconsistency between godliness and gaiety, and that secular and sacred music are twin sisters, which are then most lovely when each stands as the natural complement of the beauty which the other lacks; or, if this simile does not please, let us say that the separation between sacred and secular poetry is altogether artificial; that religion is not a separate compartment of the soul, but a consecration that possesses all the compartments; that the whole world is one living temple of the Lord, of which, though the inmost sanctuary may

[1] In a letter to me, dated June 18, 1876.

more specially represent religion, all the chambers are sacred, the outer wing and external decorations no less than the holy of holies behind whose veil the high priest enters only once a year.

WELCOME TO THE MARQUIS OF LORNE AND HIS ROYAL YOUNG BRIDE.

I.

From Scotland comes a joyful voice,
All her rugged bounds rejoice,
In the glens the pibroch thrills,
Bonfires flash upon the hills,
Banners to the wind are rolled,
And the voice of echo old
Sounds again a note of gladness,
When we deemed him sunk in sadness,
Mourning for the fallen place
Of his native tongue and race :
Now his voice is loud in song,
The glad sons of youth among.
Spirit of the Gaelic earth,
Wherefore is this wondrous mirth,
That hath waked thee from the tomb,
And to triumph turned thy gloom ?
Whence thy crown of joy so bright,
Gleaming on the dazzled sight ?

II.

Said the Spirit, shaking proudly
His bright locks of comely hair,
Gladness hath been shed around me
Like the bursting of the wave,

When the crested rollers bounding
Toss their white foam in the air;
Like cold water to the parching,
Like skilled finger on the harp-string,
Like love's breast to wretch forlorn,
Bringing balm to spirit torn,
Such hath been the news to me,
That hath stirred my soul to glee,
And my heart to joy did waken,
As when waves of wintry sea
Wildly dash in Corryvreckan.
For on Inveraray's green
Rings the shout of hosts afar,
Where the gathered clansmen muster,
And in every eye is seen,
Not the dreadful light of war,
But love's warm and kindly lustre.

III.

Raise, ye children of the heroes,
That have worn the Highland tartan,
Lusty cheer on every hillside,
From the far green glens of Cataibh,[1]
To Argyll, the nurse of valour.
As brown Diarmad, loved of women,
Slew the wild boar in the dern wood,
And won glory never dying,
While a tale is told in Gaelic,
So the golden-haired young hero
Slew the dragon, plucked the apple.
Apple noble, world's desire,
Which he bears to Inveraray.
He hath vanquished all the English,

----

[1] Sutherland.

Pomp of England, pride of Ireland,
And from German hands he carried
Off the spoil that princes longed for,
Great as is their king and army!

———

Let the waters of Awe and of Aray rejoice,
Each burnie and streamlet in song lift their voice,
With pride and with joy wakes the Muse of the glens,
When the wedding-robe decks the proud land of the Bens.
    Hail to thee, Lorne, and thy Princess together,
    Welcome are both to the hills of the heather!

Hail to thee, young chief, and yet again hail!
No wonder my darling o'er all should prevail,
For no blood of Kaiser or King ever born
Is better than flows in the blue veins of Lorne.

Thou well-favoured youth of the gold-yellow hair,
Full worthy thou art of thy heritage fair,
From the dawn of thy days thou wert pure without spot,
Thy course like the bright sun that wavereth not.

Hail to the diamond that beams in thy crown,
The Princess whose true heart and hand are thine own,
Well may the mountain-land bid her all hail,
Who is simple in greatness as flower of the vale.

Sweet blossom the flow'rets, unheeded of men,
With censers of fragrance perfuming the glen,
The bloom of their beauty unvalued doth fall,
But the peerless white Rose wins the worship of all.

O child of good Mother most royal in worth,
Whose fathers of old wore the crown of the North,
As dew to the mountains and glens of our isle,
Is thy coming in joy with the heir of Argyll!

Thou heir of great fathers, and thou, his young bride,
Fair as down of the mountain, or shell of the tide,
May the best dews of blessing descend from above,
To the end of their days, on the pair of my love !

Hail to thee, Lorne, and thy Princess together !
Welcome are both to the hills of the heather,
Hail to thee, Hail to thee, Hail to thee, Lorne !
With thy love to the land where thy fathers were born.

The translation from the Gaelic in this case is from the pen of Sheriff Nicolson of Kirkcudbright, a gentleman well known all over Scotland for the truly Celtic inspiration which he flings into his lyrical compositions, whether in the tongue of the Saxon or the Gael.

I have now to touch a sadder string. Those who are acquainted, even by the most superficial snatches, with the character of Highland music, are aware of the wonderful beauty with which it can clothe the sharpest utterances of sorrow that can be wrung from the human heart. The laments played with pipe-music are not less masterpieces in their way than their stirring *caismeachds*, full of war, and their strathspeys and reels, to which their mountain-limbs respond with such agility, emphasis, and grace. The following is a translation, I know not by whom, which I cut out of a newspaper, of a Highland lament, characterised by that intensity of genuine pathos which is one of the finest elements in the moral nature of the Gael. It relates how Donald, the young proprietor of Barbreck, was foully murdered by a false friend at the Cross of Blood above Kintra (a site still marked), after having hospitably entertained and so far accompanied him on his journey homewards.

A LAMENT FOR DONALD OF BARBRECK.

Oh for Donald! oh and aye!
Oh the dark and angry day!
When you pass the Cross of Blood,
That stands above the road,
At Kintra,
Forget not to pray
For the soul that passed away;
Oh the drearie, eerie day
That I said.

He was bonny, he was young,
Oh the day, and oh the song!
The lonesome song that I sing,
While the wild mountains ring
With my wail.
Oh the false friend that came,
Oh the hated, hated name,
Oh the cunning, stunning shame
Of the tale !

Oh the heart of my heart,
Oh the son that shared the part,
The part that was the strongest,
The fullest and the longest
Of my love.
Oh the kindness that he gave
To the traitor and the knave;
Oh the bloody, muddy grave
Of my love.

Oh ill-omened purple heather
On which they went together,

Their arms entwined so tight,
Iu the chill and frosty night—
Foe and friend.
With his black hair streaming,
His dark eyes gleaming,
One beaming—one secming—
God the end!

I will throw on thee a stone,[1]
No more, no more than one,
And with it I will throw
Myself, my joy and woe,
With my grief.
Woe is me for my loving,
That fainly would be proving
Some day may bring soothing
To my grief.

The well-known mournful air, "MacCrimmon's Lament," composed by M'Leod of Dunvegan's piper, under the strong presentiment that he was going forth on an expedition from which he would never return, appears in Finlay Dun's Collection, with a translation by Moir, the well-known Delta of *Blackwood's Magazine.* The following is by myself :—

" Round Cullen's peak the mist is sailing,
The banshee croons her note of wailing,
Mild blue eyne with sorrow are streaming
For him that shall never return, MacCrimmon!

The breeze on the brae is mournfully blowing!
The brook in the hollow is plaintively flowing,

---

[1] An allusion to the common Highland custom of throwing on the cairn piled over a person's grave an additional stone as a mark of respect. "*Cuiridh mise clach ad charn sa*" is a common Argyllshire expression, used as a promise of future help and friendship.

The warblers, the soul of the groves, are mourning,
For MacCrimmon that's gone, with no hope of returning!

The tearful clouds the stars are veiling,
The sails are spread, but the boat is not sailing,
The waves of the sea are moaning and mourning
For MacCrimmon that's gone to find no returning!

No more on the hill, at the festal meeting,
The pipe shall sound with echo repeating,
And lads and lasses change mirth to mourning
For him that is gone to know no returning!

No more, no more, no more for ever,
In war or peace, shall return MacCrimmon;
No more, no more, no more for ever
Shall love or gold bring back MacCrimmon!

I conclude with a piece of considerable length, one of
the finest of all the pathetic pieces which have been called
forth, either in English or Gaelic, by that sad process of
depopulation called CLEARANCES, which has deprived many
parts of the Highlands of blood, bone, and marrow, and
left nothing but feebleness and desolation behind.

FAREWELL TO MY COUNTRY.

BY A HIGHLAND EMIGRANT.[1]

O dear-loved glen where I was born!
And must it be that rudely torn

---

[1] I translated this from *Leabhar nan Cnoc, le Tormoid Macleoid, D.D.*
Greenock: Neill & Fraser, 1834. The Editor states in a note that the
poem was "sent to him" by the Reverend Mr. Kelly of Campbeltown;
but this does not absolutely fix the authorship.

From thee, with wife and bairns I sever,
To see thy face no more for ever?

And must I travel far away
When strength is small and locks are grey,
And years are few, that bear me down
Like a stone that rolls from the mountain's crown?

And eye with mist of age all dim,
And trailing foot, and laggard limb,
And a heart like a harp with a broken string,
And a breast that brings no breath to sing.

In vain you raise the strain of glee,
The blithe note wakes no joy in me,
My sun went down in the darksome West,
No more to lift his shining crest.

O wife of my love, so mild and sweet,
Let not thy tears flow down so fleet!
Thy grief but steals thy strength away,
When friends are far in the evil day.

I'm wae to see thee, worn and wan,
And me a helpless frail old man,
And the place where we lived on plenty's store,
A place of rest for us no more.

New people are come to hold command,
And the brave and the good must beg in the land;
The sons of the brave shall own no more
The mist-capped Ben and the wave-lashed shore!

They are gone from the land, with their deeds of grace,
And we are a headless and helpless race,
As weak as the reed in the sweep of the blast,
Or the weed of the sea on the sea-shore cast.

Go, my children! and far in the West,
New skies drop ruth on the place of your rest,
Though far from Albyn's Bens and the roar
Of the old grey sea on the old grey shore!

Away, away, across the sea,
Though the wish, God knows, was far from me;
Nearer my heart was the prayer to God
To sleep with my kin 'neath the old green sod.

And the tears from my eyes are falling hot,
When I see the grey ruin that once was a cot,
And look for the loved ones that peopled the brae;
But now they are scattered and far away.

No more a dear friend's kindly greeting
At morn or eve shall cheer our meeting,
And the glen that rung with voices of glee
Is silent, and dumb with despair to me!

Where be the lads that were gallant and gay,
And the blithe-faced lasses, where be they?
Where the old men that never looked sour,
And where the sweet song's soothing power?

Where is the hall with the liberal lord,
Who fed the hungry from gracious board?—
Banished is he far over the main,
Where host shall never see guest again!

Stranger that wanderest through my glen,
Thou lookest in vain for the haunts of men,
Thou shalt not clasp a fair maid's hand;
Nor lad nor lass remains in the land.

Thou shalt not see her wending home
At eve with her pail of creamy foam;

Thou shalt not hear her blithe song, when
She gathers the brindled goats from the glen.

Thou shalt not see in decent pride
The mild old man by the greenwood side;
Nor song nor tale shall he ask from thee,
Nor feast in the glen, nor sport shall be.

Weary with travel thou shalt not see
A door of welcome oped for thee;
No dwelling is there but the old grey stone,
With moss and nettles rudely grown.

Look for the hall where the grass is green,
Pluck the fern where the floor hath been,
And where the ingle was blazing red
Press now the heather beneath thy tread.

The grace of the knolls is gone; no more
Thou seest the seat of the elders hoar,
Where they span the praise of the good old time,
With the shrewd old saw and the wise old rhyme.

And round them the young men sat in a ring,
And their young soul floated on wondering wing,
Drinking delight from the brave old tale,
When freedom was nursed in the land of the Gael.

And why are we banished with outcast ban?
What treason was done by the sons of the clan?
Did we against the king rebel,
That in our homes 'twere sin to dwell?

No! that no tongue yet dared to say,
We lived in loyal and peaceful way;
Though many were keen to fish for blame,
In us they found nor sin nor shame.

But men were there who basely sold
Right for power and love for gold ;
And law but stronger made the strong,
That should have saved the weak from wrong.

But times may come to Britain when
They'll seek for men in the land of the Ben ;
But Ben nor glen shall yield a man
That once swarmed with the trooping clan.

Lorn and lonely the friendless thane
Shall sigh for his people back again,
Mocked by the whey-faced loons who hold
The land he basely pawned for gold.

He shall be left alone, alone,
Without a clansman, no, not one ;
Far, far are they across the wave
The wretched remnant of the brave.

He shall weep the bitter tear
For the wrong that was done by the hand that was dear,
When he banished the men, as noble a race
As e'er looked the broad-eyed sun in the face.

But though he pour his grief like a river,
He may recall them never, never ;
Who bear in their bosoms the memory keen
Of the wrongs they have known, and the things that
    have been.

He shall sit a lonesome wight,
Like a bird of the dark in a cave of the night,
And weep for the sin of his soul, when he sold
The love of his people for silver and gold.

He shall weep, till wiser grown,
He maketh the joy of the people his own,
And gladlier lives to rule brave men
Than to count ten thousand sheep in the glen.

But 'twill be long before the land
Is plenished again with a stalwarth band;
The old oak falls when the harsh winds blow,
But the tender shoots take years to grow.

When fails the seed of the mighty men,
A feebler people fills the glen,
Unpraised by bard, who live and rot,
Like their own sheep, upon the spot.

But who is he across the heather,
That hies this way?—'tis he, my brother;
He bringeth news, which I must hear,
Or good or bad with open ear.

Tell me, brother, and must we go,
With sail outspread where the breezes blow,
Or may we lay this night our head
Once more where we were born and bred?

The sail on the mast is hoisted high;
The breeze from the Ben is sweeping nigh;
Rest for us is here no more,
We must sleep mid ocean's roar.

Farewell, my children, we *must* go,
Though our will say ten times no!
The Ben and the glen, and the tree and the river
Must vanish from our sight for ever.

Farewell to the deer on the mountain heather,
I'll track them no more with my face to the weather;
No more the roe on the lawn shall flee,
Nor the silly young kid on the crag from me!

Farewell to the birds that sing in the morn,
The wood and the Ben with his old grey horn;
Farewell to the brindled goat on the brae,
The sheep with the white-fleeced lambs at play!

Farewell to the house with its liberal grace,
And the door never shut in the stranger's face!
Farewell to the cold grey stones that keep
The bones of my sires in their dreamless sleep!

Farewell, dear Albyn, with Ben and glen!
This night I must leave you, and never again
My foot thy dear green sod shall know;
Farewell, farewell—O waly woe!

It is impossible to read a composition of this kind
without having feelings stirred within us, and speculations
started that go far beyond a mere critical estimate of its
value as a poem. It is here as with the Jacobite songs;
this lament represents a social or economical fact, just as
much as the ballads represent a historical one. The
human value of these ballads, over and above their artistic
merit, depends on the high feeling of loyalty to race
which they embody; if they had been rooted in truth a
step further, that is, if the special historical fact which
they embody had been as wise as it was brilliant, and as
fruitful in good consequences to posterity as it was effective in circling with a halo of chivalrous glory the generation to which it belonged, these compositions would have
been perfect. As we have them, of course, we are willing

to forget the brilliant blunder out of which they arose; but it is alway a drawback when a cool hearer of a poetic composition can say, This is fine poetry no doubt, but it is poetry without sense, or poetry misapplied. Are we to form the same judgment on this poem of the clearances, and all similar poems with which the lyric poetry of the Gaels is so plentifully strewn? I wish for the honour of my country and the character of the great owners of the soil, that these wails might be pronounced altogether causeless. No doubt, in not a few special cases an outcry has been raised by poor people when forced to leave their native country, just as reasonable as the screaming of a schoolboy when he is taken for the first time to the presence-chamber of a dentist. It never can be a pleasant operation to pull out a tooth, and yet it must be done sometimes; and the wrench which a Highland heart feels when its roots are torn from its native soil in the glen is not less keen for the moment, and is much more enduring than any pain which the most harsh of surgical operations can inflict. Now, there can be no doubt that the Highlanders of Scotland, living as they do in a remote, secluded world of their own, and breeding, as in Ireland, not always with a salutary moderation, and this in a climate anything but favourable to a regular supply of the necessaries of life, were liable to fits of over-population and recurrent visitations of famine. To such a population, so situated, when no large draughts of young men for the army were required, periodical discharges by emigration were naturally recommended. So far well. And if poor people who had learned to cling to their comfortless homes as limpets to a rock, sometimes cursed their landlord or their factor for a misfortune which lay in the peculiarities of their situation, and for a momentary bane which would issue in a permanent blessing, this was quite natural.

But is this the whole philosophy of the clearances, the evil effects of which the noble Duke of Sutherland is now exerting himself with such Titanic preparation to counteract? I fear not. The facts of the case are these. Many of the original Highland lairds lived in a style of grand open-house hospitality, and of showy rivalry with the rich aristocracy of the South, to which their means were utterly inadequate. Their pride, too, prevented them from sending their sons to trade and commerce, where they might have made wherewithal to defray their expenditure; so they fell into habits of spending much and making little, a habit which goes on for a time speciously enough by a process which Jews and lawyers understand, but which ends sooner or later in a process which everybody understands. The laird becomes embarrassed, and creditors have no bowels. What's to be done? Law and political economy step in and say, "Turn out all the poor tenants of this spendthrift chief, who are as little able to improve the soil as their master was to keep it; ship them off wholesale to America, or let them go to Glasgow, where they will learn to be active and get higher wages than they can ever expect to earn here loafing about a crazy clachan—anywhere rather than here, where they are of no use but to raise poor-rates and breed poachers; turn them out, and bring in a big wealthy farmer from the Lowlands, who will stock the hills with profitable sheep instead of unprofitable men, and pay you a rent of £2000 per annum without any trouble to yourself or your factor, and with an increase of the gross produce of the country, which will entitle you to be looked up to as a great patriot and benefactor of your species." It was difficult for a man over head and ears in debt to see through the social fallacy or to resent the gross inhumanity of such an argument. So the people were turned adrift wholesale, and the glen lay desolate, with no population but a single shepherd and a dairymaid, perhaps from the South, to represent what had once been a chain of smoking cottages, the hive of a happy Celtic life, the seminary of a stout Celtic people, and the nursery of a brave British army. Nor was this all. By the improvements of roads, the introduction of steam-boats, and the general facilities of communication between the extremities of the land and the metropolis, the Highland lairds, even when they had not got into debt, became more and more estranged from the Highland hills; they spent a great part of the year in London, and, what was worse, allowed themselves to be carried away by the fashionable fallacy that a Highland laird required no Highland educa-tion, and that the proper thing to do with him was to send him to Eton, that he might learn to quote Horace for a Parliamentary speech, and not look stupid when some pert sprig of English nobility from the great training-school of Christ Church might make allusion to Homer, and quote the current πολύφλοισβοιο. In this way the great High-land chiefs systematically denationalised themselves, and threw themselves out of a quick and living sympathy with the people from whom they drew their rents. To young gentlemen brought up in this Anglified fashion the High-land people were not, and could not be, what they had been to their fathers and grandfathers; the tie that bound them, not being so fast, could be easily loosed; and, if it so happened that they got into expensive habits in London, or lived abroad and left their affairs at home altogether in the hands of a factor, in such case it might quite readily happen that whole glens were cleared of an honest and respectable old peasantry without any sufficient cause, and without the Earl or his Grace—who very likely were personally most excellent fellows—knowing anything par-ticular about the matter. The temptation no doubt, in such case, was in every view very great to get rid of the people; and human nature is weak. The factor was sure to be saved a great amount of trouble; it is a hundred times easier to collect a thousand pounds from one man, than the same sum from a hundred men; so the factor, on the selfish side of his heart, would naturally be in favour of big farms, and no warm friend to the crofters. And a new temptation, which in these latest times began to act permanently with great force on the lords of the soil, was even more seductive. Formerly, when the Highlands belonged to Highlanders—real Highlanders, not only with periodical display of kilt and bagpipe, but with blood and bone, and soul and substance—while there was plenty of deer in the forest, and plenty of salmon in the river, and every Highland chief was brought up as a sportsman, no proprietor had need to stand on any very strict relation with his tenantry as to game; there was enough for all, and an occasional shot at a deer was not looked on as a mortal offence. But now the Highlands having become part of general Britain, and the roads being free not only to the lords of the soil Londonward, but to rich Londoners northward, a new market has been opened up for Highland properties; and London brewers, whose pockets were turgid with gold, or English lords who wanted the variety of a little mountain air in the autumn, came down in troops upon the estates of the old lairds, and either bought or leased their land at fabulous prices, for the aristocratic dignity of landownership, or for the mere sake of sport. Those who bought the land with the intention of settling on it as resident proprietors often did a great deal of good; the money made in Liverpool or Manchester was spent in Mull or Skye, and a great deal of local life with good social economy established which had not been under the old lairds. But two evils also happened: the new proprietor knew neither the language nor the habits of the people; he knew only his own notions of improvement brought with him from the South, and these, if he was a strong-willed fellow, he would insist on carrying out with all decision and speed, without considering the habits of the people, much less their kindly claims to remain on the soil where their fathers had done faithful service from time immemorial. Farms must be let to a certain size, not an inch less; certain things must be done by the tenant in a certain way within a certain time; and the people who would not, or perhaps could not, adapt themselves to these conditions on the moment, would be turned off as cumberers of the ground, and the enemies of all improvement. But the Nimrods of whom we were speaking played havoc with the hamlet and the crofters in a very different fashion. If they paid £3000 a year to his Grace or other magnate for the shooting, they were entitled to have value for the money. Gamekeepers and crofters have always been enemies; the land bought for the sake of game would be kept for the sake of game; and if ever a quarrel arose—as such were sure to arise—between the owner of the deer-forest and the crofters who might in the old time have lodged comfortably on the skirts of the glen, the lord of the deer-forest was sure to get the better of it. Law and custom, aristocracy and fashion, and political economy too, in the narrow selfish way in which it is often taught in a mercantile country, would be in his favour; and the poor people were sent away, or went, when they found that nobody wanted them any longer. When a sturdy lad appeared in one of these depopulated districts, if his services were not wanted as a gillie or a gamekeeper, there was no demand for him; so he went to Glasgow or Otago, where muscle was required and money was to be made; and if any human beings remained in the glen, it was the feeble and the feckless, who either could not be removed, or would be of no use if they were removed. Thus notably in the midst of all the Christian civilisation of this nineteenth century the Darwinian law was allowed to rule unopposed in the moral as in the physical world; the strong man rioted in his strength, and the weak man went to the wall.

Of course I am perfectly aware that those who concern themselves to defend the clearances in all cases, and who deem the destruction of our peasant population in that part of the world a public benefit, might easily point out the reverse side of the picture, showing how the poor starving Highlanders had been blessed by their banishment, and how many rich corn-growers and wool-growers at the far ends of the earth had owed their prosperity to their expatriation. This side of the picture I have not the slightest wish to ignore; all that I am concerned to show is that the above poem, and scores to the same tune in the Gaelic language, have a root in the truth of fact, and possess a value not only as poetry but as a speaking witness of something wrong in the social economy of the country. That there were such things as " reckless and unprincipled clearances " in the Highlands, Dr. Norman Macleod, who knew well, has publicly asserted; and he were a bold man who should deny it.[1] The Darwinian law, however potent in the physical world, has little to do with the constitution of a sound social system; quite the contrary: not the overpowering of the weak by the strong, but the protection of the weak from the strong, is the principle at once of pure Christian ethics and of sound social polity. Nothing can tend more to sap the foundations of society in this country, to alienate the great mass

---

[1] Dr. Macleod's life of his father prefixed to *Curaid nan Gaidheul*, p. 30.

of the people from the landed aristocracy, and to turn our common people into Radicals, Revolutionists, and Socialists, than the doctrine that a landholder is only a land-merchant, and has done his duty to the country when he has made the greatest amount of material profit from the greatest amount of material production, without the slightest regard to the character or the distribution of the rural population. Selfish principles of this kind eat into the very core of national life; and, if we are prepared, as a people, to stand, as the Americans phrase it, on this platform, there is no hope for us. We shall certainly perish by that disintegrating force which sooner or later dissolves all societies in which purely commercial principles usurp the moral supremacy of the soul.[1]

Let us now conclude with a taste of Gaelic prose. The natural field for the exhibition of this talent in the Highlands would have been religion and theology; but great as is the preaching power of the Highland ministers, few sermons have been printed; and for the purposes of practical piety, when venturing beyond their favourite sphere of devotional verse, they seem to have contented themselves with translations from Bunyan, Boston, Baxter, Owen, and divines of what in Scotland is called the Evangelical

---

[1] The views on the great clearance question here stated do not materially differ from those in my notes to the *Braemar Ballads*, published twenty years ago, or the statement in the prose introduction to the *Lays of the Highlands and Islands* (London, 1872), p. 48, with which the present pages may be compared. The inquiries and observations which I have from time to time made on the subject have resulted in producing greater caution with regard to the judgment of individual cases, but have not in the slightest degree changed the general principles which I then applied to this subject. The clearance question is, in fact, like all political, social, and economical questions, ultimately a moral question, and, as such, depends on the existence of a delicacy of social instinct, which is as rich as the fragrance of a rose, but can neither be created nor annihilated by a tabulation of mere *pros* and *cons*. Sympathy is the salt of the moral world; but if the salt has lost its saltness wherewith shall it be salted?

school.   Their best specimens of original pulpit eloquence,
I am told, are by M'Diarmid ; but I have not read them.
But the weakness of the Highland pulpit, so far as literary
composition goes, seems evident from the fact, which I am
afraid there is no denying, that a great number of the
sermons preached in Gaelic are cooked up or simply translated from the English, and often in such a hybrid fashion
as to be utterly unenjoyable by genuine Highlanders.[1]
This wretched abuse arises no doubt from the habit, so
common among young Highlanders, of allowing their
mother tongue when at school and college to fall into
abeyance, so that, when at a later period they enter the
Church, and are appointed to a Highland parish, they find
themselves in the unnatural position of thinking in English while they are speaking in Gaelic ! Far more characteristically Gaelic than the average of the sermons, I
believe, are the *Sgeulachdan,* or prose fairy tales and other
fictitious narratives, published and translated by that excellent Celt (would there were many such !) J. F. Campbell,
whose name we have had so often occasion to mention.
These tales, that were used to entertain the long winter
nights round the cheery peat-fire by the old crofters, are a
perfect model of that graceful and unaffected simplicity of
early graphic narrative of which we have such classical
examples in Herodotus. Those who are wise enough to
seek after the truths contained in popular fiction, and who
know that an old fairy tale is often much more sound-hearted
and much more truly felt sometimes than the last new
novel, will find this book of Campbell's extremely delect-
able, though a friend of mine said to him on opening it,
as Cardinal Hippolyto d'Este did to Ariosto, in reference
to his Orlando, *Dove avete trovato tante coglionerie ?*—Where

---

[1] This is distinctly asserted by Norman Macleod the elder, in the *Caraid
nan Gaidheal,* part i. p. 11.

did you get all these blethers? The man who cannot enjoy *Cinderella* and *Jack the Giant-Killer* and *The Shifty Lad*, in Mr. Campbell's collection, has not yet reached that stage of æsthetical culture where the sage shakes hands with the schoolboy, and knows that even out of the mouths of babes and sucklings in various wonderful fashions God hath perfected praise. Next to the *Sgeulachdan*, as a part of the popular prose currency of the Highland people, we must rank the *Sean-fhocal*, or *Proverbs*, of which there is a great abundance, marked by that shrewd practical sagacity which always belongs to the current wisdom of the common people, happily preserved as they are by their position from the idle luxuries of useless learning and baseless speculation.[1] But the great work of classical Gaelic prose, which shines above the rest as the moon among the lesser lights, is the *Caraid nan Gaidheal*, by the late Rev. Dr. Norman Macleod of St. Columba Church, Glasgow, the father of the well-known divine whose memoir has recently thrown such a radiance of warm, vivifying light into the field of British biography. This work is a collection of papers originally written in two Gaelic magazines, to which Dr. Macleod himself and some other members of his noble clan were the chief contributors. The most brilliant papers are written in a dialogic form, marked by the dramatic grace of Plato and the shrewd humour of Lucian. The subjects which it discusses are such as naturally attract every man who takes an intelligent interest in the changes which have been going on in the Highlands during the last half-century, and who, while he

---

[1] As the edition of the *Gaelic Proverbs*, by MacIntosh, a nonjuror Episcopalian clergyman (Edinburgh, 1819), is now rare, scholars will be happy to learn that a new, more correct, and enlarged edition is being prepared by Sheriff Nicolson of Kirkcudbright, and will speedily be published. In connection with the Proverbs I must not forget to mention the excellent articles on them by Mackinnon in the *Gaidheal*, vol. iv.

is willing to welcome the new, so far as it is beneficial or unavoidable, is not blind to the virtues of the old.   Like Lord Cockburn's personal memoirs, this book has the great historical value of painting the best life and character of the Highlands at a time when, if it had not been fastened down by such a master pencil, it would have been lost for ever to the world.   In the author of this remarkable book we discover with delight the rich union of the humorous and the pathetic, which gives such a charm to the biography of his distinguished son.   Certainly there is no prose-writer in Gaelic at whose thrilling touch one may so lightly see a whole audience of rapt hearers either moved to tears or convulsed with laughter.   I subjoin a specimen of his powers in pathetic description, but before doing so will jot down a few of the more notable facts of his life.[1]

Dr. Norman Macleod, born in the year 1783, was the son of a brave and disinterested gentleman, who served God all his life in the remote district of Morvern, between Mull and Loch Eil, with the small recognition of £40 (afterwards £80) for his services.   What was done for the education of a large family under such circumstances it is a school of virtue to understand.   Young Norman learned Greek and Latin in the first place from his father; afterwards, as Scotch young men only contrive to do, with success at Glasgow and Edinburgh Universities; but he learned also boating, shooting, and pedestrianising, and all that manly sort of exercise which the reader will see depicted in the well-known *Reminiscences of a Highland Parish.*[2] Following his father's profession, after going through the regular course of study prescribed by the Church of Scotland for her licentiates, he was licensed to preach in the year 1806, and served his Master as a zealous but judicious

---

[1] Taken from the life by his son, prefixed to the edition of the *Caraid nan Gaidheal,* 1867, superintended by Dr. Clerk of Kilmallie.

[2] London: Strahan, 1868.

and moderate minister of the gospel ($\epsilon\pi\iota\epsilon\iota\kappa\eta\varsigma$) first at Campbelton, then at Campsie, and lastly at St. Columba's Church, Glasgow, for the long period of fifty-seven years. His services as a faithful shepherd of souls were so appreciated by a faithful people, that at the period of the great disruption in 1843, when almost all the Highlanders behind the Grampians left the Established Church, Dr. Macleod's people remained firm. But it was not the faithful performance of the routine work of a parish that would satisfy the lofty apostolic ambition of a Macleod. Though a man in every sense, and a gentleman every inch, he was more than both—a Highlander. Like Moses in Egypt, he saw how his people had been neglected and oppressed, and in some places wellnigh exterminated, by those who should have been their protectors.[1] He brought the cause

[1] The following passage shows that since the Highlands lost its peasantry and its middle class, the army can now no more be recruited from the best school of soldiers :—

" There was in my youth a company of Volunteers in every parish of Argyllshire. There were eight companies in the district of Mull and Morven, under the immediate command of Major Maxwell, the Duke's factor, afterwards my father-in-law, and a most admirable disciplinarian. I may be permitted to say that handsomer men than these Volunteers never were embodied, chosen as they were from the whole population. There existed then a most loyal and martial spirit in these counties, forming an extraordinary contrast to the spirit that now, I fear, characterises many of them. Besides the company of Volunteers in each parish, I have still in my possession the names and designations of 110 officers, natives of Mull, Morven, and Coll, who held commissions in the army, and with each of whom I was personally acquainted. Many of these were highly distinguished, and attained to high rank, and many more, alas ! perished during the great war. I lament to be obliged to admit that those clearances, which for years have been most extensively and injudiciously carried on in the Highlands, have contributed very much to bring about a very different state of things. The Highlanders have been expatriated ; and if we look for the descendants of those brave, loyal, and virtuous people who once inhabited our glens, we must look for them among the forests of America or the prairies of Australia—

' Ill fares the land, to endless ills a prey,   .
Where wealth accumulates and men decay.' "

of his unfortunate countrymen before the General Assembly, and of course had the usual difficulties to contend with, which everything relating to the Highlands always has had, arising from the ignorance, prejudice, indifference, and superciliousness of the Lowlanders. However, a good cause, firmly handled and wisely managed, carries the germs of success in its breast. With the able assistance of Dr. Baird, Principal of the University of Edinburgh, Highland schools at length were planted in hundreds of places where no schools had been before; and Bibles were published in sizeable type, which the pious old women in their peaty huts might read without spectacles.[1] But his heart was too large to be satisfied with Bibles and school primers. He, just as Norman his noble son, saw that sermons and catechisms required to be supplemented by some such literature as we now have in *Good Words*, and half a dozen serials started on its model; so the old Norman when at Campsie struck out the original idea of creating a periodical literature in Gaelic for the sake of giving his Highland friends that sort of literary culture in their mother tongue which would both be beneficial in itself and act as a whet to sharpen the appetite for the intellectual banquet which lay prepared for them in the rich and various literature of England. These periodicals came out at intervals, between the years 1830 and 1848, under the names of *Teachdaire Gaelach, Cuairtear nan Gleann.*

Never had the Highlanders been treated like reading

---

[1] A strong party in the Assembly had obstinately opposed the motion to get a quarto edition of the Gaelic Bible printed, as the only edition that existed—in 12mo—could not be read by persons in advanced age. When Dr. Macleod was pressing this grievance, as he thought, with some effect on one of the chief men of the party, he suddenly was met with the reply, *" There's the breakfast bell; just advise your Highland friends to get spectacles!"*

animals in this style before, and they were not slow to appreciate the value of such services. Pity only that on account of the continued apathy of the upper classes, the absence of a middle class, and the want of intellectual self-respect in not a few of the sub-middle and lower classes, this noble intellectual achievement has not been followed by any such growth as might have been expected from such wisely sown seed. Neither the schoolmasters nor the clergymen, in many cases, seemed to have sense enough to know that these publications of Dr. Macleod's contained a literature that, after the Bible and the Hymn-book, ought to have been part of the familiar furniture of every family and every school. They became more and more fixed in their mechanical notion of educating High-landers by external appliances alone, without attempting to touch humanly the Celtic fibres in their heart. We may, however, attribute to the intellectual contagion of Macleod's Gaelic prose works the efforts which are still being made by various patriotic persons to keep up a Gaelic periodical, the *Gaidheal*, now in its fifth year; nor less, perhaps, the sturdy manhood with which the editor of the *Highlander* newspaper, in Inverness, has asserted his right to feel and think, and write and speak, like a High-lander, in the face of no small amount of popular indiffer-ence and fashionable opposition.[1]

THE EMIGRANT SHIP.

In returning from Iona, on one of the finest summer evenings I ever remember to have seen, we landed at a snug and sheltered place on the north side of the island of Mull. I cannot imagine a harbour more effectively

---

[1] I observe the dialogic style of the *Teachdaire* appears frequently in the columns of the *Highlander*. This is a vein which they ought to culti-vate, and in which something notable may possibly be achieved.

fenced from the rage of the storm and the swell of the sea.
In front of it a long narrow island stretches out, spreading
its protecting wings around boat or ship that may be either
seeking covert here from the rush of the ocean waves or
waiting for the turn of the tide to help it round the huge
headland that fronts the broad Atlantic. On the right
hand, as we enter, the land rises sheer and steep. We
sailed in close to the lip of the crag, where the branches
of the trees were hanging quite close to our masts. The
fragrance of the fresh green leafage flowed sweetly down
on the breeze, and hundreds of little birds were warbling
their welcome to us from every bush, as we sailed in
gently beneath their haunts. All around, in whatever
direction the eye might turn, the view was full of beauty
and pleasantness. The mountains of Ardnamurchan, green
to the top, Suinart, with its lovely hills and knolls, and
the whole breadth of the adjacent coast of Morvern,
were rejoicing quietly in the flavour of the summer
evening.

> O lovely and beautiful Ben,
> The chief of all Bens art thou!   ·
> The white cloud sleeps on thy crown,
> And the stag looks out from thy brow.

When we entered the bay there was nothing to see within
its circle but ship-masts and streamers floating idly before
the breeze, and nothing to be heard save the stroke of
the oar, the murmur of the brook, and the roar of the
waterfalls, which were leaping down from many a lofty
steep into the wide bosom of the bay. On our left hand,
from side to side of the beach, rows of high houses rose up,
as white as snow; and right behind them the ground rose
up so steep that the branches of the trees—ash, rowan,
and hazel—with which it was thickly tufted, seemed to

hang over the very roofs of the houses. On the slope of the brae, higher up, you see another part of the town between you and the sky, in a fashion of which you will with difficulty find the match, whether for beauty or strangeness. And looking outward to the bay itself, a sight was presented full of animation; scores of vessels, some large and some small, many a tiny pinnace with green oars, many a trim yacht with white sails, and a war-ship with tall masts and the royal flag. And, in the midst of all, my eye rested on a ship that far overshot the rest in size and equipment; towards it I observed a great many small boats were making their way, and everything indicated that it was about to set sail. There was one of our fellow-voyagers, who joined us from the back end of Mull, and who had scarcely lifted his head since he entered the ship; this man now raised his eye, and directed his gaze with an expression of eager anxiety to this ship. "Do you know," said I to him, "what ship this is?" "Yes, I do, and to my sorrow," he replied; "I know it only too well; sorry I am that there are more of my dear friends than I wish in that ship; there too are my own brothers, and the best blood that belongs to me, going to make a long long journey to America, whence they will never return; and a pitiful wretch am I, so bound by harsh circumstance that I may not follow my heart and go along with them."

I now followed him and some others to the ship; for I could not restrain the strong desire that I felt to see those warm-hearted men who were this day going to bid a long farewell to dear old Scotland, in search of a country where they might establish a permanent dwelling for themselves and their families. It is not possible for me to convey to a person, who was not present, any idea of the sight that there met my view. That day will never fade from my memory. Here there was crowded together a great multitude, of all ages, from the babe a week old to the old man with the weight of threescore and ten years on his white locks. It was pitiful to see the deep sorrow, the pain of mind, the despondency, the despair, and the heart-breaking pangs that were depicted on the countenances of the greater part of them, people gathered together from many a remote island and corner of the Highlands, but all brothered here in one common grief.

My attention was specially drawn to one man—old and blind, who was sitting apart from the rest, with three or four little boys round about him, his old arms stretching over them, while they were trying to come as near as possible to his breast, his head bending over their heads, his long grey hair and their curly brown locks loosely mingling together, and the big tears rolling down his cheeks. Near him, close to his feet, was a handsome woman, sitting and sobbing as under some heavy affliction; and I guessed that it was her husband who was walking up and down with a short, hurried step and his hands folded. His eye had a wild and unsettled look, and the disturbed expression of his countenance showed plainly how little peace there was in his mind. I drew near to the old man, and asked him in a gentle voice if he, in the evening of his days, was going to leave his native country. " I," he said, " emigrate ! Not I. I shall not move from my earthly home till I go to that land to which we must all go some day ; and when my hour comes to go, who is there now that will put his shoulder under my head and help to carry me to my last resting-place ? Ye are gone ! ye are gone ! and I am left alone, blind and old, without brother, without son, without stay or support ; and to-day—day of my sorrow ! God forgive me,—you, Mary, my daughter, my only child, with my dear, beautiful, bright-eyed grandchildren, you are going to leave me ! . . . I shall go back this night to the old glen; but I shall not know the hand that leads the blind old man. Never more shall I hear the prattle of your sweet voices beside the stream; never again shall I cry 'Come back! come back!' though the danger was not great; but still I loved to cry 'Come back! come back from the brink of the water!' Never again, when I hear the barking of the dogs, will my heart leap up, when I shall be crying, 'They come, they come, my children!' Who now will guide me to the shelter of the hill, where we may sit down and read the Holy Book? Where will you be in the grey of the evening, when the sun sinks behind the hill, O children of my love? And who will lift up the cheerful psalm to gladden my heart at our morning devotions?" "O father," cried the daughter, coming near to him, "do not break my heart!" "Is it you, Mary?" said he. "Where is thy hand? Come near to me, my daughter, my jewel; the sound of thy voice is a comfort to me. I have nothing to blame you for, Mary, and I will not complain any more. Go! take my last farewell, and God's blessing with you. Be you, as your mother was before you, always true to your duty. For me, it is not long that I shall be here. I have been robbed to-day of the tender shoots of beauty that made my life lovely; but while I live God will stand by me; He was always my stay in every hard case, and He will not leave me now. Blind as I am, thanks to His name, He has given me to look on a Friend that is better than a brother, and on a countenance that is full of loving-kindness and grace. At this very moment I am drawing new strength from Him. His promises are coming near to my heart. Other branches may fail; but the tree of life will not wither.—Are you all near me? Listen!" he said; "we are now about to part; you are going to a far distant country; and it may be that before you have reached it I shall be in a bright, sunny land, where I hope that we shall all meet again, and there will never be parting or separation any more; no, for there is no poverty there, and no harsh, unfeeling taskmaster to drive us away from the soil which we have subdued with the brawn of our arms, and watered with the sweat of our brows. We shall be there for ever with one another, and for ever with God. There every tear shall be wiped from every eye, and the day of sorrow shall be past. Be ye mindful of the God of your fathers, and fall not away from any godly practice that ye have learned. Every morning and every evening bend the knee as was your wont, and lift up the psalm of praise. And you, my children, who were my eyes to see, and my staff to lean on; you who I looked to that ye should put the green sod upon my head, from you I must now part. God help me!"

I was not able to wait longer; a yawl to bring the old man to land was coming alongside of the ship, and he was told that the time had now come when he must depart. I slipt aside; I felt utterly unable to stand and witness the final separation.

In the back part of the ship was a company of people whom, from their dress, I knew to be from the country, and from their accent conjectured to be from some of the northernmost islands. They were looking with great eagerness out in the direction of a little boat that was coming in under sail and oar. As soon as the boat was fairly within the harbour, and was approaching the ship, they all called out—"*It is he! it is himself! blessings on his head!*" There was one man in that company who to all appearance was of higher degree, and seemed to command more respect than the others. As soon as he recognised the little boat he went up to the captain; and I noticed then that the captain called to the men who were upon the masts and astride the spars to come down and suspend the preparations which were making to set sail. The boat approached, and there stood up in it a tall, old man, as handsome a gentleman as I ever beheld, and, though his hair was as white as the moor cotton, he mounted up the ship with a steady, firm step, needing no man's help. The captain welcomed him with much honour. He cast his eye around, and forthwith perceiving the dear company that was at the far end of the ship, he walked up to them. "Now, God be with you," said he; and each one rose with bonnet in hand to give him welcome. He sat down in the midst of them, and for a while leant his head on the staff which he had in his hand, and I perceived that the big tears were rolling down one of the finest countenances that I had ever set eyes on. All the company gathered round him, and some of the children crept close up and sat at his feet. There was something about the whole appearance of this patriarchal man that could not fail to attract every beholder; there floated such an atmosphere of goodness and gentleness about him that the most faint-hearted felt courage to approach and to speak to him; while, at the same time, there was a power in his eye and in his brow that repelled the slightest tendency to undue familiarity or forwardness. "You have come, as you promised," said they; "never did you desert us in the day of trial, and we knew that you would not do it now. This night we must set our face to the great ocean; and before the sun shall set behind yonder mountains we shall be for ever cut off from your sight. That is the cause of our weeping to-day—day of our sorrow!" "Let me not hear," said the minister, "this sort of language; be of good cheer; no time is this for faint-heartedness; put your trust in God; for assuredly it is not without His knowledge that you are making this long journey. It is by His providence that everything takes place, or near or far; and will you be talking as if you were to go beyond the government of the All-powerful and be drifted to a country whither His fatherly kindness may not reach?   Alas for you if this is all your faith!"   "This is true," said they; "but the sea, the mighty ocean, the ocean that is broad and long."   "The sea!" replied he; "why should that discourage you?—is not God to be found on the waters as well as on the dry land?   Under the guidance of His wisdom and the protection of His power are you not as safe on the ocean as ever you were in the bosom of your own sheltered glen?   Did not He create the ocean, with the swell of its impetuous waves, not one of whose billows can rise without His will? and He it is that can lay its gathered fury with a word.   He rides the waves on the chariot of the winds as certainly as He sits enthroned in heaven.   O ye of little faith, wherefore did ye doubt?"   "We are leaving the dear old country," said they.   "You are indeed," said he, "the dear island in which you were born and bred; you are going a journey from home, far far away, and there is no use of concealing that much hardship awaits you there; but this did not come on you without your knowing.   Leave your country, did you say? Is there any fixed bond to bind any human being to one country more than another?   We have no abiding country on the face of this earth; we are strangers and sojourners here; and in this changeable world which God has granted us for a habitation there is no home to us from which we are not to expect a removal."

"That is true," said they; "but we are wandering far away like sheep without a shepherd; without any one to whom, in the hour of need, we could turn for advice.   Oh, if only you were going with us!"   "Hush!" said he, "give no breath to language of this kind.   Consider: are you going further from God than ever you were before? The same God who opened your eyelids when you first learnt to look on day, even He it is who worketh everywhere wonderfully, at the other end of the world as well as here. Who went with Abraham when he left the land of his fathers? Who revealed himself to Jacob when he went from his father's house, and laid him down to sleep with a grey stone for a pillow? Shame on you, my dear friends! Where is your faith? Did you say that you were like sheep without a shepherd? Is there one of these little ones beside me here that could not repeat these words—

'The Lord's my shepherd, I'll not want?'

Is not He the great shepherd of the sheep, He who said— 'Fear not, little flock, be of good cheer, for I go to God.' There is no church, I know, where you are going; and likely enough you may seldom see the face of a minister; but remember the day of the Lord. Gather yourselves together under the shelter of the rock, under the shadow of the tree, and lift up there in melody the songs of Zion together, that ye may know how the presence of God is not confined to one place more than another; that He is to be found in every place by every one that seeks Him sincerely in the name of Christ, on the top of the highest Ben as well as at the bottom of the lowest glen, in the dust and sweat of the reeking town no less than beneath the pictured dome of the most stately cathedral. Each one of you is able to read the Word of God with his own eyes; were it otherwise my heart would be heavy indeed, and my sorrow inconsolable at this separation. Whithersoever you go, I know that the Bible goes with you; and take from me here these new Bibles, newly printed in a little volume easily carried, and you will not value these the less that your names are written in them by the hand that baptised you, and was many a time lifted up to heaven in earnest supplication in your behalf, and will still be lifted up in good hope in the name of Christ for you till the day of death shall lay it low. And you, my dear little ones, lovely lambs of the flock that I fed, for you I have brought some small memorials of the great love which I bear you. God bless you!" "Oh!" said they, "how thankful are we that we have seen your face once again, and depart with your latest kind word in our ears."

The people of the ship had been gradually drawing nearer to the place where he was standing, and, though they were only sailors, most of whom did not understand the words which he spoke, they were evidently moved deeply at the solemn and touching style of the words to which he gave utterance. There was an earnestness, a flavour, and a kindliness about his person and his address that hushed them into reverent attention; and I observed tears trickling down from many a withered cheek, which the harsh conflicts of life had long weaned from that use of tenderness.

The good old man then took his hat from his head and stood up. Every one knew what he meant. Some of them fell on their knees, and every one looked on the ground, when he said with a firm voice, "Let us ask God's blessing; let us pray!" Oh! hard were the heart that would not have melted, and not to be envied the spirit of the man that would not have given heed, while this earnest warm-hearted man was sending up his prayer to heaven, and whose spirit in the act was lifted above the earth and its concerns. Many a poor downcast soul plucked courage from his words; words that fell like the evening dew with fresh strength to the dry and drooping branches. Sharp were the pangs which shook their breasts as they were on their knees, and heavy were the sobs which they vainly

strove to suppress; but when they rose up I could see
new courage in their faces, new light of hope shining
through the mist of bitter tears that were now drying on
their cheeks. Then he opened the book of Psalms; and
they raised a sacred melody, which, while it expressed fully
the deep sorrow that then possessed them, seemed to carry
with it tones of the sweetest comfort and consolation.

The sound of this thrilling hymn reached every vessel
in the harbour. There was no boatman that did not rest
on his oar; no pipe was heard; no sound but the soothing
notes of sad resignation, as they parted singing the well-
known verses of the forty-second Psalm :—

> " My soul is poured out in me,
>   When this I think upon;
> Because that with the multitude
>   I heretofore have gone;
>
> With them into God's house I went,
>   With voice of joy and praise;
> Yea with the multitude that kept
>   The solemn holy days.
>
> O why art thou cast down, my soul ?
>   Why in me so dismayed ?
> Trust God, for I shall praise him yet,
>   His count'nance is mine aid." [1]

And now I have brought to a close this attempt which
I have made to break down the middle wall of partition

---

[1] There is a translation of " The Emigrant Ship" in the *Reminiscences
of a Highland Parish*, by the late Dr. Norman Macleod; but I rather
courted than shunned the profitable exercise of doing into English a piece
of Gaelic prose, which, for graceful simplicity and profound pathos, is
second to nothing that I know in any language, unless indeed it be the
account of the death of Socrates in Plato's *Phædo*, and some well-known
chapters in the Gospel of St. John.

that has hitherto separated the Lowlands of Scotland and the whole of Saxon England from the soul of the Highlands. What I have done in this cause has been an episode in my life into which I was drawn by external circumstances over which I had no control, and by deep moral instincts that are stronger than circumstances. It did not lie at all directly in my way either to study the Gaelic language or to agitate the country for the erection of a Celtic chair. I have taken an infinite deal of trouble in a matter with which I had nothing directly to do, and which carried me forcibly away from the tract of my own proper work; but there is no act of my life on which, now that the thing is done, I look back with greater satisfaction. It was a sad thing for me to hear the poor Highlanders, just because they were poor, hardly ever mentioned except to be made the subject of vulgar jests and shallow slanders; it was a sad thing to see the systematic desolation of our beautiful glens, and the dwindling away of our stoutest population; and saddest of all, to contemplate the ingratitude of Britain to the men who had fought her most critical battles, and performed her most glorious achievements in war, in commerce, and in geographical exploration. If there were who could console themselves for these losses by reflecting that there were more deer in the forest, and more London people for three months in the year looking at mountains and waterfalls, and more Highland mutton on the groaning boards of rich Glasgow merchants; and who had brought themselves to believe in selfish earnest that the commercial bond of cash payment in all things is a far better cement to hold the classes of society together than mutual love and respect, I could derive no comfort from such considerations. I wanted Highlanders in the Highlands, and a lusty peasantry in the breezy glens; and both had been swept away. I wanted a human life in harmony with the life of external Nature, and I found it not. Rents had risen immensely, I was told; and Highland estates were sold at three times the sum for which they were bought thirty years ago; but I did not believe in money; I believed in men. There was only one consolation left for me: as I could not rejoice with those that rejoiced (for joy had perished out of the land), I might fulfil the other half of the apostolic law of sympathy, and weep with those that wept. More pleasant always to weep with Greeks than to triumph with Turks. Thus arose the present book. In it I have paid the debt of human sympathy to a most ill-treated and ill-starred race of my fellow-countrymen; and if it may have any issue beyond that, so as to restore in the breasts of some who have it not the lost idea of a moral bond between class and class, to recall one here and one there from the idol-worship of glittering externalities called wealth, and to deepen the faith in a few thoughtful breasts that the one thing seriously to be sought for in all sound-hearted societies is not money, nor anything that money represents, but love, and truth, and devotion, and wells of living water from within; in such case I shall have had my reward.

PRINTED BY T. AND A. CONSTABLE, PRINTERS TO HER MAJESTY,
AT THE EDINBURGH UNIVERSITY PRESS.

www.ingramcontent.com/pod-product-compliance
Lightning Source LLC
Chambersburg PA
CBHW031146120726
47905CB00006B/1836